The Woman in the Muslin Mask

The Woman in the Muslin Mask

Veiling and Identity in Postcolonial Literature

Daphne Grace

Pluto Press

LONDON • STERLING, VIRGINIA

First published 2004 by
Pluto Press
345 Archway Road, London N6 5AA
and 22883 Quicksilver Drive, Sterling, VA 20166–2012, USA

www.plutobooks.com

British Library Cataloguing in Publication Data
A catalogue record for this book is available from the British Library

ISBN   0 7453 2005 8 hardback
ISBN   0 7453 2004 X paperback

Library of Congress Cataloging in Publication Data
Grace, Daphne,
    The woman in the muslin mask : veiling and identity in
postcolonial literature / Daphne Grace.
        p. cm.
Includes bibliographical references.
    ISBN 0–7453–2005–8 — ISBN 0–7453–2004–X (pbk.)
    1. Veils in literature. 2. Muslim women in literature. 3. Literature,
Modern—20th century—History and criticism. I. Title.

PN56.V44G73 2004
809'.933559—dc22

                                                           2003022873

10   9   8   7   6   5   4   3   2   1

Designed and produced for Pluto Press by
Chase Publishing Services, Fortescue, Sidmouth, EX10 9QG, England
Typeset from disk by Stanford DTP Services, Northampton, England
Printed and bound in the European Union by
MPG Books, Bodmin, Cornwall, England

This book is dedicated to my mother

Contents

List of Illustrations

Acknowledgements

My interest in the subject of women and the veil (and the concept of female space) began through visits to the palace harems of Topkapi and Dolmabahçe in Istanbul – cool, quiet places where the voices and laughter of centuries of women are forever silent. My interest developed through a series of friendships, conversations and experiences – especially with colleagues and students (although none of them veiled) at Eastern Mediterranean University. Other friends in North Cyprus from a variety of countries including Turkey, Iraq, Palestine, England and the United States provided 'real life' as well as academic insights and inspiration.

Those to whom I owe gratitude include my colleagues in the Faculty of Arts and Sciences (the departments of English Literature and Language) at Eastern Mediterranean University, especially Nicholas Pagan, Peter Malekin, Ahmet Hidiroglu, Robert d'Alonzo and Lorraina Pinnell; Feliz Çermen and the library staff, and other faculty friends throughout the university (many of whom did not realise how much they were helping me as we sat talking on Salamis beach); and all the students I have had the joy of teaching in Cyprus. My Turkish and Cypriot friends especially gave me an insight into the world of politics and gender relations, as well as into the beauty of their cultures. I must also thank Valérie Orlando for the initial spark that got me started and the e-mailed enthusiasm that kept me going. Also appreciation and thanks go to dear friends Awad and Enthazar, Sheniz and Yilmaz, Matthew Gould and Beth Schneider (for all the music); to Özkul Mük, whose constant friendship inspired me to keep working in present reality while also appreciating the finer details of the Ottoman past; to Philip, Joanna, and Annabel Blair, for their hospitality, friendship and support, intellectual, social, and spiritual; and to Geoffrey Clements for his unfailing help and encouragement.

A deep gratitude is owed to my colleagues at the University of Sussex, most especially Minoli Salgado, Denise deCaires Narain and Stephanie Newell, and to Ralph Yarrow at the University of East Anglia. I would like to express my gratitude to William S. Haney II, without whom this project would have been impossible.

Most of all I offer thanks to my family, my father, Edward, my sister, Jennifer, and her husband, Craig, my brother, Nigel, and his wife, Jacqueline, for their unending support, encouragement, and love.

1
Background to the Veil: History, Theory and Culture

The veil remains one of the most controversial issues in postcolonial and feminist studies. In both academic study and the popular press, it has taken centre stage as a symbol of both oppression and resistance, while in cultural studies veiling has been thrust into the forefront of arguments surrounding identity, colonialism and patriarchy. Yet, despite its continuing resonance in the western imagination, 'the veil' remains a confusing and controversial topic, one which is frequently 'attacked, ignored, dismissed, transcended, trivialised or defended' (El Guindi, 1999: xi). While social scientists discuss its cultural significance and argue over the meaning of its expansion into western cultures, and the media spreads fear about the Islamic threat, western feminists locate the veil as emblematic of an oppressed minority within patriarchal structures. From this perspective, the veil is seen as symbolic of the suppression and exploitation of the 'oriental' woman both by man and, conversely, by the gaze of the western colonialising and neo-imperialist world powers.

The image of the veiled woman is not in any way neutral, but is an ambivalent and shifting signifier, redolent with 'orientalist import'. The Eurocentric view of Europe's south-eastern neighbours has for centuries been one of fascination and repulsion, one in which a western lifestyle was of necessity superior and in which 'veiled women were necessarily more oppressed, more passive, more ignorant than unveiled women' (Mabro, 1991: 3). Many debate the continuing significance and presence of the veil in modernising societies. Does the visible upsurge of 'new' veiling arise from the fear of loss of identity in a changing society, a demand for privacy perhaps, or from an ideological revival/revolution, a protest against western values, or are women now veiling because they have something 'immoral' to hide? Differing perspectives cite various cultural reasons for wearing the veil, many of which raise disturbing questions.

While there exists much generalised discussion on the veil, little work has been done on what – or who – lies beneath the veil. While, for the western voyeur veiled women still remain 'mysterious', the conflict in understanding is not only a problem of history and colonialism but is also conceptual and cultural, encompassing religious bias and preconception (Lazreg, 1994). As Nancy Lindisfarne-Tapper and Bruce Ingham conclude, veiling (and head covering) must be understood in terms of how images of veils are used, 'to persuade which audiences of what political advantages, and why?' (1997: 16).

This study seeks to expand upon current scholarship with an aim to elucidate a concept that has been grossly misinterpreted in the past. It attempts to determine how far literature (most importantly, works by women in cultures where veiling occurs) is able to express the problems and experiences of women beneath the veil. My analysis seeks to redress the 'invisibility' of the woman beneath the veil, while examining whether fictional representations confirm or negate the involvement of the veil in the oppression of women. Exploring the veil as both reality and symbol, and the multiple cultural inscriptions of veiling, this book brings together previous cultural arguments on the veil from both 'western' and 'eastern' perspectives in order to analyse the phenomenon within its patriarchal, religious, and political contexts.

Egyptian sociologist Leila Ahmed writes of the imperial nineteenth century, 'Veiling to Western eyes – the most visible marker of the differentness and inferiority of Islamic societies – became the symbol [in colonial discourse] of both the oppression of women (or, in the language of the day, Islam's degradation of women) and the backwardness of Islam' (1992: 152). The range of literature examined in the following chapters exposes how far attitudes have developed or changed during the last century.

Encompassing literary representations of orientalist attitudes in England, and veiling in turn-of-the-century and post-independence India and in contemporary Arab contexts in Africa and the Middle East, the book reveals how veiled women have negotiated issues of identity, mobility, and independence. It argues that the veil is by no means ineluctably oppressive. A comparison of gendered viewpoints indicates the ambiguity of the veil as cultural articulation, and confirms the impossibility of a simple reductionist explanation or 'solution'. The veil, chosen by writers for over a century as a trope of varying symbolisms surrounding women's identity, conceals fundamental and disturbing elements of misogyny, patriarchal denial and fear.[1] I suggest that within these parameters the veil acts to eliminate expressions of both difference within and unity of female identity; it both defines and disguises the individual self.

Locating the veil as simultaneously a site of colonial fantasy, nationalist ideologies (both traditional and revolutionary) and discourses of gender identity, my discussion of veiling is not limited to a Muslim/Arab context, but encompasses class contexts of veiling in the Indian subcontinent, and compares Islamic and colonial locations of the gaze. While considering the proposition that 'positive' concepts, such as women's space, are embedded within the more 'negative' readings of segregation and suppression, the next chapters will show that the veil, while from a western feminist perspective a 'universally' denounced institution and a symbol and instrument of the refutation of women's individual identity and the means of restricting agency, is in fact nuanced and ambiguous. Oppositional viewpoints revolving around binaries of oppression/opportunity, incarceration/insurrection, denial/expression of identity, and entrapment/agency, are contingent upon cultural and individual positioning. The analysis of literature here examines to what extent they are also determined by gender. My discussion of these problems of identity and agency incorporates psychoanalytic theory, cultural theory, postmodern and postcolonial studies and feminism.

The majority of texts analysed here are by female writers, chosen for their particular insights into experience 'behind the veil' or into the role that the veil takes in their own cultures. Rather than being a purely sociological or cultural work – as most of the writing on the veil has been to date – this book will focus on literature from a range of contexts: Victorian Europe, twentieth-century Egypt, the contemporary Middle East, North Africa (particularly Algeria), the Arabian Gulf (Saudi Arabia), the eastern Mediterranean (Lebanon, Palestine), and India. As well as being pertinent to the topic, these places have been selected for the accessibility of their literature in translation.[2] They also represent a wide diversity of cultures, many of which are all too often subsumed under the heading of 'Islam'. India strikes a point of contrast here since in India veiling is associated not only with religion but also with class, caste and traditional values (often adopted and endorsed by religious practice). India – a country of contrasts in itself – perhaps holds a key to the veil in its other roles, paradoxically perhaps, in 'erotic' allure, and spiritual awakening.

CHAPTER OUTLINE

Following a consideration of the veil as a social and literary construct and the critical theories of relevance to my argument, the next six chapters examine the veil across two centuries and three continents. Each chapter discusses the socio-historical background to a particular region, the theoretical framework for debating the issues involved, and the works of literature (whether novels or short stories) that shed light on the theme of veiled women.

Chapter 2 discusses the western imaginings of the veiled woman from the late nineteenth to the early twenty-first century. Detailing how the eastern veiled woman has been imagined in the west, this chapter questions whether portrayals of the 'covered woman' have much changed over a hundred and fifty years. Also debating the (mis)conceptions regarding the veiled world of the harem in Ottoman society, this chapter explores the foundations of twentieth-century prejudice and xenophobia. Taking fictional texts from a diversity of authors, ranging from Oscar Wilde to Hilary Mantel, I examine prevailing attitudes of orientalism and cultural stereotyping. This analysis forms a basis against which writing from 'oriental' societies on veiled women can be juxtaposed. Taking as a starting point the rise of imperialism in the Victorian period (which coincided with the repression of emotion, the subjugation of women, and the crushing of early attempts for women's rights), texts such as Oscar Wilde's *Salomé* and some of Rudyard Kipling's short stories of India are indicative of both Victorian attitudes towards 'eastern' woman and their subversion. Significantly, the Victorian period was the last in which veils were habitually worn in England – and they are often cited by writers such as Wilde and Dickens as symbols, or the practical means, of secrecy, deceit, perversity and entrapment. As the 'imperial gaze' turned inwards towards 'the other' at home (forging links between imperialism, misogyny, and the 'othering' of women) the figure of the veiled Victorian woman can be as revealing of middle-class 'white' European attitudes, fears, and bigotries as the more stereotyped alterity of the veiled Islamic woman. Veiling and unveiling are terms through which the east has long been devalued and the west has constructed itself as superior. This hierarchy 'imagined' out of nineteenth-century imperialism is still prevalent in today's society, riddled as it is by conflicting strains of Islamophobia and orientalism. In the latter part of this chapter, I argue that several contemporary texts embellish and promote stereotypes of the veiled, oriental woman as either an erotic image of 'forbidden' male desire or as an oppressed and trapped victim within stifling, 'backward' societies. I examine European attitudes towards the veil, questioning Manichean and orientalist discourse of the west through, for example, the analysis of a novel by an English woman writer depicting her 'veiled sisters'.

Chapter 3 is the first chapter that focuses on the Arab Islamic world of the Middle East. Geographically, I divide the Arab world into three areas and deal with each in a different chapter. My discussion of the Islamic world covers a broad range of fictional texts in order to delineate the multiplicity of voices and the variations of culture. It seeks to explore women's veiling while questioning whether the veil is primarily a religious, political, nationalistic or patriarchal phenomenon. Chapter 3 highlights literary texts that reveal how women and nationalism are linked within the context of the Islamic religion, bringing the debate on veiling up to date with consideration of the contemporary challenge of 'new' veiling. Analysing the veil from its role in early twentieth-century nationalist debates to its part in contemporary issues of religious and cultural identity, this chapter deals primarily with Egypt, where veiling and the feminist movements have been inextricably linked for more than a century. An exploration of issues raised by both male and female authors, ranging from Naguib Mahfouz to Ahdaf Soueif, in relation to veiling in the Egyptian context reveals the centrality of religion, politics and economics, and exposes the relationship between class and the availability of choice.

Chapter 4 moves eastwards to examine the role of the veil in the most rigidly theocratic of Islamic cultures, in Saudi Arabia and the Gulf States, debatably a particularly volatile area, especially where women are concerned. Focusing on the veil as primarily a religious phenomenon, this chapter analyses novels and short stories from local writers. It highlights the role of gender politics and morality codes, and their utilisation in Arab women's victimisation by patriarchal laws in the name of 'cultural authenticity'. Many Arab feminists emphasise religion as sanctioning a gendered discourse of inequality: the institution of veiling is one method of secluding and restricting women both in private and public spheres of life. The fiction analysed here, however, indicates a broader awareness of the problems facing both men and women within these 'desert' cultures, suggesting that the imposed veil is only a part of an extensive cultural and patriarchal system of domination of women *and men* through the restriction in women's roles and mobility in society, and the prohibition of social contact between the sexes. Arab women writers explore the possible avenues available as outlets for female creativity and personal fulfilment, structuring a penetrating examination of both social and spiritual roles. While change may seem desirable, many Arab writers themselves regard veiling as an inherent part of the Qur'anic requirements for strict gender segregation and for modesty and piety. Here, writers such as Hanan Al-Shaykh, women short-story writers, and the Sri Lankan writer Bandula Chandraratana, expose diverse aspects of life in Saudi Arabia and the problems of living within strictly segregated social space.

Chapter 5 extends the discussion of the veil within the Islamic world to look at the politics of veiling, particularly in the Maghreb (North Africa). Using as a critical framework the issues of veiling elaborated by Frantz Fanon, this chapter explores the multifaceted meanings and symbols of woman and veil in colonial and postcolonial discourse. The women of Algeria struggle to find a place of agency within the Islamic regime and within the framework of turbulent political events. Here, the veil can be a sign of not only religious piety, but also political protest. The shifting significations of the veil were apparent during the Algerian war of independence when it became a symbol of resistance to colonisation, of emerging nationhood and traditional values. Women's veiled bodies quickly became the disputed site of national meaning and the veil took on a central role in liberating Algeria from French colonial occupation. In the analysis of how these historical events are dealt with in literature, the Moroccan sociologist Fatima Mernissi and fiction writer Assia Djebar are contrasted with male writers. Within this complex setting of Franco-Arab-Berber culture, Djebar, along with other women writers, such as Leïla Sebbar, have brought the issues of women's identity and freedom into a contemporary context, in which women seek to define themselves as more than a colonial or patriarchal 'other'. With other writers, the veil also plays a role of access to transgressing gender boundaries. My analysis concludes with a discussion of the controversial notion of veiled 'female space', the traditional harem (women's quarters of the house) and the *hammam* (public bath) in Muslim societies.

Chapter 6 turns to India, analysing veiling during the Raj, in the struggle for independence, and in contemporary India. Through discussion of novels and short stories that depict the uses of the veil in disguise, punishment and allure, it brings to the forefront different facets of the veil, including class and caste implications. An initial analysis of early-twentieth-century writers relates veiling with the nationalist cause, and the identity of women's body with 'Mother India'. Questioning the continuing involvement of religion (both

Muslim and Hindu) with the iconisation of veiled woman as upholder of family and national honour, the discussion focuses on a selection of texts which serve as examples of how women are controlled by 'traditional' codes of behaviour in patriarchal society. A number of recent stories by Indian women writers explore the varied experience of veiled women and the 'purdah mentality' that still pervades the lives of Indian women even as they search for new modes of female awareness. This chapter also includes a detailed analysis of novels by Salman Rushdie. Dominant themes in Rushdie's novels are identity, migrancy and exile – topics relevant to a consideration of how women are positioned in society. Moreover, several of his novels are rich in allusions to veiling and the trope of women beneath the veil. A discussion of his novels *Shame, Midnight's Children* and *The Satanic Verses* reveals how the veil is used as a self-conscious literary device and a means of social and political comment. The shrouded but nevertheless real involvement of women in history is highlighted by frequent references to concealment by veils and *burqas*. Both history and women are 'partitioned' from and by narrative. My discussion also addresses Rushdie's problematic depiction of masculinist stereotypes of veiled woman as mysterious, erotic, and dangerous.

Chapter 7 consolidates the various theoretical positions analysed in relation to veiling and assesses how useful such theories have been in the light of historical and contemporary experiences of veiling. This chapter summarises the varied and often ambiguous representations of veils observed in this study. It also poses some final questions, such as why, at the start of the twenty-first century, the wearing of the veil particularly by young women seems to be more popular than ever. Chapter 7 also considers how recent political events in central Asia have impacted upon our understanding of the role of the veil in society, literature, and world events – and how the veil continues to be a paradoxical and highly emotive subject of debate.

Chapter 7 includes a discussion of the possibility of a 'women's space' that transcends the problems of patriarchy. If men build their world upon fear is it not possible for women of the new millennium to find an alternate space of their own making, where they may regain agency? My own conclusion as to whether or not veiling indicates or eradicates agency and identity involves the important question of women's ability to make choices. Both veiling and unveiling can be liberating or suppressive, depending on the context and on where and how women see themselves dominated. I argue that the veil, subject to negotiation and multiple (mis)interpretations for over a century, while an overdetermined signifier, nevertheless frequently represents a site of women's oppression – a situation that Arab and Indian women writers strive to define and ultimately ameliorate.

THE VEIL IN LITERARY AND CULTURAL PRACTICE

The title of my book is a playful – yet provocative – reference to Alexander Dumas' *The Man in the Iron Mask*. The main horror of the (historical and) fictional man in the iron mask was that his mask could never be removed. That it also obscured and denied his identity – which was its chief purpose apart from punishment – was a slightly less horrible reality. Yet how easy is it to remove the mask made of muslin, the veil? What are the ramifications of trying to do so, the implications and punishments both overt and subtle?

The image of the mask for postcolonial critic Homi Bhabha is one of an identity of 'no presence', a trope of 'unrepresentable identity' (Richards, 1994: 294). In terms of the anthropology of art, David Richards also concludes that the mask has 'an aura of ambivalence and ambiguity about it. It is a disguise, it hides what we most need to know' (Richards, 1994: 295). This study of veiling in different cultures aims to look at multiple representations of the phenomenon, both positive and negative (supportive and critical) with a view to determining why women veil – and what are the implications of their doing so for society as a whole. My analysis of the veil aims to create a new discursive argument that forges links between historical, cultural and literary readings.

A comparison of creative writers, while not representing stereo-typical viewpoints of either 'east' or 'west', also provides an insight into the problem of cultural impenetrability. While women's issues in western culture have evolved at their own pace, with questions of universal suffrage and women's right to education and work now consigned to history, the development of women's concerns in eastern cultures has followed a different historical path. (Although predating western articulations of women's rights, women's struggle in the Arab world, for example, still revolves around negotiating issues of identity, mobility, and independence.) Now, in an age of instant global communication and the multicultural society, these paths have to some extent converged, with the possibility of discourse between local and global established. The increasingly globalised and hybrid nature of cultures necessitates the analysis of a broad range of cultures and literatures in my present discussion of veiling, a phenomenon no longer exclusively assignable to 'other' cultures or peoples.

In line with this globalising trend, this work collects together a number of writers from 'west' and 'east' (as well as others who defy such compartmentalisation) and spotlights a number of women authors from the Middle East and North Africa (Hanan al-Shaykh, Nawal El Saadawi, Assia Djebar), and writers from Palestine and Saudi Arabia (Zeina B. Ghandour, Sharifah Ash-Shamlan, amongst others) and from India (such as Rama Mehta, Ismat Chughtai and Ginu Kamani) many of whom appear for the first time in a comprehensive work of literary analysis. Examples drawn from a range of writers' voices and experiences will expose the limitations of previous readings, while suggesting that there can be 'positive' concepts embedded within the more 'negative' readings of segregation and suppression.

This study of the veil in literature will seek to answer several questions. What do we mean by 'the veil'? Where does it occur? Why do women persist in veiling? (To assume that the veil is exclusively female attire, however, is to misrepresent the range of cultural meanings and occurrences; 'male veiling' is discussed in Chapter 5.) Lastly, what is it that is being veiled? Analysing these questions will also address controversial issues on the definition of identity.

Literature plays a key role in answering these questions. Homi Bhabha argues that the study of world literature involves strategies whereby cultures can recognise themselves through their projections of 'otherness' (1994: 12). Literature, while arguably the means for imperial (and patriarchal) powers to propagate their version of culture, also, as Edward Said has argued, encompasses narratives which challenge dominant hegemonies and through which colonised people can assert their own identity and history (1994). However, although much postcolonial literature *is* concerned with interpreting a specific political or historic reality in its own terms, an analysis cannot presuppose that such literature is purely 'social comment'. By extension, in my present analysis, much of the literature written by women in the Arab Middle East or Hindu India cannot be prejudged as necessarily 'feminist protest' citing the veil as the foremost indicator of social ills. For many writers, the veil is a given fact: it is not highlighted as a specific issue but passes as part of the traditional milieu.

While it is both necessary and informative to juxtapose texts from social science with literary fictions, it is important to clarify the connections between cultural and literary practice. The relationship of self to other is the concern of both disciplines: 'getting to know the other' has long been the raison d'être of anthropology, while a literary text both enunciates the cultural collision and allows the 'other' a voice of resistance (Daniel and Peck, 1996). Although both ask questions about the way meanings are constructed, literature allows on a subjective basis for the 'other' (whether gendered or racial) to find a space of freedom in which to express his or her identity. Nonetheless, literature and literary criticism are products of and interventions in particular moments in history. Moreover, the study of literature can involve moral and ideological assumptions, and can be complicit in both colonial and neo-colonial discourses (Viswanathan, 1989). The discussion here aims to overcome these dangers by drawing upon a range of textual representations: literary, cultural, and visual. Interdisciplinary and multidisciplinary, my approach will incorporate the fields of orientalism, anthropology, women's studies, cultural studies, semiotics and history. Placing the topic within a historical context also reveals how concepts and symbolisms of the veil (and the seclusion of women) change over time and across cultures.

(RE)PRESENTING THE VEIL

The veil, as Judy Mabro (1991) warns, is such a powerful symbol that it can blind us into generalisations. Any writer taking on the vast theme of 'veiling' is also warned that 'confusing and contradictory statements about what veiling "does" abound' and of the dangers of analysing 'the veil' as a unitary phenomenon (Lindisfarne-Tapper and Ingham, 1997: 15). It is important from the outset to understand that to speak of 'the veil' in fact engages in a misleading reductionism; the phenomenon of veiling cannot be reduced to a single explanation or 'solution'. Similarly, while it is possible to argue that veiling is an indicator of class identity, gender inequality and/or opposition to the west, it is important to clarify who is speaking and by which standards they are measuring. Everything depends on 'who is describing the phenomena of veiling, for whom and to what end' (Lindisfarne-Tapper and Ingham, 1997: 14). Ultimately, any interpretation – including my own – is contingent upon the socio-historical situation of the writer or observer.

The power of the imagery of the veil 'lies in its vacuity' (Lindisfarne-Tapper and Ingham, 1997: 15), a concept which in itself indicates a palimpsest open to theoretical and semantic reinscription. Indicating the problematic nature of cultural preconceptions that abound on this issue, the following comments reveal the deeply-ingrained, and erroneous, nature of our assumptions. Azizah al-Hibri questions, 'Why is it oppressive to wear a head scarf but liberating to wear a mini-skirt?' (in Okin, 1999: 45). In Oman, where the veil is a symbol of high social status, Unni Wikan argues it is 'as much a symbol of male oppression as Western women wearing a blouse' (1982: 106). Due to the volatile and highly interpreted nature of veiling, the rhetorics of veiling have also proved a versatile political tool.

Writers such as Marnia Lazreg advocate an understanding of women's experience beneath the veil, to eliminate the preconception that the veil is simply a symbol of women's identity. She complains,

> Ironically, while the veil plays an inordinate role in representations of women in North Africa and the Middle East, it is seldom studied in terms of the reality that lies behind it. Women's strategic uses of the veil and what goes on under the veil remain a mystery. (1994: 14)

While taking into account recent arguments on the dangers of generalising on topics of race and gender, the present study examines both the symbolism and practical uses of the veil in the lives of women, simultaneously attempting to avoid a stance of 'victim feminism'. The ambiguity surrounding discourse on the veil is both in terms of reality and metaphor. This problematic ambiguity is highlighted by the many interpretations that women themselves give to the veil and to their varied reasons for its use.

The roots of European notions about veiling lie in nineteenth-century attitudes on both women and the 'orient'. In the Middle East and beyond, since the beginning of the twentieth century, the veil has been a symbol of national identity and resistance. At the present time, the issue of veiling is still at the cutting edge of political and social change. Fadwa El Guindi has argued that 'a reaffirmation of tradition and culture might be played out in the near future through the idiom and politics of the veil' (1999: 185): a prediction that has been confirmed in the recent political rhetoric of American and British 'global interventionist' foreign policy towards Afghanistan.[3]

In Britain, with both Islamophobia and traditionalism on the rise, the veil has become a symbol of tradition and religious identity. With globalisation and the all-devouring 'McDonaldisation' with its imperialist ambitions, we are witnessing a simultaneous rise of religious fundamentalism in Arab countries as well as within Great Britain, South Africa, and elsewhere. Tribalism and globalism, paradoxically interdependent forces, are reshaping the world, as Benjamin R. Barber explains in his illuminating book *Jihad Versus McWorld*. 'Jihad', he writes, 'pursues a bloody politics of identity, McWorld a bloodless economics of profit. Responding to McWorld, parochial forces defend and deny, reject and repel modernity wherever they find it' (1996: 12). At the same time, according to many western commentators, the perceived 'Islamic threat' (epitomised by the *fatwa* against Salman Rushdie and the current rise in terrorism) has set Islam and the west on a collision course. In a confrontation often portrayed as a clash of civilisations, Islam is seen as a triple threat: political, cultural and demographic (Esposito, 1995a). Indeed, Margaret Thatcher has described Islamic extremism today as the new bolshevism, 'and like communism, it requires an all-embracing long-term strategy to defeat it'.[4] The veil is central to the discourses of west versus east, democracy versus 'fundamental' Islam, and still remains an icon of the otherness of Islam and a symbol of Muslim women's oppression.

The international crisis which followed September 2001, and the ensuing focus on Afghanistan, associated the oppression of women and 'fundamentalism' with terrorism. The persecution of the population – especially through the strict rules of conduct and punishment imposed upon women – within extremist regimes, such as the Taliban, was perceived elsewhere as the 'violation of human rights'. The all-encompassing view of what constitutes such regimes (a fundamentalist Islamic regime that denies human rights and democracy to sections of its population, especially women) became inextricably linked with what constitutes sponsored terrorism. The popular media's perspective was fuelled by western governments wishing to portray the view that an Islamic state persecuting its people is inevitably linked to global terrorism. According to this view, if the pernicious regime is removed, at one stroke the cause of terrorism and oppression of the people is also removed. Those who subscribe to this naive understanding of Muslim states perceive the internal problems mainly as cultural repression (epitomised by veiling) and the external symptoms as terrorism. Fundamentalism, repression of the people, and terrorism are pinpointed as the *cause* of the problem. The identification of terrorism as both symptom and cause of these problems exposes the flawed logic behind the 'war of terrorism'. To imagine that regime change will stop terrorism, ignores the fact that there are many other factors – social, religious, cultural, and historical

– that underlie both social customs and the current polarisation between the world views of 'terrorist states' and the anti-terrorist western alliance.[5]

In Iraq, which had (until the recent overthrow of the regime) had a socialist government since 1958, women had equal rights with men in relation to education and employment and tended not to veil. However, young women were increasingly appearing in full body veils (the *chador*) because of the danger of attractive women being abducted by Saddam Hussein's National Guard. Such women simply disappeared and were never seen again. Following the devastating April 2003 war on Iraq, the future of women in Iraq and indeed the future of the whole society, now one of the poorest on earth, remain uncertain. The religious and political future of Iraq and the redefinition of its nationhood may well involve the discourse of veiling/unveiling and the iconisation of women as the representatives of national and religious or sectarian identity.

Contrary to western-based negative and negating depictions of the veil is another that presents it as a symbol of liberation, both individual and cultural. In a world of increasing systematised and political violence against women, the veil can stand as a symbol of the protection of public honour (as well as being the practical means of providing obscurity, as outlined in the case of Saddam's Iraq). For Muslim women living 'between worlds' in Britain or elsewhere, the veil becomes a symbol of their religious identity as well as providing a practical means of protection against unwanted harassment. In a recent BBC documentary on the veil in Britain, a young Muslim woman remarked that 'the more I cover, the less fear I feel'. The veil (in this case the total black covering of the *chador*) was like a wall protecting her; without it she felt naked. Another woman in London felt that 'you have to cover the face to be identified as a Muslim, otherwise you don't have an identity'. One Asian woman commented that ultimately the veil is 'only a construct that can be used either to mask or to liberate'.[6] Writing of earlier decades, Clifford Geertz discusses how in Morocco the custom of veiling provides a 'language for assertion of social identity and status' (1979: 331).[7] The new trend in Egypt of veiling in 'designer headscarves' similarly defines the 'new aristocracy' in Cairo.

Thus, political, social, religious and gender factors all play a part in determining the reasons for and symbolism of veiling. Structuring concepts of both religious 'identity' as well as indicating new social hierarchies, the veil remains a primary site of national and political negotiation.

THE SOCIO-HISTORICAL ROOTS OF THE VEIL

Several studies have discussed the traditional roots of veiling and traced the development of the veil through different civilizations, both Mediterranean and Mesopotamian, arguing that the veil predates Islamic and Christian cultures.[8] Although in popular perception the veil has long been associated with Arab women, evidence shows that it has existed for longer outside Arab culture than within it. It has been suggested that veiling originated with slavery, a system perpetrated by all three monotheistic religions that developed in the Arabian desert, and even that justification for the veil goes back as far as the myth of Adam and Eve. (All three religions cite Eve as responsible for the fall of man and the origin of sin. Veiling is often associated with the need to cover her corrupt nature and shameful body.) However, contrary to expectation:

in the Middle East the veil was historically worn to distinguish women of high status; it was in the Hellenic, Judaic, and Christian systems to which the West traces its roots [that] veiling was associated with seclusion in the sense of the subordination of women. (El Guindi in Esposito, 1995b: 109)

By the time of the birth of Christianity, however, Jewish women were veiling both their heads and faces. References to veiling appear in the Old Testament (see Genesis 24: 65 and Isaiah 3: 32). One, in Genesis Chapter 38, is made in the story of the patriarch Judah who encounters his daughter-in-law, Tamar, but mistakes her for a road-side prostitute *because* she is veiled. (The episode is evocatively illustrated by Emile Vernet's 1840 painting, now popularly considered to epitomise the orientalist imagination and women's pivotal role in the sexualisation of the orient.) In the New Testament, St Paul insists on the veiling of women during prayer, describing those who do not veil as shameful and concluding that 'if she refuses to wear a head covering, then she should shave off all her hair' (1 Corinthians 11: 3–17). Christian connotations of 'taking the veil' with religious seclusion and celibacy are not widely cited, however, in the west's current trend for Islamophobia.

Why the veil? – origins of *hijab*

While in the west, dress in general is mostly a secular phenomenon, in Arabic, the term *libas*, 'dress', encompasses both material/social

1   Judah and Tamar, by Emile Jean Vernet (1840). The biblical story of Judah and Tamar associates the veiling of Jewish women with prostitution. Endorsing the fantasy of 'forbidden' erotic voyeurism, the imagery here, based on the biblical story, can also be linked to the association of veiling with slavery. (The Wallace Collection, London, UK/Bridgeman Art Library)

and sacred realms – with symbolism that embodies both the visible and invisible. Similarly, the veil has been seen to have both sacred and secular origins and uses (El Guindi, 1999: 70), and as such has symbolic as well as practical implications both for the wearer and for society.

In terms of clothing, *hijab* refers to the 'modest dress' that is prescribed, and often compulsory, in Islam. However, as Fadwa El Guindi points out, *hijab* is not the Arabic word for 'veil'; in fact there is no one word which describes the various head and body coverings. Numerous words are used to describe the diverse articles of women's clothing, including: *abaya* (Saudi Arabia), *chador* (Iran), *gallibiyyah* (Egypt), *burnus* and *haik* (Algeria), *jilbab* (Indonesia); while others such as *burqa*, *niqab* and *qina* refer to the face masks worn, for example, by Bedouin and other desert tribal women (El Guindi, 1999: 7). Such linguistic variations highlight differences in both regional and religious connotations, based on a multitude of complex social arrangements articulated through the symbolism of clothing.

In Arabic the *hijab* is a barrier, literally, a 'curtain'. (The word *hijab* itself is formed from the two words *sitr* and *hajaba*, which mean 'to hide with a curtain'.) The *hijab*, as Fatima Mernissi, the influential Moroccan sociologist, explains, can be an outward symbol of a woman's religious faith and a marker of her modesty, and is also in its wider connotation, a partition that protects the secular from the profane.

Yet veils are not exclusively a feature of Islam. Moreover, the new generation of Islamist women fighting for women's rights in Egypt claim that it is traditions prevailing from before Islamic times that are responsible for discrimination against women (Al-Ali in Chatty and Rabo, 1997: 184). Some writers, such as Nawal El Saadawi, have argued that veiling is not part of Islamic or Egyptian identity, and have utilised the trope of the veil in fiction as indicative of patriarchal oppression. Trained as a medical doctor, El Saadawi documents the mental problems of her veiled patients, victims of the 'oppression and contradictions' of the veil in Egypt today. To understand veiling, El Saadawi argues, we must locate its historical origins in slavery. 'Why did the veiling of women start? It is not Islamic ... it goes beyond that, we must look back in history. It started with patriarchy' (1999).

Contrary to popular belief, the veiling of women is nowhere explicitly prescribed in the Qur'an. It is claimed that the custom of veiling arises from the verse in the Qur'an telling believers to 'cast down their eyes ... and reveal not their adornment save such as is outward; and let them cast their veils over their bosoms'. El Guindi elaborates on the translation of this passage to reveal that the original meaning was to 'cover the cleavage of the breasts' (1999: 136). The passage has been interpreted (by men) in some countries to indicate the requirement of the full veil, a head-to-toe covering such as the *abaya* or *chador*, while in other countries (such as Egypt) a fashionable headscarf suffices. (It is worth noting that the cover outlined in the Qur'an was intended to prevent the public flaunting of sexuality, and a parallel verse prescribed an equivalent modest dress code for men.)

Fadwa El Guindi (1999) also discusses the original use of the veil to distinguish the status and identity of the Prophet's wives, 'so that they may be recognised and not molested' (Qur'an, 33: 59). Another mention of the *hijab* is in Chapter 33, Sura 54: 'When you ask any of the wives of the Prophet for something, ask from behind a curtain.' The historical origin of 'the veil' was a curtain, not between man and woman, but between two men. The descent of the *hijab* is an event mentioned in the Qur'an (Sura 33, Verse 53) and refers to the occasion when Mohammed called for a curtain to be placed between himself and his newly-married bride and his male companions. He was eager to be alone with his new wife, Zaynab, and to be rid of a small group of tactless friends. Mernissi concludes that in drawing down the curtain and revealing the verse on the *hijab*, Mohammed was to make a proclamation that split Muslim space in two (Mernissi, 1991: 86). The boundary between forbidden space, which is hidden by the *hijab*, and permitted space, was to become a key concept in the Islamic world. As Mernissi argues, however, 'reducing or assimilating this concept to a scrap of cloth that men have imposed on women to veil them when they go out on the street is truly to impoverish this term, not to say drain it of its meaning' (1991: 95).[9] Mernissi concludes that the imposition of social, spatial and religious restrictions on women was never inherent within Mohammed's teachings:

Paradoxically, and contrary to what is commonly assumed, Islam does not advance the thesis of women's inherent inferiority. Quite the contrary, it affirms the potential equality between the sexes. The existing inequality does not rest on an ideological or biological theory of woman's inferiority, but is the outcome of specific social institutions designed to restrain her power: namely segregation and the legal subordination of the woman to the man in the family structure. (Mernissi, 1975: xvi)[10]

This important statement of Mernissi's will inform much of my analysis in the forthcoming chapters. As we shall see, whether in the context of the Middle East or India, it is legal and social (including family) codes and rules of behaviour that determine and control women's freedom and access to fulfilment – sought through either education, employment, or emotion/relationships. For me, Mernissi's work in cultural feminism also holds a key to why women are veiled in and by patriarchy. She continues elsewhere:

> If women's rights are a problem for some modern Muslim men, it is neither because of the Koran nor the Prophet, nor the Islamic tradition, but simply because those rights conflict with the interests of a male elite. The elite faction is trying to convince us that their egotistical, highly subjective, and mediocre view of culture and society has a sacred basis. (1991: ix)

Many of the concepts in Mernissi's book *Islam and Democracy: Fear of the Modern World*, although relating to a Muslim context, can be applied to an extended cultural picture. The word 'fear' is pertinent to an examination of patriarchy regardless of cultural context. Sharon Spencer, giving a European example, outlines the origins of the process whereby

> Man denies and represses woman's natural intimate connection to the instinctual life process that in ancient times endowed women with power and wholeness. Man 'veiled' woman in order to conceal from her and from himself this power. Then ... man redefined woman to suit his own ends. (1981: 96)

Tariq Ali's analysis of early Islam corroborates this masculine fear of women. An 'anxiety that regarded women's desire as untameable, dangerous and thus requiring repression' was at the root of the strict codes of conduct (and dress), violation of which led to brutal punishment (2002: 63).[11]

Most Euro-American feminists and Asian feminists agree that the veiling of women is a result of oppression and domination of women by patriarchy *in the name of* religion.[12] I will now turn to an area, which, for many in the western world, is regarded as the most important cultural reference point of the veiling of women: that of so-called 'fundamentalism' or Islamism. Following the creation of the extremely arbitrary and alarming signifier of the 'post-9/11 world', the veil has taken on a hitherto undreamed of political and religious significance as a corroboration of the righteousness of the western alliance's 'crusade' against Islam. With the powers of fundamentalist Christianity now at their most influential in the United States, the increasing oppression of women within the US goes unreported, while the liberation of 'under-cover woman' becomes an inflated issue of global importance. Meanwhile, the word 'fundamentalist', used originally to denote a religious conviction, has become synonymous with the word 'terrorist' – but only when associated with Islam.[13]

'Fundamentalism' and the veil

The word 'fundamentalism', as Bernard Lewis points out, is derived from the history of American Protestantism, and is ill-chosen to refer to recent Islamic movements. The more appropriate term 'Islamism' indicates not the revival of a trend in religion, but the assertion that religious belief should be involved in all aspects of daily life, most specifically in politics. The central concern of the Islamist movements is not the interpretation of religious texts (the Qur'an or Hadith: the associated sayings of Mohammed) but rather the resistance against alien and 'oppressive' secular states and the establishment of control of the state. Nonetheless, there is no one simple definition of an Islamist regime. Political options range from military dictatorship (Libya, Pakistan and Sudan) and tribal oligarchies (Saudi Arabia) to clerical dictatorship (Iran) (Halliday, 1994: 94). In some countries, the growth of Islamism has been in response to colonialisation (Algeria) or to the establishment of secular governments (Turkey).

Within these contexts, women are frequently placed as the victims of the struggle for state and religious definition. Akbar S. Ahmed suggests that Muslim women

> seem to be squeezed between Islamic fundamentalism and modernity, and between modernity and postmodernity ... Muslim women are frequently perceived as the most vulnerable to radical change and outside influence, the more so since the front door and the compound wall are no longer effective barriers to such forces. (Ahmed and Donnan, 1994: 14)

In Islamism, veiling has become not only a religious but also a politicised act, 'whose meaning shifts depending on the articulation of the local with the global in any particular setting' (Ahmed and

Donnan, 1994: 15). In seeking to transcend the polarised western view (veiling as oppressive) and Muslim view (veiling as liberating), it is imperative that we realise that veiling is as much a response to change in the world as it is an expression of 'religious tradition'. While both western and Arab feminists are critical of Islam for imprisoning women in their own homes, it is important to note the conflicting arguments within Islamic feminism. One side of the debate argues that Islamic rules have created problems for women in the Middle East; the other claims that Islam and the current resurgence of religion are responsible for the *liberation* of women, protecting and honouring their status and role rather than treating women as sex objects, as in the west.[14] Fatima Mernissi delineates the position within arch-patriarchal/religious systems, where women

> have been, are, and continue to be the targets of intimidation and violence, whether from regimes in power or oppositional movements that hark back to the past. It happened in Pakistan in the 1980's; it is still going on in Iran; and today [in the early 1990s] it is happening in Algeria. Tomorrow the same thing can happen elsewhere. (1993: 174)[15]

Cultural differences

Local variations of 'the veil' range from the black cloaks (the *abaya*) worn in Saudi Arabia and the *chador* in Iran, which provide total covering, to the white *haik* of Algerian women, to the brightly coloured scarves worn in Turkey and Egypt. This continuum of veiling stretches from state sanctioned modest attire to individual fashion accessory. Veils cover the hair, the head, very often part of the face, and sometimes the arms and the rest of the body including hands and feet. In Egypt, the *hijab* is now worn mainly by upper-class and educated intellectual women, although in the rural villages fundamentalist young men have been found to pressure their sisters to veil fully and stop engaging in 'un-Islamic', 'superstitious' practices. Farzaneh Milani has described how the veil is a physical representation of both charm and shame (*sharm*): attributes most valued in a woman. She refers to the situation in Iran, where the more a woman conceals herself, the more she indicates her privileged social status (in Naghibi, 1999: 557). (Interestingly, the word *chador* in Persian means 'tent', implying that the veil, in effect, is a mobile enclosure.) In a country such as Saudi Arabia, where the upper classes may enjoy enormous wealth, the veil fabric itself may be a statement of superior class.[16] These few examples contradict western discourse, in which the 'veil' is politically charged with connotations of the inferior 'other', implying an inferiority of Muslim women.

It is relevant here to question to what extent dress defines identity. Even in the west, fashion critics examine how far 'a piece of cloth' can define and expose identity.[17] In Turkey and Iran the fact that dress identifies national and social identity lay behind the national dress reforms (which centred around the illegalisation of veiling) instigated by Kamal Atatürk and Risa Shah. Contradictions are inherent in any discussion of veiling: veils have been described as representing a woman's sexuality, or as a means of distancing women from their sexuality. Muslim women in South Africa, for example, regard the veil positively as a symbol of their religion, while some find it 'makes them feel sexy' (Ridd in Ardener, 1997: 190). Veiling may be argued to protect the woman from becoming the object of the man's desire, or to protect the man from the strong sexual impulses of the woman. The veil is a 'double shield', protecting women against society and protecting society against the 'inherent evil' of woman.

For the majority of the Islamic world, wearing *hijab* indicates that a woman is a good Muslim, and that she takes pride in her religion and culture. Younger women who report a sense of insecurity in today's changing world (whether in Pakistan, Turkey or Britain) find covering up gives a certain security and sense of identity. Wearing *hijab* also allows women freedom to leave the house or to work without criticism, harassment or violence from men. At another extreme, in countries such as Saudi Arabia and Iran, the religious police maintain a strict control over women's appearance in public: if *hijab* is not worn (or in the case of *bad-hijabi* not properly worn) or in any way reveals the face or hair, the woman may be publicly beaten or jailed. The current sentence is up to 74 lashes (El Guindi, 1999: 175).

From a different point of view, women within countries where *hijab* is strictly upheld also report a sense of freedom in that they do not have to be constantly concerned with their appearance: the obsession with appearance often denounced as western and un-Islamic. Condemning the western equation of 'beauty with truth' as corrupt, deceitful and delinquent, Zahra Rahnavard, an Iranian writer, argues that the *hijab* removes woman from being 'an object whose value lies solely in her looks'. Furthermore, she regards western criticism of veiling as part of a wider imperialist stratagem designed to attract the Muslim to the rotten surplus goods of Western capitalist economies, clothes, makeup, fashion-accessories none of which are marketable unless there are unveiled female bodies to wear them ... [Hijab] is not a prison ... it is a weapon, a fortress, a sanctuary of decency and chastity, which enshrines not only your physical attributes ... but also the divine essence of your womanhood. (1990: 9)

Meanwhile, Patricia Holton's account of life in the desert of the United Arab Emirates appreciates the burqa and abaya for their practical use as protection. When she sees the face of an old Bedu woman uncovered, she is amazed how youthful the woman's face is, protected as it has been from a lifetime of exposure to the sun and wind (1991). This is one practical – and positive – use of the veil that western feminists do not mention. (The veil as part of the beauty myth after all, perhaps.) Use of the veil as protection from the sun is not unrelated to the association of pale skin with beauty (and superior class) in many nations (Japan, the Philippines, and India to name only a few Asian examples) and the designation of 'pale skin' as a marker of cultural superiority. Unni Wikan cites attitudes in Oman, where face veiling is not associated with Islam but identifies a conservative middle class. The burqa is thought to be an integral part of a woman's self: 'it is not that we wear the burqa because it is shameful to go without it', she quotes, 'but because it is beautiful to go with it' (1982: 104).

THEORETICAL APPROACHES

Positioning veiled woman within rigid limitations imposed on her by patriarchal discourse, it is important to acknowledge that national and geographic variations, as well as class and education, account for subjective differences in and experiences of such positioning. In order to broach the discussion of the impact of the veil upon female identity, it is instructive to explore if any valid theory exists that may elucidate the cross-cultural phenomenon. While theoretical approaches are not exhaustive, they may offer penetrative insight into the veil as mask of identity, as secluded space, and as means and symbol of female oppression. My analysis of literary texts utilises aspects of several theories that shed light on the problematic of veiling: Euro-American and Arab-Asian feminisms,[18] postcolonial theory (including orientalism), psychoanalytic theory (Freud's theory of the gaze), and postmodern theory. In the remainder of this chapter,

I briefly outline some main trends and concerns in feminist and postcolonial theory, as well as introducing some of the concepts within psychoanalytic theory that are of relevance to a critique of veiling. These concepts will be elaborated in the following chapters in relation to literary texts and specific cultural analysis.

East/west, north/south feminisms: women, identity and agency

To what extent can it be argued that the veiled woman acts within a sphere of agency? Is she free to initiate action, or is her action determined by the way her identity has been framed within the discourse of the veil, whether by Islamic men or western women? In her work on 'subaltern identity', Gayatri Spivak discusses the impossibility of women, particularly those in the 'third world', having agency or a voice. The history of women, she argues, can be reconstructed but not reclaimed. In the classic essay 'Can the Subaltern Speak?', Spivak cites the case of the *satis* in India (women who have immolated themselves on their husbands' funeral pyres) whose voices will remain forever unattainable. She argues that the figure of 'Third World Woman' disappears into a 'pristine nothingness' since her displaced figure is 'caught between tradition and modernisation' (1988: 306). Similarly, the figure of the veiled woman is in danger of becoming a palimpsest written over with the desires and meanings of others. It is imperative that we let 'veiled woman' speak for herself, if possible. Spivak, however, argues that to retrieve the lost voice of the subaltern subject is to risk complicity in an essentialist, and western, model of subjectivity that ultimately keeps the subaltern woman muted, because her speech is always improperly interpreted. Nonetheless, even if subaltern identity is irretrievable, it can be recreated through fictional texts that function to subvert rather than duplicate dominant phallocentric discourse. Fiction does recreate the historical – and contemporary – subaltern voices that otherwise might be lost. Short stories and novels (and biography) act like the 'handprints on the wall' of the dead *satis* – evidence to bear witness to the importance of the veil in relation to the identity of women.

Even in the early days of the new millennium, feminists are still struggling to resolve two basic questions: how to free women from the iconic function to which phallocentrism has confined them, and how to express a different, positive vision of female subjectivity. Feminism, while mainly critical of veiling as a denial of women's identity, also offers a theory of 'female space' which arguably could be a place of women's agency. The concept of women's secluded space (the veiled world of the harem) can – like the veil itself – be interpreted from supportive, critical or ambivalent viewpoints. Within diverse cultural contexts, female space is traditionally an inner space, as opposed to 'outer' male space. Women (in India, for instance) are placed in the space of home/spirituality which is in opposition to the male and material world of the marketplace. The concepts of 'home' as nation and as a feminised spiritual space that must be kept unpolluted have roots in ancient texts and were revived by the nationalist movement in the twentieth century. Yet the home may also be the site of feminism and resistance to nationalist ideals, a site of struggle rather than of resolution. In the traditional Islamic world, a sharp division separates the gendered space of the household between the domestic space where related men and women may mingle, and an outside space forbidden to women. If women must venture into 'public' space, methods of 'fictive invisibility' such as the veil must be adopted to ensure segregation of the sexes and a 'separate space' for women. The segregation into male and female space underlines discrepancies between discourses of female incarceration in patriarchal space and women's locus of independence and feminist insurrection.

Within a Eurocentric framework, responding to the sense of being relegated to the domestic sphere and denied access to 'male' public spaces, feminists since Virginia Woolf have urged that a woman must have a space of her own. Billie Melman, however, persuasively documents how women within harems in the Ottoman Empire actually had more rights and enjoyed greater freedoms than married women in Europe (see Chapter 2). In the context of women's captivity within patriarchy, Gilbert and Gubar emphasise the importance of women's liberation from social and literary confinement in both 'male houses and male texts' (1979: 58). Elaine Showalter argues that oppressive patriarchy has forced women to forge a new reality for themselves. While seemingly trapped within male-ordered society, women constitute 'a muted group, the boundaries of whose culture and reality overlap, but are not wholly contained by, the dominant male group'. Her conceptualisation of the 'wild zone' – an area of female lifestyle and agency that is outside of and unlike the male sphere of activity – is a place for both revolutionary women's language and interpersonal experience (Showalter, 1985). In an Indian context, critics conceive of a place for women's writing and creativity, 'a sort of female enclave, untouched by masculinist assumptions' (Tharu and Lalita, 1993: vii). Within the parameter of 'female space' women are placed outside the suppressive elements of patriarchy. If we view the location of veiled women (outside male space) as equivalent to a 'wild zone', then through veiling women may gain access to an area of inner experience that is a psychological life force of women, a prerequisite for regaining rather than losing self-identity.

2   Three generations of women outside the Sultanahmet Mosque, Istanbul, May 2001. In countries such as Turkey, the older generations tend to cover up more than the young. (Here, the grandmother wears a more traditional shawl, while the young mothers wear fashionable headscarves.) In other countries, factors such as increased sexual harassment, a loss of cultural identity, and protest against 'western' values have initiated a reverse trend in which younger women have returned to the symbolic protection and meaning of the veil – one that both affirms and challenges tradition. (Photo: author)

The symbolic role of the female body and clothing is paramount in any analysis of the representations of the veil. Feminist writers such as Judith Butler stress the importance of the signifier of the body to a feminist analysis of power relations in societies that are founded through a set of violations. European feminists such as Hélène Cixous and Julia Kristeva claim that the whole basis of women's writing, *l'écriture féminine*, *is* the female body. All women, according to this argument, regardless of geo-historical position – and behind a veil or not – have been effectively silenced. Teresa de Laurentis has expanded upon the problem: 'Feminism discovered the non-being of woman: the paradox of being at once captive and absent in discourse, constantly spoken of but of itself inaudible or inexpressible' (1990: 115). Luce Irigaray, meanwhile, insists that women's difference must be written into culture and the Symbolic Order in order to challenge woman's 'othering' by western patriarchal culture and thus her absence as woman (1985).

Reviewing these feminist critics reveals a cross-cultural concern about women, the female body, and phallocentric power relations. Arguing from a more postcolonial stance, Kadiatu Kanneh writes that the place of the body in feminist or cultural debate has become so complicated in contexts of gender and race that words like 'identity', 'subjectivity' and 'desire' are anything but simple. ('Agency' could be added to this list of terms, since what constructs and comprises agency must also be determined by culture and to some extent class.) Kanneh tackles the problematic figure of the 'third world woman' arguing that contradictory representations by Europeans have misrepresented the colonised black woman, and made her body 'an unstable arena of scrutiny and meaning' (1999: 145). In cases of Islamic nationalism (as we shall see in Chapter 5 on Algeria) the veil becomes a substitute for the female body – just as the female body becomes a synecdoche for a nation.

Yet why do men assign such importance to women's bodies and clothing in the context of nationalism, and why is such ideological weight given to the veil? Cynthia Enloe identifies five major reasons why the veil and sexual purity are important in terms of nationalist causes. She suggests that women are: 1) the community's/nation's most valuable *possessions*, 2) the principal *vehicles* for transmitting values to the next generation, 3) *bearers* of the next generation ('nationalist wombs'), 4) the members of the community most vulnerable to defilement and exploitation by oppressive alien rulers, and 5) the most susceptible to 'assimilation and co-option by insidious outsiders' (1990: 52). She notes that in every case women are passive vehicles for male-imposed meaning.

Demonstrating their affiliation with the postmodern trend of rejecting any theories of essentialism, feminists in the last decades have grown wary of any mention of an 'essential' nature of the female, and advocate a feminism that seeks to reflect the wide diversity of women's experiences and views. Since Simone de Beauvoir's ground-breaking work *The Second Sex*, in which she voiced the now famous phrase 'One is not born, but rather one becomes a woman' (1973: 301), gender has become a cultural rather than biologically-given entity. Judith Butler endorses de Beauvoir's condemnation of universalist theories arguing: 'When the essential feminine is finally articulated, and what we have been calling "women" cannot see themselves in its terms, what then are we to conclude? That these women are deluded, or that they are not women at all?' (in Benhabib and Cornell, 1987: 142).

Viewing identity as indeterminate allows the flexibility and the opportunity for negotiating new identities, and for the possibility of change. This paradigm would respond to the problematic position of veiling/unveiling, rationales for which are numerous, contradictory and changing (even within one cultural location). As individual women and men recognise the need for change in worldwide inequalities (from gender and class inequalities to those in religion, philosophy and science), identity will correspondingly be reassessed in terms of unity (conjunction) not difference.[19]

Black and Asian feminists are among the main advocates of rejecting any universalist theories of women's identity, which are generally seen as unjust and oppressive. ('Essential woman' is most likely to be white, middle-class, and heterosexual.) Importance is placed on individuals within categories of difference, whether racial, sexual, ethnic. Moreover, recent antagonisms and distinctions between 'first and third world' feminists (such as arguments put forward by Kanneh, Kabbani and others) are fast being eroded. Afro-American feminist writer bell hooks has long advocated a solidarity that will embrace differences. In her important essay 'Sisterhood: Political Solidarity between Women', hooks argues that

> women do not need to eradicate difference to share solidarity. We do not need to share common oppression to fight equally to end oppression. We do not need anti-male sentiments to bond us together, so great is the wealth of experience, culture and ideas we have to share with one another. We can be united by our appreciation for diversity. (in Kouramy et al., 1995: 104)

Other recent arguments have put forward a concept of transnational feminism, refusing to accept difference as an absolute value and suggesting that it must be understood as *relational*. New forms of connection and solidarity across nations will do justice to the differences that force women apart while they attempt to speak and act together. Women's agency 'anchored in the practice of thinking of oneself as part of feminist collectives' is now discussed in terms of the *relationship* between local and universal, so that:

> To talk about feminist praxis in global contexts would involve shifting the unit of analysis from local, regional, and national culture to relations and processes across cultures. Grounding analysis on particular, local praxis is necessary, but we need to understand the process in larger, cross-cultural processes.[20]

This international dimension of the feminist preoccupation with identity, transcending cultural boundaries, is significant to my present study especially as cultures become increasingly hybrid. Within this dynamic, the problematic of the veil has far-reaching importance, both individual and national.

These concepts and arguments in recent feminist thought will be referred to throughout my argument, and used in comparison with and contrast to the issues and problems emphasised by Arab and Indian feminists. I shall now discuss the other area of theory central to an understanding of the socio-historical reading of the veil, that of postcolonial studies. The postcolonial argument too will be elaborated in further chapters as a constructive tool in the analysis of literary representations.

Postcolonial theory: *orientalism* and beyond

The veil, in the current climate of juxtaposed globalisation and Islamophobia on the one hand and the rise of Islamism (or 'fundamentalism') and nationalism on the other, is an important icon in cross-cultural processes. The field of postcolonial studies challenges universalist and imperialist notions and focuses on marginality, alterity and agency as aspects of power. The theme of the veil brings into dialogue the two sides of relevant debate: orientalism and Islamophobia. The inherent and inevitable paradoxes within these viewpoints in themselves provide a point of negotiation. Although we can view the veil as a boundary between points of contact, east/west and male/female, it also acts as a meeting point for confrontational perspectives, providing a contentious image to initiate debate.

Edward Said's formulation of 'orientalism' refers to the imperialist discourse in which cultures 'make representations of foreign cultures the better to master or in some ways control them'. These representations 'developed and accentuated the essentialist positions in European culture proclaiming that Europeans should rule, non-Europeans be ruled'. As Said points out, 'no area of experience was spared the unrelenting application of these hierarchies' (1994: 120–1). The erroneous (and imperialistic) depiction of the 'east' as a realm of the exotic, the seductive and the mystical, is nowhere more clearly seen than in the trope of the veil.[21] In Said's terms, the veiling of women, depicted as suppressive and 'backward', also shapes the negative representation of the east as cruel, inferior and sensual. Uma Narayan has similarly commented that in the political struggles between 'western culture' and the 'culture of the colony', veiling, polygamy, and *sati* were all 'significant points of conflict and negotiation'. In these conflicts such indigenous practices were symptoms of backwardness and barbarity of the third world cultures and were contrasted with the 'progressiveness' of western cultures. The figure of the (veiled) colonised woman became a 'representative of the oppressiveness of the entire "cultural tradition" of the colony' (Narayan, 1997: 17). The orientalism of the west (and of western literature) has also been criticised for its depiction of non-European peoples as homogeneous anonymous masses, whose actions are governed by instinct and raw emotion rather than by logic and intelligence. (One can find many examples of these attitudes in literature. They are brilliantly satirised in E.M. Forster's novels on English attitudes and behaviour abroad, such as *A Passage to India* and *Where Angels Fear to Tread*.) Said particularly cites European attitudes towards the Arabs in which any suggestion of individual identity is obliterated. The Arab, in history and literature, has been projected as the 'other', a threat and a challenge to Eurocentric morality and, of course, the Christian church. He/she is also, paradoxically, a figure of romantic and sexual allure.[22] Said points out the inaccuracies of this situation, 'Direct observation or circumstantial description of the Orient are the fictions presented by writing about the Orient' (Said, 1979: 34).

It is relevant to mention the recent conflict in Afghanistan here, since it amply illustrates the dichotomy of eastern and western world views. During this recent crisis the trope of the veiled woman behind the *burqa* was central to debates raging around 'first versus third world' ethical values, religion, politics (and political religion, that is, 'extremism'), terrorism, and nationalism. Nancy Lindisfarne cites the 'liberation' of the woman behind the grilled *burqa* as one of the pretexts for the bombing of Afghanistan; this focus on oppressed veiled woman disguised the US's previous financial and political support of the Taliban and continuing US interests in central Asia. The positioning of Afghan women as either victims or as complex agents of change depends on various competing discourses. These grand narratives of both eastern and western cultures neutralise the possible articulations of identity, whether through voiced opinion or written word, of the women themselves. The focus on the veil, ethnic divisions and poverty also served to confirm further stereotypes of Afghanis/Arabs as primitive, backward and naturally brutal (all orientalist suppositions about the east, as we have seen previously), stereotypes that were used to justify destruction by the Americans of their former allies (Lindisfarne, 2002: 2–3).

Frantz Fanon, a hugely influential writer whose work pre-dates that of Said (and whose use of the veil as an icon of nationalism is problematised in Chapter 5), refutes the racist stereotyping by colonial powers. In his ground-breaking work *The Wretched of the Earth*, he urges the silenced and misrepresented peoples under colonial rule to find a voice and identity by reclaiming their past. Fanon advocated active and violent political opposition – an opposition that in Algeria was symbolised by the figure of the veiled woman.

The postcolonial emphasis on the search for identity has more recently been superseded by Homi Bhabha's concept of culture being 'less about a pre-given identity ... and more about the activity of negotiating ... often conflicting demands for collective self-expression' (1999: 38–43).[23] Bhabha regards people in cultures today as living in an 'in-between state', in a state of suspension of time, space and identity. This state of both physical and temporal 'in-between-ness' could also describe the position of the woman behind the veil, who is always located in in-between space, an interloper or a 'thief in male space' (Djebar, 1980: 138). Yet, as Bhabha emphasises, 'we should remember that it is the "inter" – the cutting edge of translation and negotiation, the in-between space – that carries the burden of the meaning of culture' (1994: 1–2). The veil creates such an ambiguous space; it defines identity and yet simultaneously removes any identity.

This conceptualisation of the veil as a borderline, a barrier between spaces and between identities could be argued to provide a possible site for women's agency. Some writers have advocated the veil for its associated sense of privacy and freedom, the liberty of seeing while remaining unseen.[24] Yet, often made of translucent muslin, the veil can be a permeable membrane (as revealed in the etymology of the word), one that can filter, purify, and clarify. In this context, the veiled woman can be seen as a purifier of her environment, someone who acts to absorb and reduce the family stress, one who in the Hindu tradition in India maintains the spiritual purity of her society. Anees Jung, an Indian journalist brought up in strict purdah, discusses the *havelis* (women's quarters) in India as 'energy-filled spaces of silence' where women fulfil a role as 'the silent centre, the point of unity' of the collective consciousness of their societies (1987: 20).

Any discussion involving postcolonial theory includes an analysis of the distribution of power within society. Can a female role such as the one described above (which included key terms such as 'silence') be a source of power and creativity to women, or is this just another example of women *being* silenced? It is time for women to act as agents of change, in redefining social space and the artefacts of culture and tradition. Social space has traditionally been branded by the binary logic of inside/outside, female/male, trivial/important; now women can redefine their areas of agency to upset, or even reverse this logic. Referring to the cultural context of Iran, Farzaneh Milani (1992) discusses how the veil both polarises and delineates boundaries, consigning power, control, visibility, and mobility to one social category at the expense of the other. Yet both men and women are responsible for the perpetuation of this formulaic division. It will take a quantum shift from a level of life more fundamental than that of social rules and religious prejudices to alter this tyrannical status quo. Since experience itself comprises both external and internal, subjective and objective phases of activity, this shift could come about through a prioritisation of internal, subjective space as a place of agency.

Psychoanalytic theory: Freud, fear, and the gaze

Freudian psychoanalytic theory was arguably the basis of many masculinist attitudes to women in the late nineteenth century and the twentieth century. This discussion will take notions of veiling out of any limited religious or cultural context and involve ideas that lie at the basis of patriarchal psychology. Sigmund Freud belonged to the world of late-nineteenth-century Vienna. Yet his ideas have become commonplace throughout the western world, the concepts of psychoanalysis becoming entrenched in European culture and its terminology entering common parlance. Interestingly, his concepts regarding women and their role in society are comparable to some of the basic tenets of Islam.

Freud's discussion of the gaze in particular relates most centrally to the problematic of veiling. To summarise briefly: in an essentially patriarchal theory, Freud claims that the exclusive rights of the gaze belong to men. In his 'Three Essays on Sexuality', he isolates woman's basic quality as one of lack. In the patriarchal subconscious, the woman, because of her lack, symbolises a threat of castration. In this situation, based on both fear and obsession, man is able to play out his fantasies and obsessions, since he is the bestower of meaning, the rightful owner of language and the symbolic order.

Freud discusses 'scopophilia', the pleasures inherent within other people being treated as the objects of a controlling gaze. Woman is the silent image upon which man superimposes his own meaning through control of the gaze. While man seeks to define and control woman through the gaze, woman becomes the silent spectacle, the passive object of desire. The male pleasure-in-looking projects both a role for woman as erotic object while also giving the man a satisfying sense of omnipotence. Woman goes 'on display' for the gaze and the enjoyment of men. For feminists, Freud's analysis of woman is both frustrating and oppressive. Yet it reveals one explanation of the roots of oppression under the phallocentric order.

Alexandra Warwick and Dani Cavallaro have discussed the veil in its paradoxical role of both concealing and exposing: concealing the truth by giving 'familiar realities an unknown turn' and as a means of exposing since 'defamiliarisation enforces discovery' (1998: 134). In two texts that can be analysed in terms of Freudian theory, 'The Sphinx without a Secret' by Oscar Wilde and *She* by H. Rider Haggard, the veil's fascination lies in the prospect of *un*veiling. The male characters in the stories long for this moment, both for the revelation it affords, and the opportunity to gaze unrestricted upon the object of desire – since (if we follow Freud and, later, Foucault) the gaze secures power over the object gazed on. Yet this enjoyment hides the basic fear that man feels – fear of the power of woman both to castrate and to reproduce. Thus, the gaze oscillates between a masochistic scopophilia and sadistic voyeurism. Gaylin Studlar notes that, 'Unlike sadism, which depends upon action and immediate gratification, masochism savours suspense and distance' (in Mast et al., 1992: 785).

Freud argues that fear is generated by the fact of woman being an indecipherable 'problem', different – the enigmatic 'other' (1961: 113). Oscar Wilde's short story 'The Sphinx without a Secret' (written in a culture contemporary to Freud's) usefully illustrates this theory. A man contemplates the mystery and strangeness of a woman with whom he thinks himself in love. The narrator sees her as a 'beauty molded out of many mysteries', a *'belle inconnue'* (Wilde, 1966: 215–18). The protagonist, Gerald, falls in love with her *because of* the atmosphere of mystery that surrounds her, describing her in terms such as 'like one of those strange crystals one sees in museums, which are in one moment clear, and at another clouded' (217). One day, determined to discover her secret, he follows her when she ventures out into the streets of London 'deeply veiled'. Later, she denies having gone out and Gerald confronts her, demanding the truth. When she responds by asking him, 'What right have you to question me?' he denounces her for not telling the truth. He abandons her, and soon afterwards she dies. He is left to contemplate whether or not her mystery was real, or whether she 'had a passion for secrecy' and was merely a woman who enjoyed the liberty of 'going with her veil down and imagining she was a heroine' (218).

A Freudian reading suggests that woman as the other harbours a secret, a mystery that is both desirable and dangerous for man. The signifier of 'woman' negates the 'reality': an enigma that raises the question 'is there any reality behind the female facade at all?' The signified seems to be ultimately deferred, or an empty void. In Wilde's story, the woman is denounced as having 'no truth', which equates with 'no reality'. The female stepping outside (here, literally) the female sphere threatens men, since women have no right to partake in the liberties of society that are open only to men. While Gerald enjoys the erotic voyeurism and masculine power of his gaze, he denies 'his beloved' the right to action, truth and language (all three belonging to man). The woman is permitted to be concealed beneath the masquerade of femininity, the mask or 'decorative layer which conceals a non-identity' (Doane in Mast et al., 1992: 765). She is in fact allowed to be a sphinx – mythically the androgynous creature, half woman and half lion, that had access to enigmatic knowledge – as long as she *does not have* a secret. Rachel Bowlby similarly argues that 'as long as the Sphinx can maintain her illusion of posing a question and withholding an answer ... she has her lover in her power ... The appeal is in the illusion of a concealed true identity' (in Freedman, 1996: 180).

Woman as sphinx, woman as the veiled *femme fatale* (also exemplified in Oscar Wilde's play *Salomé*, to be discussed in Chapter 2) – these are images that conjure up the Freudian notions of erotic voyeurism and sadistic fetishism. In Mary Ann Doane's analysis of the role of the veil in psychoanalysis, she discusses the relations between truth, vision and the woman sustained by patriarchy (1989). She argues a disparity between seeming and being, between deception and unpredictability of woman. Again, woman represents the pre-cariousness and instability of reality; for man, the veiled woman represents the horror of that precariousness. In cinema in particular, Doane argues that the veiled woman is a trope of uncertainty and instability of vision, making graphic the question of what can and cannot be seen. The veil acts to conceal, cover, hide and disguise, but – through its opacity it simultaneously conceals and reveals, both allowing and disallowing the gaze (Doane 1989: 107). The veil's dialectic of vision and obscurity is related to the male desire to hide woman. While the owner of the gaze, according to Freud, may desire to see, his overwhelming urge is to conceal, to contain, and to obscure woman as lack and as threat. Fearful that the female may eventually threaten to return the gaze, men place the veil over the female face to keep it from contaminating the male subject.

A brief extract from the text of H. Rider Haggard's *She* illustrates this overriding male fear of woman's gaze and woman unveiled (1887, 1994). The narrator is Horace Holly, a self-professed misogynist, who has accompanied the hero, Leo Vincey, to the lair of She (Ayesha), a mysterious African queen of timeless beauty. Here, at the request of the two men, she finally unveils:

> She lifted her white and rounded arms – never had I seen such arms before – and slowly, very slowly, withdrew some fastenings beneath her hair. Then all of a sudden the long, corpse-like wrappings fell from her to the ground, and my eyes travelled up her form, now only robed in a garb of clinging white that did but serve to show its perfect and imperial shape, instinct with a life that was more than life, and with a certain serpent-like grace that was more than human ... I gazed at her face, and – I do not exaggerate – shrank back blinded and amazed. I have heard of the beauty of celestial beings, now I saw it; only this beauty, with all its awful loveliness and purity, was *evil*. (152)

A closer look at some of the negative terminology used in connection with Ayesha: 'corpse-like', 'serpent', the oxymoron 'awful loveliness' and so on – reveals words associated with the ultimate 'evil'.[25] Added to this, the narrator is 'blinded' by her beauty – the ultimate danger for man inherent in the gaze. In his exploration of the symbolism of the eyes, Freud relates blindness to the fear of castration, as in the Oedipus legend. To be blinded by woman's beauty is for a man to fear her Medusa-like power, where the eye of woman becomes the source of castration (Jay, 1994).

In Rider Haggard's novel, Holly concludes in looking back upon the experience that night:

> it was not safe for any man to look upon such beauty ... Curses on the fatal curiosity that is ever prompting man to draw the veil from woman, and curses on the natural impulse that begets it! It is the cause of half – ay, and more than half – of our misfortunes. (156)

Again here, sadistic and masochistic impulses alternate in the male gaze. Exposing the form behind the 'protecting veil' although referred to as a 'natural impulse' also carries the implications of revealing something very unnatural. Freud defines the uncanny (*das Unheimlich*) as 'the name for everything that ought to have remained secret and hidden but has come to light' (Freud in Jay, 1994: 332). In *She*, Ayesha represents the uncanny nature of woman, with all its implications of horror, death and unnaturalness. The novel also is rife with instances of 'orientalist' attitudes towards the exotic and dangerous African subcontinent – as personified by Ayesha – where Islam meets 'the heart of darkness'.

This fear of the female return of the gaze is found in Islam as well as in the work of Freud. (Nawal El Saadawi's short story 'The Death of His Excellency the Ex-Minister' (in El Saadawi, 1987) is analysed in this light in Chapter 3. In this story, the minister is driven to madness and death through a woman usurping the power of the gaze, which is legitimately male.) The perceived female aggression – in the example of El Saadawi's 'Ex-Minister', suggested in a woman's refusal to acknowledge shame and inferiority – is threatening both to the man as individual and to society as a whole. In Islam, woman is the symbol of *fitna*, 'the embodiment of destruction, the symbol of disorder, the polarization of the uncontrollable, the representative of the dangers of sexuality and its rampant disruptive potential' (Mernissi, 1975: 130). Women must be restrained (and veiled) to protect men from an irresistible sexual attraction that will inevitably lead to social chaos. The Freudian concept is directly comparable: 'the placement of a veil over a woman's face works to localise and hence contain dissimulation, to keep it from contaminating the male subject' (Doane, 1989: 141).

Men are vulnerable to the dangers inherent in female sexuality and in particular to the dangers of the female gaze. Freud's interpretations of the uncanny and the threat of the female to patriarchal society are parallel to the Islamic tenets of women and *fitna* – and these ideas are still prevalent today, in the Judeo-Christian world just as much as within the Islamic world. Psychologists in fact have concluded that 'the use of the gaze in human social behaviour does not vary much between cultures: it is a cultural universal' (Argyle and Cook: 1976: 169).[26]

The *Encyclopaedia of Symbols* notes that 'Persons making sacrifices frequently wore veils over their faces ... as a sign of awe or fear in the presence of the Holy One' (Becker, 1994: 318). Here, one could argue in Freudian terms that woman must be veiled in the presence of the phallus, the Symbolic Law of the Father. She is the potential victim captured within the confinements of the symbolic male order. Freud saw Medusa as the 'veiled woman', and finally concluded that psychology 'will never solve the riddle of femininity'. He coined her sexuality as the obscure 'Dark Continent' never to be understood or conquered. Patriarchal society, with its desire for power and control over the other, bases its viewpoint of women, and by extension its colonies, on such concepts.

The next chapter explores the expansion of these nineteenth-century concepts into the twentieth century through the analysis of the 'western gaze' onto the east. Instances of the European imagining of the eastern woman, quintessentially a veiled woman, document how attitudes and fantasies pervade our 'knowledge' and perception of the east even today.

2
Imagining Veiled Woman

This chapter explores how veiled women of the east have historically been imagined in the west, and enquires whether recent depictions of the veiled woman are more culturally informed than earlier depictions. Have contemporary authors managed to shed or shun the prejudice and culture stereotyping of past centuries? Revealing the links between imperialism, misogyny, and the 'othering' of women in England and abroad, I argue that the figure of the veiled woman, with its symbols and connotations, exposes middle-class 'white' European attitudes, fears, and bigotry otherwise hidden behind the mask of English sobriety. This chapter identifies stereotypes of 'the veiled woman' that have prevailed in the European imagination.

The west's historic relations with and understanding of the east have informed western scholarship and literature forging an underlying predilection to orientalising eastern cultures and peoples. Misinformation and misleading cultural connections or associations have infiltrated both the mass media and popular culture (stereotyping still maintained for example in Hollywood) as well as academia. Erroneous associations of the veil with practices of polygamy and female genital mutilation have generated widespread moral and ethical debates in which cultural, traditional, or religious rituals and behaviours have been indiscriminately condemned as 'backward' and degrading. Women's own attitudes to such practices have largely been ignored, as has the fact that they are found worldwide (polygamy and FGM exist in the US, for example) and not only in the 'exotic east'.

This chapter aims to serve the dual function of exposing some of these misconceptions, while also outlining how imperialist and orientalist attitudes in the west developed, and how the situation of women in both Europe and the east was influenced by such attitudes. My discussion is centred around several examples from literature, taken from contexts ranging from Victorian England to contemporary India and all written from the 'imperial' or western perspective.

IMPERIALISM AND THE FICTIONAL EAST

Edward Said claims that the high age of imperialism began in the 1870s, a time when 'nearly everyone in Europe and America believed him or herself to be serving the high civilisational and commercial cause of empire' (Said, 1994: 266) – although imperialism itself had been a continuous process for hundreds of years. What we could term the 'fictionalisation' of the orient has been credited largely to the nineteenth-century writer, translator and explorer Richard Burton. Through his works, especially his translation of (and commentary on) *The Thousand Nights and A Night* (1885), Burton both revealed and created a mythos of the east as a land of intrigue, forbidden pleasures and sexual possibility. As Rana Kabbani describes, 'The European ... entered an imaginary harem by entering the metaphor of the Orient' (1994: 2). Burton's travelogue and conceptualisation of the east epitomised the British attitude: a desire to know in order the more effectively to rule. For Burton, the orient 'was chiefly an illicit space and its women convenient chattels who offered sexual gratification denied in the Victorian home' (Kabbani, 1994: 7). Women were demeaned as both female and as 'orientals'. According to Edward Said, 'The Orient was linked thus to elements in Western society (delinquents, the insane, women, the poor) having in common an identity best described as lamentably alien' (Said, 1979: 270). Oriental woman became a symbol of the secret and the obscure. Meyda Yegenoglu explains, 'the process of Orientalisation of the orient is one that intermingles with its feminisation', stressing that 'the typography of femininity as enigmatic, mysterious, concealing a secret behind its veil is projected onto the iconography of the Orient' (1992: 48).

Historically, the areas of the world discussed in the following chapters – together with western attitudes towards them – have undergone continual change in terms of national identity over the past several hundred years. The French scholar Maxime Rodinson traces how, dating back to the Middle Ages, 'Western Christendom perceived the Muslim world as a menace long before it began to be seen as a real problem' (1991: 3). Over time, the 'east' became renowned for its luxury and hospitality as well as for the depth of its learning. By the eighteenth century, the west had begun to assimilate the 'myths' of an exotic east, which soon swamped art and literature – with the flowering of orientalism influencing all aspects of culture. After the first translation in 1717 of *The Arabian Nights*, 'the Muslim world no longer appeared the province of the Antichrist, but rather an essentially exotic, picturesque world' (Rodinson, 1991: 44). This trend of exoticism shifted emphasis with the nineteenth-century rise of imperialism, however – and the need to create a cultural scapegoat for Europe. By the early twentieth century, the Middle East, including Turkey and Iran, was the 'sick neighbour' of Europe, with the colonial powers waiting to take control. In order to counteract any opposition to Eurocentrism, a resurgence of hostility towards Islam occurred, particularly following the First World War. 'A triumphant Europe saw all resistance to its domination as a sinister conspiracy ... whenever there was any show of anti-imperialism, pan-Islam was blamed. The very word itself suggested an attempt at domination, aggressive ideology, and international conspiracy' (Rodinson, 1991: 67) – a trend that has striking correspondences to today's Islamophobia. Even in more recent years, Islam 'has been made into the religion that the West loves to hate; a seething cauldron of sexism, and a dumping ground for all blame' (Kabbani, 1994: viii).

WOMEN AND EMPIRE

In the British colonial era, women as ambivalent symbolic constructs had always been regarded as dangerous and corruptive within western religious, social, and medical discourses (Suleiman, 1986). As argued in Chapter 1, woman is seen as dangerous to the stability of society, that is to say male homosocial society, in discourses ranging from Freudian psychoanalysis, to Islam, to Christianity to the Greek Apollonian/Aristotelian ideal of civilisation.

In imperial India, indigenous women wearing the veil or the *burqa* were 'invisible'; other women, although visible in the public realm and to the colonial gaze – nautch dancers, lower-class workers, courtesans and household servants – became merely representatives of the bodies hidden within the fantasy of the harem (or *zenana* in India). An illogical configuration of colonialist reductionism saw both veiled and unveiled women in terms of sexual symbolism. The more overt eroticisation of public space by the female dancer or performer merely corroborated and exacerbated the frustrated male gaze in its denial of the body of the veiled, private woman. Indian women homogenised into either of the two categories, those in public view or those confined in purdah, met with the moral approbation of the ruling British (Suleri, 1992a: 92). As Bhattacharya emphasises, the colonial gaze projected a monolithic 'bestial' essence of subaltern woman behind the veil (1998: 132).

THE VEIL AND THE HAREM

Victorian England witnessed the height of Empire, the height of British confidence at home and abroad, and the height of patriarchal expressions of misogyny. Literary works (from around 1850 to the end of the nineteenth century) expose the undercurrent of both misogyny and 'orientalism' in male attitudes towards women, who together with the orient were perceived and rationalised as 'other'. The relationship between Empire and England created a double discourse, one characterised by the apparent repression of the sexual along with sexual anarchy: 'all the laws that governed sexual identity and behaviour seemed to be breaking down' (Showalter, 1992: 3).

A brief account of life in the *seraglios* (palaces) of the east is instructive here in order to contrast European and Asian attitudes and lifestyles at the time, as well as to highlight erroneous beliefs of the veiled world of the 'harem'. In a male-dominated hierarchical world view, representations of women were central to the exoticisation of the conquered eastern lands.[1] While Victorian men may have regarded the orient as a site of sexual freedom – a 'libidinous space of fantasy' with the harem as a symbol of mysterious eroticism, and female suppression/inaccessibility – for Victorian women, the harem appeared a place where women gained rather than lost their freedom. While the Victorian woman was led into the orient by the perhaps exaggerated sense of practical liberty formulated in (the eighteenth-century) letters of Lady Mary Wortley Montagu and other travel writers, the Victorian male was lead by an erotic fantasy depicted in Burton and the paintings of the orientalist artists. For the Victorian male, the eastern woman was indolent, naked, lesbian, and tantalisingly unavailable except to the sultan who had access to his harem. Whereas the word 'harem' for the western mind connotes a sexualised space, where a plethora of semi-naked women await the pleasure of the sultan or pasha – an image elaborated in orientalist paintings, such as Ingres' *Bain Turk* (1862) – the '*haremlik*' merely denoted the women's area of the house or palace. (The men's quarters were the *selamlik*.) In fact, in the Ottoman imperial harem, only a small percentage of women were concubines or odalisques (*odaliks*: literally 'for the chamber'); the majority were employed in the household tasks in the kitchens, laundry, storerooms, the infirmary, baths, and so on. Slaves were also given a rigorous training in etiquette, Islamic culture and religion, writing, sewing, dance, poetry, and singing, and they were often freed into prestigious marriages (Croutier, 1989: 24–33).

These contrasting representations and connotations of the harem in eighteenth- and nineteenth-century England reveal the difference between appearance and reality. Setting aside male fantasies of the harem, Billie Melman suggests that, for the oppressed Victorian wife who had few rights to own property or money – nor to restrict her husband's 'conjugal rights' over her body – the harem women seemed to possess many rights denied to them (1986). When English women visited the Topkapi Serai (palace), they were amazed at the freedom enjoyed by the women. Many of the harem women, especially the sultan's mother, had enormous power and autonomy. For Lady Mary Wortley Montagu (who visited Istanbul in the early eighteenth century), the liberty offered by the veil constituted freedom of movement, sexual freedom and economic independence.[2] According to Montagu, in her letters from the Turkish Embassy:

> 'Tis easy to see they have more liberty than we have, no woman of what rank soever being permitted to go in the streets without two muslins, one that covers her face all but her eyes ... You may guess how effectually this disguises them, that there is no distinguishing the great lady from her slave ... and no man dare either touch or follow a woman in the street. This entire masquerade gives them entire liberty of following their inclinations without danger of discovery ... Upon the whole I look upon the Turkish woman as the only free people in the empire. (1716, 1993: 96–7)

Montagu delighted in veiling herself in the *yashmak* in order to explore the cities she visited and it is relevant to note that her association of the veil with liberty (physical, moral and sexual) is related to the inability to distinguish class. This was also a feature that both shocked and delighted female visitors to the *hammam* (or Turkish bath), a female space like the harem where women mixed freely regardless of race, class or colour.

One text depicting harem life that can not be accused of orientalist attitudes is Leyla Saz Hanimefendi's memoirs of her life in the harem of the last sultans of the Ottoman Empire.[3] Her book *The Imperial Harem of the Sultans* describes daily life in the imperial harem. She confirms the luxury in which the women lived, yet the book is essentially an affectless piece of writing. Yet, as such, it serves to counteract erroneous western notions of harem life. Herself a poet and musician, Leyla Hanimefendi documents the lifestyle of the women of the harem, their occupations and pastimes (including learning both Turkish and European music in the palace orchestras, dancing and caring for their children). Most noteworthy is the lack of class distinction within the harem. Both slaves and their mistresses shared a common lifestyle, different ranks within the harem often being indistinguishable. Her account exposes that life was far from the idle eroticism depicted in orientalist art, but one of strict discipline.

Neither were the women cloistered as in a monastery. The harem often moved to the countryside, and excursions and visits to other residences were frequently organised. During such excursions, the women wore the traditional *ferace* and *yasmak*, the headdress and veil made of light, transparent muslin or gauze. Leyla details how the *ferace* and *yasmak* would often be made from exquisite fabrics to match the dress being worn, with different styles for day and evening wear. Her nostalgic memoirs paint a picture of a time of great peace and contentment, of moon-lit boat rides on the Bosphorus accompanied by musicians, of great men and beautiful women, when 'the only thing which was banished from the Serail [palace] was ugliness' (1994: 163).

Alev Lytle Croutier's 1989 account depicting life in the Turkish harem is based on her own family history. (Although she unquestioningly illustrates her findings with an array of orientalist paintings, she also includes several original photographs, including family portraits, which undoubtedly shed more light on the harem women than the romanticised and fictionalised art works.) Outlining the fascinating history of the harem and the life of the sultans and their odalisques, Croutier also provides a detailed explanation of the etiquette of veiling. Describing the harem as 'the world behind the veil' – since the veil *signifies* 'harem', sanctuary – she contrasts the elaborate and sumptuous costumes worn by the women inside the harem to the uniform drabness in which they were concealed when outside (76). Outdoors they always wore the veil:

> The yashmak was a diaphanous veil exclusive to Istanbul made of two pieces of fine muslin ... One piece was bound across the head like a bandage, over the forehead down to the eyebrows, knotted just above the nape of the neck ... The other covered the lower part of the face and was tied together in such a way as to give the illusion of a single veil ... The translucency partially and tantalis-

ingly revealed the facial features behind it. However, a woman was extremely careful not to expose the nose, lest she be taken for an infidel or a prostitute ... For a man to approach or talk with a woman on the street was unthinkable, since her veil and cloak were as sacred as the doors of the harem. (78)

THE VICTORIAN VEILED WOMAN: FACT AND FANTASY

Despite the quotidian reality of harem life, in literature it is the male 'fantasies' of the orient and oriental woman that predominate in the Victorian imagination. By extension, the Empire becomes a male space of safety, a place of male bonding, where homosocial desire 'acts as a kind of textual unconscious for the entire discussion of empire' (Donaldson, 1992: 8). Beyond this place of safety is 'the other': the uncharted territory of the feminised orient. The west is rational, moral, and just, while the east is irrational, exotic, erotic and unruly (R. Lewis, 1996: 13).

Wilde woman as colonial other: western gaze/male power

Arguably an early postmodernist, Oscar Wilde exemplifies many of the nineteenth-century attitudes towards veiling outlined above. His works propagate Victorian orientalist discourse whilst simultaneously being concerned with 'deconstructing' the mores of English upper-middle-class society.[4] His (in)famous play *Salomé* can be read as an example of Victorian stereotypes regarding the sensual nature of 'oriental woman', the dangerous aspects of 'woman' when unveiled, of the feminisation of the orient, and as a questioning of gender identity and a postcolonial text. Wilde's play exemplifies the themes both of the fear of woman and the role of the orient as the locus for sexual 'perversion'.

Oscar Wilde was, being Irish, a colonial minority within English society, and he was moreover the son of a famous Irish nationalist poet.[5] As such, it could be argued that he, although for many years the highly acclaimed centre of English theatre and society, assimilated the hegemonic terminology of 'Englishness' in order to negate any sense of being an 'outsider'. Wilde himself, while seeming to be *within* the ethos of male Victorian values – which Elaine Showalter refers to as the misogynist world of 'clubland' (1992: 11) – was nevertheless famously denounced as foreign 'other' on the basis of his preferred sexuality.[6] Just as his creation Salomé was condemned as the 'Goddess of Decadence' (Showalter: 1992: 149), so Wilde was imprisoned for

3   *Stallholder Selling Spiced Delicacies at the Bazaar*, by Adolphe Bayot (1810–66).
While Victorian men saw the oriental woman as a symbol of mysterious
eroticism and inaccessibility, Victorian women found that their eastern
counterparts enjoyed greater freedom. The veil provided anonymity and
protection as well as access to outside the home. (Stapleton Collection,
UK/Bridgeman Art Library)

being the dangerously visible manifestation of the desire for the male body that lurked beneath the veils of socially acceptable woman.

Aubrey Beardsley's famous illustrations to Oscar Wilde's play *Salomé* include a picture entitled 'The Toilette of Salomé' (1893, 1967: facing 56). In this picture, a masked dwarf powders the face of Salomé. Both masks and the 'mask' of makeup are important Wildean symbols of Decadence, being as they are symbols of the absence of the natural and a celebration of the artificial.[7] At the end of the nineteenth century, the artistic and literary movements of Decadence and Aestheticism grew out of a reaction against the Romantic belief in nature and metaphysics. They emphasised the omnipresence of evil and the grotesque, and relied on extreme artifice, the anti-natural (including masks, cosmetics, hot-house orchids, green carnations – which became the closet symbol for homosexuality – peacocks, fans, and the male dandy), in an attempt to escape the human condition.[8]

To look beyond the artifice, to lift the veil, is – according to Freud – to risk a glimpse of death itself. As Showalter explains, 'The veiled woman who is dangerous to look upon also signifies the quest for the origins of life and death' (1992: 145).[9] This fear of going beyond was prevalent in Victorian England – as manifested in both misogyny and homophobia – and was represented by the 'otherness' of the orient, the heart of darkness that lurked in the vast expanse of the Empire, epitomised here by Salomé.

Salomé: a nineteenth-century veiled woman

Wilde's play *Salomé* can be read as a stereotyped portrayal of the orient as the female other (dangerous, seductive, erotic), or as a depiction of the orient as a locus for homosexual encounter. In either case, Wilde's exoticised depiction of the east subsumes his identification of the other as national as well as sexual. Since Wilde's identity was as colonised subject, it could be argued that he looked to the east (albeit a stereotyped east) as an alternate mode for the expression of a suppressed self. In this sense, to use the locale of the orient for the 'expression of self' is in itself a socially acceptable – although simultaneously subversive – way of 'unveiling' the colonial subject.

In Robert Ross's introduction to the play, he writes that 'Wilde used to say that *Salomé* was a mirror in which everyone could see himself.' To my mind, the key to interpreting Wilde's version of the story lies in a comment he wrote on Aubrey Beardsley's illustrations. In an inscribed copy of *Salomé*, Wilde claimed that apart from himself only Beardsley 'knows what the Dance of the Seven Veils is and can see that invisible dance' (Hart-Davis, 1962: 348n). Tantalisingly, critics do not seem to have penetrated what Wilde meant by this. Many critics have focused their attention on the homosexual, homophobic and sexually perverse aspects of the text, or on its autobiographical content. The suggestion that 'Wilde had in mind a more inward meaning ... Imagery of veiling and unveiling is frequent in Wilde's prose writings and it usually associated with some kind of spiritual exploration' (Worth, 1983: 66) points to a fascinating line of further study.

Showalter argues that the key to Wilde's ambiguous text lies in Aubrey Beardsley's illustrations.[10] For me, however, the most arresting portrayal of Salomé is not the Beardsley drawings, wonderfully evocative and provocative as they are, but the painting by Gustave Moreau, *L'Apparition*.[11] This painting shows the already unveiled, near-naked Salomé pointing at John the Baptist's decapitated head suspended in the air in a mystical blaze of golden light. Around the high-arched cavernous room of the otherworldly palace, the figures appear faint and ghostly, none of them looking in the direction of the head, suggesting that it is seen only by Salomé. John's eyes glare down accusingly at her. The picture raises the question, is it a representation of Salomé's inner lust and desire for vengeance, or is it the vision of a disembodied desire for something spiritual, beyond the body? This interpretation would be more in line with Worth's analysis, and Ross's comment, mentioned above.

Wilde wrote the play in French, within the contextual framework of the movement of French Decadent literature and symbolist theatre. He never saw the play performed, however, as it was banned by the London Lord Chamberlain on the basis that it represented a biblical topic.[12] By the time the play received its first performance, Wilde was in prison. Since then, it has become a favourite play, with a wide range of interpretations from Russian Formalist versions to Lindsay Kemp's transvestite staging in 1977. Performances of the play have remained controversial up to the present time.[13] A comparison could be made here to Charles Dickens' Gothic short story 'The Black Veil', in which a doctor fears that a veiled woman client may in fact be a man in disguise. Hence, the 'woman behind the veil' may still turn out to be 'the man in the mask'. (In the 1977 Lindsay Kemp production of *Salomé*, the dance of the seven veils *did* reveal *Salomé* to be a man in drag.)

Wilde might have approved of Jean Baudrillard's comments on seduction, that 'the strength of the feminine is in seduction ... the feminine is not what opposes the masculine, but what seduces the masculine' (1990: 7). Salomé, with her seductive dance of the seven veils and her lust after John the Baptist, is in many ways the triumph of the female over conventional patriarchal structure. The beheading of John, the result of her seduction of Herod, arguably represents 'mastery over the symbolic universe, while [masculine] power represents only mastery of the real universe' (Baudrillard, 1990: 8). The fear of unveiling, and what it might reveal, is represented in Salomé's dance of the seven veils, the archetypal representation of these destructive forces, and a symbol of woman's greed, cruelty, and lust.

The play opens with the discussion of three male sentries, one of them a young Syrian, standing on a balcony overlooking the hall of Herod's palace.[14] They compare the beauty of Salomé to the moon, but the metaphor is immediately distorted into more evil connotations. She is like 'a woman rising from the tomb' (obviously a foreshadowing of Jokanaan's [John the Baptist] entry), a 'dead woman' and a vampire 'looking for dead things'. The normal world is already defamiliarised. Salomé has 'a strange look'; she is like 'a little princess who wears a yellow veil', a 'princess who has little white doves for feet', she is 'like a woman who is dead' (1–2). As the Young Syrian continues to gaze at Salomé, another sentry, the Page of Herodias, warns him of the dangers of his fascination: 'You are always looking at her. You look at her too much. It is dangerous to look at people in such fashion. Something terrible might happen' (3).

This concept of the danger of looking at Salomé is repeated throughout the play. According to a Freudian psychoanalytic interpretation, the gaze is linked with the ability of woman to castrate, with the eye as source of castration (Freud, 1962: 18). The terror of Medusa arises from this fear of castration. Medusa with her snakehair can kill at a glance; she represents the *vagina dentata*, and therefore reflects male terror of castration/decapitation. For men to look at the head of Medusa, to unveil her gaze, is to confront the dread of looking at 'Nature' as an unveiled woman. Salomé, however, does not usurp the masculine ownership of the gaze until her encounter with Jokanaan. Until then, she is particularly aware of the discomfort of being the object of the gaze. (Aubrey Beardsley's illustration 'The Climax' captures an image of Salomé with wild snaky hair resembling Medusa.)

It is Jokanaan's strange voice emerging from the depths of his prison (representing the underworld/unconscious), not his gaze, that arouses and corrupts Salomé into womanhood.[15] She persuades the infatuated Young Syrian to bring the prophet out of the dark cistern, so that she may see him. Beginning to realise her own power, and playing upon the tantalising combination of secrecy and exposure, she promises that: 'I will look at thee through the muslin veils, I will look at thee, Narraboth, and maybe I will smile at thee' (16). When she at last sees Jokanaan, her transformation to *femme fatale* is complete. Yet if Salomé is the 'symbolic incarnation of undying Lust, the Goddess of immortal Hysteria' and so on (Huysmans, 1884, 1959),[16] then Jokanaan is the embodiment of misogyny and homosexual loathing of women – to the extent that they are the direct cause of his death (Knox, 1994: 34).

As Salomé gazes at him, remarking 'Ah, but he is terrible, he is terrible!' (19), she reverses not only the male power inherent in the gaze, but also the experience of terror embedded within that power. The more Jokanaan tries to repel Salomé, the more she is fascinated by him, until he cries 'Daughter of Sodom, come not near me! But cover thy face with a veil, and scatter ashes upon thine head' (21). But by now, Salomé is irrepressible:

> I am amorous of thy body, Jokanaan! Thy body is white, like the lilies of a field that the mower hath never mowed. Thy body is white like the snows that lie on the mountains of Judea ... There is nothing in the world so white as thy body. Suffer me to touch thy body. (22)

Jokanaan attempts to repulse her, referring to his body as 'the temple of the Lord God' (23); he is the sacred male who refuses to be violated by woman. But the incantatory nature of Salomé's speech makes her seem like a woman in an orgasmic trance, so powerful is her absorption in her desire for Jokanaan. She continues to desire his hair, and then his mouth. 'There is nothing in the world so red as thy mouth ... Suffer me to kiss your mouth' (24). Although cursed again and again by Jokanaan, the vampire-like Salomé is determined that 'I will kiss thy mouth, Jokanaan' (26).

Herod and Herodias appear and comment on unnatural events in nature – Herod hears 'the beating of vast wings' in the sky (31) and the moon ominously turns 'as red as blood' (53). Herod then demands that Salomé dance.[17] It is Salomé's progressive and erotic unveiling, the famous dance of the seven veils, that symbolises the danger and unnaturalness of women's assertion of sexual power. Salomé, like Sybil Vane in *The Picture of Dorian Gray*, is casting aside the layers of false identity that are projected onto woman by patriarchy.[18] If, as Dijkstra proposes, Salomé is Everywoman, then the dance can be taken to represent a symbolic unveiling of woman. (However unpopular the idea of an 'essence' of woman may be today, one cannot ignore that for Wilde, the concepts of surface/depth, and essence/artifice were central in the new ideas evolving in Aestheticism and Decadence.)

Masks, veils, and mirrors are all-important here, and are dwelt on at length in Wilde's essays 'The Truth of Masks' and 'The Decay of Lying', which celebrate art for rejecting truths and faces in favour of lies and masks (Ellman in Freedman, 1996: 29). For the Aesthetic movement, surface was everything: Salomé's unveiling both revealed everything and nothing. The veil represents Art: it is artifice, the play of surface, the 'illusion' of truth and beauty. Art is not a mirror of nature, since, as Richard Ellman explains, it 'never expresses anything but itself; 'it is "a mist of words", "a veil"' (Ellman in Freedman, 1996: 30). As Wilde writes, 'In art there is no such thing as a universal truth. A truth in art is that whose contradiction is also true ... The truths of metaphysics are the truths of masks' (1948: 1016–17). Thus the dance of the seven veils reveals neither the 'essence' of woman nor metaphysical truth, while at the same time being shocking and perverse in physically revealing 'everything'. Yet, since contradictions are also true, the concept of 'essence' seems clearly part of what Wilde meant by the 'invisible dance' of the seven veils. As mentioned earlier, Salomé's unveiling has also been described as:

> an appropriate image for the activity which Wilde regarded as the artist's primary duty: self-expression and self-revelation. In performing the dance of the seven veils, Salomé is then perhaps offering not just a view of the naked body but of the soul or innermost being. (Worth, 1983: 67)

Just as the artist (and as a dancer, Salomé is an artist)[19] is a prototype rather than an exception – since, according to Wilde we are all insincere, masked and lying – *she* rather than Jokanaan is the real martyr of the play. Only she is prepared to go beyond the masks to 'unveil' the real Salomé.[20]

The dance of the seven veils can be interpreted both for its socio-historical as well as sexual/symbolic import. As previously mentioned, the opening of the play emphasises that Salomé is a virgin, and compares her to the moon. As Showalter points out, the association of the veil with women was originally related to female sexuality and the veil of the hymen (1992: 145).[21] If this is so, then the 'unveiling' of Salomé in her dance is also symbolic of her ritual deflowering and entry into sexually-experienced womanhood. Since she performs this dance in her state of 'frustrated deflowering' (after being rejected by Jokanaan), the dance becomes auto-erogenous. While critics have pointed out the significance of the beheading as a substitute for her deflowering, her unveiling carries similar symbolic import. Salomé's dance is sexual and macabre at the same time, since 'her dance is delirium inspiring, and causes the unleashing of evil' (Kabbani, 1994: 68). The dance of the seven veils can also be seen as a dance of gender, in which Salomé breaks down the barriers between male and female through the permeability of the veil, which separates 'masculine from feminine, licit from illicit desire' (Showalter, 1992: 152).

Wilde unfortunately left few directions as to how the dance should be staged (Tydeman and Price, 1996: 138). Yet what is clear in the imagery of a young girl unveiling, is the gradual revelation of both her physical body and her 'inner nature' as woman. Wilde as well as his audience might well have been familiar with the famous work *Isis Unveiled* by H.P. Blavatsky (1877, 1976), in which the author explains how the illusory nature of the world covers the reality beneath. Above the temple of Isis the inscription reads, 'I am all that is, that was, and all that will be, and no mortal has lifted my veil.' Hence, perhaps the shocking nature of the unveiling of earthly woman.

Salomé's dance is also her *rite de passage* from childhood into woman – one explanation of Herod's horror at Salomé's independence and failure to imbibe the required notions of patriarchy into her conception of self and morality. For the Victorians, her unveiling, representing as it does both moral and sexual rebellion, would have been shocking. Victorian dress, especially for women, was rigidly conservative, restrictive and all covering: if women were not already trapped inside their homes (or attics) they certainly were trapped in their clothing. For Salomé to disrobe would have been a violation of a strict Victorian taboo: and a feat worthy of a female Houdini for the average Victorian woman to achieve unaided.[22]

After she has delighted Herod with her dance (and presumably the sight of her exposed body) Salomé asks for the head of Jokanaan upon a silver charger (55). Horrified, Herod attempts to make her change her mind, but she persists, asking not for her mother, but for her own pleasure. Herod blames her beauty for his own weakness:

> I have looked at thee over much. Nay, but I will look at thee no more. One should not look at anything. Neither at things, nor at people should one look. Only in mirrors is it well to look, for mirrors do but show us masks. (58)

Masks for Wilde, as already mentioned, are the 'truth' of metaphysics. Similarly, in Freudian theory, the mirror reflects back the male subject, the legitimate owner of truth. (In the illustration by Beardsley 'The Dancer's Reward' when Salomé looks at the severed head of Jokanaan, she is looking at her own mirror image.)

Salomé remains unflinching in her desire for Jokanaan's head, and finally it is brought to her. Her enraptured speech as she grasps his head and kisses it has been interpreted variously in terms of lesbianism (seeing her as an example of the Victorian New Woman),[23] Freudianism (decapitation as castration), and women's 'bestial' predatory nature.

Dancing on blood, she kisses the severed head in an erotic and ecstatic state of arousal. At last she is able to satisfy her frustrated lust for Jokanaan:

> Ah! I have kissed thy mouth, Jokanaan, I have kissed thy mouth. There was a bitter taste on thy lips. Was it the taste of blood? ... Nay; but perchance it was the taste of love ... They say that love hath a bitter taste ... But what matter? What matter? I have kissed thy mouth, Jokanaan, I have kissed thy mouth. (66, ellipses in original)

Herod realises his mistake and his repulsion at the scene overwhelms him. He yields to Salomé's sexuality, but the play ends with Herod's brutally ordering her execution. For Herod, the power and enjoyment of the voyeuristic male gaze have reached their limits. He calls for the torches to be extinguished, for 'I will not look at things, I will not suffer things to look at me. Put out the torches! Hide the moon! Hide the stars!' (66). Salomé's dance has the effect of undermining both Herod's power and the natural order of the universe. When she finally kisses the head, she violates the forces of patriarchal power of both Jokanaan and Herod, and thus undermines both spiritual and political authority. Since Jokanaan represents the power of the male 'intellect' celebrated as the antidote to dangerous female 'emotion' (as epitomised in the Perseus–Medusa conquest, or the Apolonious–Lamia defeat) in order for Salomé to defeat Jokanaan symbolically, she must have his head, the seat of the intellect.

In a final act of retribution, Herod orders: 'Kill that woman!' (67). The stage direction indicates, 'The soldiers rush forward and crush beneath their shields Salomé, daughter of Herodias, Princess of Judaea.' In Herod's act of brutality, the restoration of patriarchal authority (which had been usurped when Salomé danced) is achieved. He is crushing not only the usurpation of his power but also the 'instinctual life process' which Salomé represents: the essentially female power, which men deny, repress and envy. Salomé's 'crime' therefore was not only in her macabre choice of gifts, but in her unveiling of her feminine power.[24]

Ultimately, Salomé has to be 'redefined', re-veiled through the iron mask of the soldiers' shields. Fascinatingly in this context, the word for 'veil' in Arabic derives from the word 'to conceal or render invisible by use of a shield' (see Almunajjed, 1997: 47). The fact that Salomé is *crushed* beneath the shields is significant, indicating the need to stamp out her crime of gross insubordination, the upsurge of female power gone out of control. At the end of the play, Salomé's execution redresses the balance in nature, and returns man to his position of imperial dominance. Dijkstra concludes that with Herod's cry 'Kill that woman' we witness a more tortuous process of

> turn-of-the-century culture completing its long, fantastic, ritualistic indictment of woman for crimes she never planned, for outrages she committed in the skittish, nerve-wracked minds of economically ever more marginalised men. Salomé's hunger for the Baptist's head thus proved to be a mere pretext for these men's need to find the source of all the wrongs they thought were being done to them. Salomé, the evil woman, became their favourite scapegoat. (1986: 398)

Patriarchy, as represented by Herod and Jokanaan, both fears and denies Salomé's identity, as it is unveiled/revealed, whether taken in a literal 'individual' or 'essential' sense. Whether it is Salomé's daring to express her individuality through her sexual rebellion that is a threat to society, or her exposure of the 'essential nature' of woman as predatory vampire, either way she cannot be tolerated and has to be destroyed.[25] The very last words of the script – 'Princess of Judaea' – reiterate (at least for the reader) that Salomé is 'oriental', originating in the Middle East. The Victorian audience would have been conscious of Salomé being the exotic 'other' and, moreover, Jewish. This would have combined with the fear already lively in Victorian male minds of the 'oriental woman' (a feature played upon in many representations in art).

As Kabbani summarises, the turn-of-the-nineteenth-century attitudes towards the 'east', had become 'the seraglio of the imagination disclosing itself, with its veiled women, its blind musicians, its black eunuchs and jealous princes; it is the impossible other, the bourgeois drawing room's secret foil' (1994: 78). How far this 'myth' of the orient with the veiled woman as its central trope is cross-cultural (and therefore to some extent transhistorical) and perpetuated into the twentieth century and in the Middle East will be my next focus.

INDIA

The imagery of the 'mysterious veiled woman' as a trope for the east pervades discourse in Indian as well as Middle Eastern contexts (as exemplified in writers as diverse as Richard Burton and, as I shall discuss shortly, Hilary Mantel). Critics such as Sara Suleri and Sunder Rajan place 'third world woman' at the centre of discourse on colonial India. Edward Said makes explicit how the colonialist cultural, temporal and geographical distance is expressed in metaphors such as the inscrutability of the veiled eastern bride. At the heart of Anglo-Indian colonialist discourse was the subaltern women's ornamented but veiled body, a site of colonial rivalry and desire.

Representations of the eastern woman depict her exotic allure bound up inextricably with the western fear of the savage nature of the east, inherent within the west's 'orientalist' vision. The orient suggests 'not only fecundity but sexual promise (and threat), untiring sensuality, unlimited desire' (Said: 1979). In *Imperial Fictions* (her gender-orientated reading of Said's *Orientalism*) Rana Kabbani explicates how the 'east' was both a place of 'lascivious sexuality' and a realm characterised by inherent violence (1994).

To illustrate the attitudes of Empire at the turn of the century, Rudyard Kipling wrote his extraordinary story 'Beyond the Pale' (1900), which depicts the east as erotic, mysterious and violent. The figure of the colonised woman in this story is suitably confined in purdah and yet accessible to the desires of the western man. The story opens with the narrator's warning, 'A man should, whatever happens, keep to his own caste, race and breed. This is the story of a man who wilfully stepped beyond the safe limits of decent everyday society and paid for it heavily' (171).

Exposing the colonial British fear of miscegenation, these lines introduce the reader to the story of Trejago (a European), who is lured by a woman's singing to embark upon a clandestine love affair with a local Indian girl. He in fact pays lightly, compared with the woman with whom he associates, who suffers a terrible fate. The young woman, Bisesa, lives in purdah behind a screened lattice window in the Muslim quarter of town and epitomises 'oriental passion' (176). Trejago continues to have relationships with more suitable western women, so that Bisesa becomes jealous and Trejago neglects her for some time. When he finally returns to her alley, she appears at the window, thrusting out her arms to show him the stumps left after her hands have been severed. Trejago is slightly wounded in the ensuing scuffle, but although he tries to return, he never finds her house again. He loses her in the city 'where each man's house is as guarded and unknowable as the grave' (178). He never discovers why the violence happened; it is as mysterious and brutal as the east itself.

Ultimately 'walled up alive' in her uncle's house, Bisesa comes to represent the colonial territory as a 'heart of darkness': the terrifying yet obscure power at the core of both woman and orient. Trejago's penetration of the forbidden space of both the Indian home and Bisesa's body is equivalent to the violation of the lair of She in Rider Haggard's eponymous novel, or the 'rapine' that Said associates with all imperialist domination of alien lands (Said, 1994: 267). Not surprisingly, the chief victim of the story of illicit east–west liaison is the Indian woman.

Bisesa's ghastly maiming has been linked with her uncle's intent to castrate Trejago – again associating women's sexuality with man's fear of castration. In being both Indian and female, Bisesa is 'doubly other' and, in this doubleness, she represents the point at which two parallel discourses – one masculinist and the other orientalist – meet. In Kipling both Indian and English women are 'othered', since they distract men from their great work as administrators of Empire.[26] The Indian women in particular '[present] the direst possible threat to the homosocial solidarity' of the imperial men (McBratney, 1988: 54). These women must be 'shifted to the periphery of men's vision' – a conclusion suggesting Kipling's approbation of Bisesa's fate of perpetual purdah, and subtle, if culturally naive, endorsement of the practice of veiling.

Kipling's orientalist approach to India is further illuminated by referring to Homi Bhabha's formulation of the stereotype. The stereotype is 'a form of multiple and contradictory belief [that] gives knowledge of difference and simultaneously disavows or masks it' (Bhabha, 1994: 77). For example, as one of the main 'stereotypes' of the east, the veil acts as a repeated fetishistic image of otherness, and could be argued to be a projection of western superiority. Here, like an infinitely deferred signified, the veiled woman as stereotype depends on 'a continual and repetitive chain of other stereotypes' in a process of 'metaphoric masking', where the 'image' is identity and is always threatened by a lack. Although Bhabha uses this concept within the confines of colonial discourse, we must acknowledge the collusion between racism and sexism, the similarities between colonial and phallocentric discourse, and not restrict the 'stereotype' within the boundaries of colonialism.

Yet how far has the stereotypical imagery surrounding 'veiled woman' changed since India gained its independence? Harking back to the traditional and often romanticised past, a most telling 'orientalist' description of veiled woman from the recent past is that of Paul Scott:

The writer encountered a Muslim woman once in a corner street of a predominantly Hindu town, in the quarter inhabited by moneylenders. The feeling he had was that she was coming in search of a loan. She wore the *burkha*, that unhygienic head-to-toe covering that turns a woman into a walking symbol of inefficient refuse collection and leaves you without even an impression of her eyes behind the slits she watches the gay world through, tempted but not tempting; a garment in all probability inflaming to her passions but chilling to her expectations of having them satisfied. Pity for her the titillation she must suffer. (1968: 9)

Said sees 'the will to sexualise' as one manifestation of the anxiety of Empire, arguing that the issues of race, class and gender were conflagrated in the orientalist language of imperialism. Here, Scott maintains a firmly Eurocentric 'imperialist' viewpoint. He reiterates national stereotypes: the downtrodden and fraudulent Semite in need of money; the Indian colonial subject associated with dirt and lack of hygiene. What kind of misogynist mind, one can only ask, equates any woman with 'inefficient refuse collection'? The woman is moreover immediately portrayed as a sexually frustrated being – a state being somehow compounded by the asexual nature of her dress. Presupposing the sensual nature of oriental woman, Scott fails to ascribe any identity beyond that of a highly-sexed female body. He maintains the imagery of the exotic east as opulent and luxurious – a realm to be plundered – while projecting onto her blank figure both a character and a history of his own imagining: 'she had a rebellious spirit ... on the other hand she may merely have been submissive to her husband, drenching herself for his private delight with a scent she did not realise was also one of public invitation' (Scott, 1968: 9). While the narrator initially refutes the attractions of the woman, associating her with 'refuse', he now repeats the orientalist and sexist notion of the hidden treasure of the harem being for a sole man's delight. He envisages violating that sanctity, supposing that a woman's wearing of perfume (which, strangely, he is able to identify as Chanel No 5) constitutes a 'public invitation' to other men (presumably himself). It is useful to compare these twentieth-century attitudes with those in the eighteenth century in which:

> [Indian] woman's greatest defects lay in the defining weaknesses of her moral nature: a tendency to wasteful expenditure and a love of profligate spending and luxury, an innate carnal promiscuity trembling ever close to the surface, a sexual nature that allied her to barbarians and colonial natives and other lower species. (Bhattacharya, 1998: 16)

In the Scott passage quoted above, the author finds nothing amiss in his scopophillic harassment of the Muslim woman, his insult in debasing her religion, nor in the contradiction inherent in his attitude, first finding her 'not tempting' and then luxuriating in the forbidden spectacle of her sexual availability. As Bhattacharya suggests, Indian women 'both aroused and frustrated desire because they suggested a splendour that was mostly veiled, segregated, physically circum-scribed and confined, inaccessible' (1998: 17).

Islam in general has long been targeted by the west's 'inferiorising gaze' for its degrading treatment of women. Much western condemnation of the Islamic world of women remains the same while fashions themselves change over time: when western women were 'civilised' Victorians because they covered up, exposure was deemed 'uncivilised'. (Missionaries throughout the twentieth century regarded part of their civilising mission to cover up scantily-dressed women, particularly to conceal the barbarity of naked breasts.) Today, the covered veiled woman has replaced the exposed woman as the signifier of the 'other', indicating western woman's superiority (Bulbeck, 1998).

This contemporary notion is often cited by Arab and Asian feminists as indicative of western feminists' myopic cultural bias. This unfortunate attitude is demonstrated in the American feminist Kate Millet's account of when she visited Iran in 1979. The sight of the veiled Iranian women at the airport horrified her:

> The first sight of them was terrible. Like black birds, like death, like fate, like everything alien. Foreign, dangerous, unfriendly. There were hundreds of them, spectres crowding the barrier, waiting their own. A sea of chadori, the long terrible veil, the full length of it, like a dress descending to the floor, ancient, powerful, annihilating us. (1982: 49)

Nothing, it seems, could be further from a vision of 'feminist sisterhood' than this threatening imagery of alienation and danger. Millet's description of the veiled Iranian women locates the veil in a time and space of 'radical otherness'. It provides a striking example of the paranoid Islamophobia rife in the United States, which, if anything, has increased in strength since the time of Millet's comments and is more than ever influential in determining American foreign policy and in forming domestic attitudes towards Muslims.

FICTIONAL INTERPRETATIONS OF THE ISLAMIC WORLD: AN 'ENGLISH PERSPECTIVE'

Fiction is often valuable in its exploration of cultural attitudes. Hilary Mantel's 1997 novel *Eight Months on Ghazzah Street* provides a fascinating view of the culture of Saudi Arabia from a 'foreigner's' perspective. (Mantel herself lived in Saudi Arabia for four years.) The novel deals with the conflicts experienced by the British overseas, highlighting cultural clashes of ethics and understanding, and the problems of cultural impenetrability. Described in review as 'a Middle Eastern *Turn of the Screw*', the novel deals with a tale of 'disorientation and discovery', depicting the terror and secrecy apparently rife in Saudi society. Mantel's fictional rendering leaves the reader to judge the validity of the sinister view of society. The novel culminates with the female protagonist questioning the very nature of reality. Throughout, the veil is a central motif in the protagonist's search for the truth, in her attempt to fathom the Arab women that she meets, and it is also a symbol of the covering of reality by illusion, dream, or fantasy.[27]

The story relates the devastating psychological impact of life in Jeddah on the young English wife, Frances Shore, who has joined her husband, a consultant for a Saudi construction company. As ex-patriots, they are warned against disturbing the status quo of their host society and their lives are lived within a sealed vacuum of the dark, cold silence of their apartment. The novel opens with the (English) company's list of rules circumscribing behaviour, which immediately throws the reader into this polarised world through hints of sinister events, such as that referred to in 'Point B: "Refrain from public speculation about the recent deaths – remember that the matter is still under investigation by the Saudi police and Her Majesty's representatives"' (11).

In response to their sense of cultural alienation, the foreigners indulge in meaningless dinner parties and brewing illicit alcohol in the bathroom: maintaining the behaviour of life in the homeland, although some aspects of it (brewing and consuming alcohol) are illegal. From an orientalist point of view, they plunder the resources of the country (by accepting high salaries) while unwilling to understand, appreciate or fit into the country they are exploiting. In fact, many of the English characters in the novel, Andrew's boss, Eric Parsons, for example, openly deplore Saudi Arabia and mock its people, while still fearing them. This sense of moral superiority and lack of inclination to expend any energy in trying to understand the 'worthless alterity' of the foreigner exemplify Abdul JanMohamed's definition of Manicheanism, in which 'the world at the boundaries of civilisation' is perceived as 'uncontrollable, chaotic, unattainable and ultimately evil' (in Ashcroft et al., 1995: 18–19).

Unlike her husband and his male colleagues, Frances attempts to get to know and understand the culture – initially through her neighbours, two other wives: Samira, a Saudi, and Yasmin, a Pakistani. Yasmin in fact summarises the English attitude: 'It is the mentality of the West, to discredit the Eastern people', and Frances initially responds by defending a world view that she blindly holds as superior and insuperable. Frances finds herself debating cultural issues from a polarised perspective, unlike her former liberal viewpoint in England. Together with her husband, Andrew, she is bemused by the paradoxes and contradictions in the Saudi mentality: 'the Saudis hate the Americans. Because they support Zionism. They've banned

Ford cars. They've banned Coca-Cola. They'll just have weaponry, thank you' (73).

As weeks of boredom pass, Frances suspects clandestine, if not illegal, activities in the empty apartment above theirs. Her suspicions, pieced together through disparate clues, however lack the basis of a motive. She knows that 'something is wrong', but without understanding the culture, is unable to fit the pieces of the puzzle together – the noises overhead in an officially empty apartment, the unnecessary redecoration of the building, and, above all, the appearance of a crate, 'just big enough for a man if he didn't mind some pain' (217) on the balcony of the empty apartment.

As the evidence for a terrible conspiracy and crime builds up, Frances prides herself on her powers of perception. Yet her 'western' analytical form of intelligence fails her, as she is unable to see beneath the facade of appearances. The crate on the balcony moves, scraping a track through the mud and dust, but there are no visible footprints – it can only have moved, as Frances points out, 'if someone is inside it' (221). But in response to her worries, Andrew complains, 'You don't seem to have grasped ... even the fundamentals about living in this place' (224). While warning her against looking into things too deeply, he assumes her anxieties arise from ill-health, from being 'overwrought' and lonely, and urges her to spend more time with the other ex-patriot wives in the only activity open to them – shopping.

In Frances's attempt to understand her women neighbours, and in her search for illumination, the symbol of the veil is central. She realises that Yasmin, whom she had first thought of as liberal, is 'really a fundamentalist'. Yasmin explains to Frances that veiling is 'the essence of Islam' (229):

> Many Muslim women are doing this [veiling]. Once they thought it was a great thing to get rid of the veil, but now they are not so sure. They see how men exploit them. They want to have their dignity back. (208)

Here, the veil is firmly linked to women reclaiming 'dignity' and agency in defiance of male exploitation. This positive attitude towards veiling is similar to the pro-veil stance expressed by women in pre-Revolutionary Iran, in which the *chador* could be a tool for reasserting a woman's human dignity by forcing people to respond to her talents and personality rather than her body. Ironically, Frances also lacks such a response from her husband; he ignores her needs and her intelligence and ridicules her perceptions.

Frances soon makes the connection between veiling as an obfuscation of the real with concealment as 'the essence of Islam' (a concept discussed in the previous section). She also begins to appreciate how her 'western gaze' predisposes her to conceptualisations alien to the Arab world. 'You see,' one of Yasmin's friends explains, 'everything that you hold self-evident ... that democracy is good, that liberalism is good in itself ... we have never taken these ideas as naturally true' (229). Asian feminists have similarly criticised generalisations made by western feminists about 'women', 'patriarchy' and 'democracy', concepts that cannot be applied universally or cross-culturally (Mohanty et al., 1991: 51–80).

Frances's suspicions are confirmed when she encounters someone in a black *abaya* coming out of the 'empty' apartment. Challenging the covered figure, Frances grabs at the concealing *abaya*, and feels something cold and metallic under her hand. She reaches up with her other hand, and claws at the veil: 'But a veil is not something you can pull off. You can dream of doing it, but you cannot just accomplish it' (234). The figure pushes past her, and Frances is left feeling the imprint of the gun on her hand like an 'invisible stigmata'. She now has proof: the veil is disguising something tangible – an armed man. Yet Frances is unable to voice her discovery to anyone else, even her husband. She dreams of 'unveiling the truth' but she cannot accomplish it. She feels that her knowledge and experience have placed her out of a normal dimension of existence.

The theme that the veil (and the smothering of women that it represents) cannot be easily removed pervades the rest of the novel. Frances is a qualified cartographer and the text's frequent references to maps and disorientation mirror the veil's symbolism: 'She had stepped into a parallel world whose existence she had suspected for so long, and she could not say, now, I have lost my map, and I did not mean to trespass, I will never do it again.' As the boundaries of her world shift, she admits to Andrew that she has lost her bearings, but that 'She has been looking at the external city; but the internal city is more important, the one that you construct inside your head' (243).

Frances's experience henceforward significantly duplicates that of veiled third world woman, whose existence is always at the periphery of society – thus destabilising the normative east/west binary. Forced to the margins of discourse by her husband, and the margins of society by being both female and foreign, Frances is in a similar position to marginalised Arab women who must write themselves not merely into history (as Fanon urges colonised subjects to do) but into society. Fighting both to maintain and to express her identity, Frances is comparable to the Arab women struggling to avoid the annihilation of their identity who write themselves 'out of prison' through a 'multiple translation of the darkness' (Faqir, 1998: 22). According to the Egyptian novelist Salwa Bakr, many women who fall victim to the 'political illusions' propagated by men end up with psychological problems: they drift towards madness, attempt suicide or, 'in cases of extreme retreat ... put on the veil and hide behind the doors of their homes' (in Faqir, 1998: 37). In this novel, Frances's reaction to the 'illusions' of Saudi culture is to comprise exactly these reactions, either literally or symbolically.

The comparison is corroborated by an episode in the novel when a colleague is found mysteriously dead, and Frances must visit the hospital to identify the body. Once outside, she 'took a cotton scarf out of her pocket and slowly shook it out. "My hair is full of dust. I should have done this before." She folded the scarf into a triangle and flipped it over her head' (292). This symbolic covering of her head paradoxically comes at the moment of her greatest revelation. It represents, perhaps, her own desperate reclaiming of human dignity, an affirmation of knowledge even as she faces dissolution:

> She would never know more than she knew now; would never know, for instance, the name of the man who had been crated up alive. What had he done? What had he known? ... But what's one body more or less? Life is cheap enough. (292)

When Yasmin, the Pakistani neighbour, is arrested at the airport trying to leave the country without her husband (which is illegal), Frances feels utterly powerless to help, and suspects all her neighbours of being involved in the conspiracy. She falls into a state of 'willed annihilation', a state that at the end of the novel verges on a complete mental breakdown. Dream merges with reality and the reader is left to question how much has been in her mind all along. The prose in the final chapter changes to first person narrator present tense, in which no past or future exists, where 'the present moment draws itself out for ever' (299). For women, time and space are mutually dependent spheres of reality. Women traditionally do not control physical or social space directly, so that an exclusion from physical space can also affect perceptions of time (Ardener, 1997: 6). Once

Frances's identity is lost, she becomes a migrant in time as well as space. Even her sense of identity is threatened. In the heat, she feels 'I seem to flicker, I am whited out.' Catching sight of her reflection in the patio door, she describes how, 'My face is black, deeply shadowed, with empty eyes, and a pale ragged aureole encircles my head. I have become the negative of myself' (299).

European (and some Arab) feminists argue that it is patriarchy itself that demands such a negation of the woman's self. According to Luce Irigaray, woman is always seen as a lack, an absence, a default (1977). Women are enclosed behind the mirror, behind the image, that can only reflect back an empty identity: the very image that Frances sees of herself in the above quote. Woman is invisible: merely the back (the *tain*) of the mirror in which man views himself as the 'same', so that woman is always the 'other'. Irigaray claims that patriarchal discourse situates women outside representation, she is absence, negativity. Frances sees in her reflection the 'negative of herself'. Women remain devalued as inferior versions of the male subject, *imprisoned* in the male ocular world as mere objects because they are un-representable and silent.[28] Similarly, in the Islamic world, women are constantly reminded of their 'lack', 'incompleteness' and 'fragility', a cultural discourse that goes beyond controlling women to using them as a means of control for the whole society.

Veils thus, it could be argued, hide women and construct their total negation of self required by patriarchy. Yet veils also hide what women themselves are unwilling to see. Veils hide the 'real' through the 'ideal'; for women, perhaps the veiling of truth is a barrier to the responsibility inherent within knowledge. For Frances, removing the 'veils of mystery' to reveal the truth brings with it a loss of reason, and a breakdown of her marriage (she is alone at the end of the novel) as *all* life loses its sense of reality. Yet why does this have to be the conclusion to the story?

In western literature, madness has long been an escape for powerless women trapped within patriarchy.[29] In *Ghazzah Street*, Frances's husband, Andrew, is greatly to blame for her retreat from reality. Throughout, he makes her doubt her observations and above all her intuition, increasing her inability to communicate with him, along with her sense of insecurity and fear. When she attempts to confide in him, he laughs at her. Frances can only flippantly respond, 'I wish you could believe me. But if you can't, you can't. I'm only a woman after all' (246). Like other women seeking a space free from male domination, she resorts to writing – confiding her inner world in her journal, creating that 'internal city in the head ... that is subject to no planner's control' (243). It has been proposed that the power of the patriarchal order depends for its regeneration on a disconnection from women, and a process of dissociating women from what they intuitively know is 'right'. The process of inner division that has been inculcated in women 'makes it possible for a woman not to know what she knows, not to think what she thinks, and not to feel what she feels' (Gilligan, 1995: 123). These are not just problems faced by women but they are problems that face humanity. This dissociation, 'cuts through experience and memory, and when these cuts become part of cultural history, women lose the grounds of their experience and with it, their sense of reality'. Such a disconnection with caring leads 'people to abandon themselves and others: by not speaking, not listening, not knowing, not seeing, not caring, and ultimately not feeling by numbing themselves ... against the vibrations and resonances which characterise and connect the living world' (Gilligan, 1995: 125). Interestingly, in this novel, it is Frances who is the victim of this 'dehumanisation', not the physically veiled women of Arabia. She becomes metaphorically veiled, outmanoeuvred by both English and Saudi patriarchal rules of the game.

As an adjunct to this discussion, it is important to note that the influence of 'invisible veils' is a tangible reality in many cultures. While the western media/politicians locate restriction to women's freedom in the physical artefact of the veil, they may fail to appreciate that 'the purdah mentality' prevails even where veiling is absent. In countries where a greater trend of secularisation has occurred in the past decades, and the veil has been either discouraged or made illegal, such as Turkey, women are controlled by invisible boundaries and symbolic shields. New forms of discipline and self-control uphold moral and religious requirements for chastity and modest behaviour. Even within social frameworks of 'modernity', notions of family honour are maintained through the chastity of women. Anxieties over sexual morality mean that families still maintain control over potential marriages and perceived violations in the codes of monogamy are punished. Revenge killings, where a woman is perceived as having violated the strict ideals of sexual conduct, are tolerated if not endorsed by both regional and nation governments. The 'veil mentality' prevails without visible veils. In contrast, the 'new' veiling allows women greater freedom of movement in public, and ensures public respectability and social conformity.

A culture in which veiling is abolished (or at least in which the government adopts a pro-western stance) is not necessarily one in which 'liberal' 'western' attitudes prevail. In a recent biographical account by Norma Khouri, the young Jordanian author documents the type of familial morality that endorses and enacts revenge killings. *Forbidden Love* (2003) exposes how all women live in fear under the 'law' of the patriarchal members of the family, often living under the daily threat of possible violence and death. Honour killings are classified as an immoral act, not as a crime. The penal code condones the murders and protects the killers, since the laws allow men to kill any female relative even suspected of immoral behaviour. Such murders are perpetrated on the basis of suspicion or rumour or for financial reasons, in order to secure an inheritance for instance. Only a small percentage of honour crimes are reported, and fewer still ever come before the law: the murderers are treated as heroes for upholding family honour. Paradoxically, as women in countries such as Jordan gain more freedom, the numbers of such killings are on the increase.

A novel that deals with some of the repercussions of a forbidden liaison is James Buchan's *A Good Place to Die* (1999).[30] This novel also relates to a 'male perspective' on veiling. Buchan's insightful and well-researched text relates the love affair between a young Englishman teaching English in Iran in the 1970s and a beautiful girl who attends one of his classes. The girls are permitted to attend the language school since they are veiled, a situation that initially disallows communication – until John's eyes meet Shirin's. The fact that John does not see Shirin's face until some time later does not prevent him from falling in love with her, nor does it prevent their 'veiled words' from connoting their erotically-charged attraction and desires. Her invisibility is contrasted to John's visibility: on the streets of Isfahan he feels himself observed – especially by the unseen women – and vulnerable. He initially meets the unknown schoolgirl in an antique shop full of 'the relics of commerce of a differently oriented world' (13); the black-*chador*'ed Shirin herself is viewed as one of the artefacts of an exotic and remote civilisation. The erotic/exotic aspects of the culture are juxtaposed with the innocent and child-like. (As Shirin pulls the *chador* to cover her face, the hem rises to expose the white socks of her school uniform.) Her black eyes belie her innocence, however, and the girl beneath the *chador* is quickly transformed in John's mind to an adult aware of her power as a woman. Shirin 'took the cigarette [of hashish] in her thumb and fingers, gloved by her chador, and passed it to me ... Then she turned, and I felt cotton on my mouth, and through it her lips' (19). The shock of this physical contact is heightened since John has still not seen her face. When they momentarily meet in private and she allows him to kiss her, the episode is charged with the eroticism of 'the unknown' beneath the veil. He kneels to raise her *chador*, and the nudity of her face fills him with panic 'at its strangeness and unearthly pallor' (40). With her combination of helplessness and ruthless independence Shirin personifies, perhaps, both the state of Iranian culture before the fall of the Shah and the perceived personality of twentieth-century 'veiled woman': intelligent, brave, outspoken, and yet a victim of a society beyond her control. The scene above also involves numerous images of the veil, both literal and symbolic – most significantly John violates the protective veil that shields eastern woman from the imperial gaze, just as he penetrates too far beneath the veneer of cultured society.

Despite his initial orientalist attitude towards both the country and its people, the character of John is portrayed as being sympathetic to women and the cause of women's freedom – for which he ultimately risks his own life and liberty. John reads and recites a female Persian poet, he admires beautiful *objects d'art*, and works for hours in the shop 'on a tottering throne of carpets ... between the soft canyons, effeminate, luxurious and insecure' (17). His liberal and artistic personality soon comes into conflict with the traditionally patriarchal authorities of Shirin's father and her 'arranged' suitor, a major in the army. Once married and hiding from both Shirin's family and the law, John lives in a reversed purdah. While he must remain hidden in the house, Shirin is able to visit the market for food, to collect messages, and to listen out for news. She is safe only because of the covering of the *chador*, the modest clothing, that, as John perceives, also becomes a token to him of her femininity and inextricably associated with desire and its fulfilment:

> Certain words – *pushidegi* – covering, and by extension the mental attitudes in girls that are the effects or counterparts of veiling, such as ambiguity, inversion, concealment, intrigue or deceit; *eish*, meaning the delights of this worldly existence; *kamrani*, the attainment of a young man's desire – made maddening calligraphic shapes in my mind ... I thought: If we make it to the house, I am not going to stir from her bed for a year. (87)

When Shirin disappears, it is as if she vanishes back into the blackness of the *chador*, absorbed back into an impenetrable culture, one which John will literally be imprisoned in (as a spy) and yet metaphorically excluded from. The veils of the chador become the ubiquitous and impenetrable curtains blocking full cultural understanding or participation for the foreigner – despite a lifetime of learning and longing.

CONCLUSION

Both the contemporary novels discussed here conclude with the portrayal of the breakdown of the protagonist following their experience of contact with an Islamic culture. Frances Shore suffers a mental collapse, while John Pitt reflects at the end of *A Good Place to Die* that, 'I think my self is gone, and what remains is my frame and a promise I once made to a girl of this town' (340). Both characters suffer from this loss of self, a disintegration both mental and physical. Their attempted contact with the 'eastern' culture, despite good intentions to understand the 'other' and to befriend or love the 'veiled woman', ends in disaster. These representations of the veiled world of the Middle East, although written from different gendered viewpoints – by a female and male author respectively – largely replicate the disastrous attempts at cultural contact depicted a century earlier by Kipling (and to some extent by Forster). In Kipling's 'Beyond the Pale', the attempted love affair between Christian and Muslim ends in the mutilation of the woman and the misery and frustration of the man. Although written from a standpoint of greater cultural understanding and sympathy, James Buchan's novel follows a very similar plot, describing the devastating consequences of an inter-faith and inter-cultural sexual liaison – where, in this case, it is the European man who is tortured and mutilated (and possibly poisoned by gas during the Iran–Iraq war) as his punishment for daring to breech the cultural divide.

Veiled woman, as symbol of the desirability of eastern culture – the icon for which it is worth risking all – remains mysterious and obscure. Although in *A Good Place to Die* she is represented as the erotic and sentimental, ultimately she is the locus of the danger of the orient – an image that has prevailed in literature and the arts for over a century.

How far these representations are supported or negated by writers from the Middle East and India will be the subject of the next chapters. They will seek to investigate whether an analysis of Islamic writers, with presumably a radically divergent perspective, exposes the fallacies of these western viewpoints.

3
Revealing and Re-veiling: Egypt

Although the veiled woman remains a stereotyped image of patriarchal oppression in 'western eyes', the literature of the 'Middle Eastern' woman reveals contradictory and paradoxical symbolisms of the veil. While the veil itself cannot be universalised ideologically, the religious and cultural background of 'Muslim identity' provides a pivot around which 'western' concepts of the veil traditionally revolve.

The 'Middle East' has for centuries been a site of fascination for the European mind.[1] In the eighteenth and nineteenth centuries, the 'orient' was romanticised as the 'Holy Land' in a reductive vision that, paradoxically, stereotyped the region negatively as everything the west was not. From the Maghreb to Persia, oriental society was defined as a system of absences, which in turn perpetuated, as Said has argued, one of the deepest and most recurring images of 'the other'. As glimpsed in the previous chapter, while European influence in the region originated in economic interests, the myth of the orient developed though the work of eighteenth- and nineteenth-century writers, artists, and travellers, who flocked to the region. Writers as diverse as Robert Browning, George Eliot, Walter Scott, and Lord Byron, amongst others, produced a body of work that was to become the 'reality' of the orient in the English mind. By the end of the nineteenth century, British and French primacy in the area was assured, and with the break-up of the Ottoman Empire at the beginning of the twentieth century a new Middle East was carved out. New states were created that took no account of the natural demographic, ethnic, linguistic, and religious makeup of the territory (Milton-Edwards, 2000:20).[2]

Within the Middle East, several of the countries we know today only gained their independence and sovereignty after the end of the Second World War (countries such as Jordan and Lebanon having been 'invented' by the British and the French respectively after the First World War). When the First World War ended, Britain (and to a lesser extent France) remained firmly established as the dominant power in the Middle East, although the involvement of the British was 'an imperialism of interference without responsibility' (Lewis, 1994: 61). As the British gradually withdrew power (which happened alongside their loss of India), both America and the Soviet Union sought to extend their influence through various pacts and alliances. This foreign influence eventually backfired in a series of Arab revolutions, the first in Egypt in 1952, followed in 1958 with a strongly anti-western revolt in Iraq.

Gradually, in the eyes of the Arab world, the 'west' came to be regarded as the source of evil, particularly by those regimes that have been referred to by the misnomer of 'fundamentalist'. As Bernard Lewis explains,

> The protest of the so-called Muslim fundamentalists is not against liberal theology or scriptural criticism ... Their protest is directed against the entire process of change that has transformed a large part of the Muslim world during the last century or more, creating new structures and proclaiming new values. (1994: 118)

The links between orientalist discourse, the rise of imperial consciousness and attitudes that promoted the oppression of women as part of the patriarchal power motive, become particularly overt in examples of British imperialism in the Middle East. This chapter examines texts that highlight the situation of women within nationalist struggle against British rule as well as within contemporary patriarchal social structures. Fictional texts range from the work of the Egyptian Nobel Prize-winning author Naguib Mahfouz, to that of the controversial feminist writer Nawal El Saadawi and the recent historical novels of Ahdaf Soueif. These texts facilitate an explication of the historical, social, and cultural aspects of the veil from points of view as diverse as psychoanalysis, anthropology, and recent feminist debate.

THE VEIL AND NATIONALISM IN THE MIDDLE EAST

Woman's body is used in many cultures as a site and symbol of nationalist meaning. The links between the rise of feminism and nationalism in Egypt suggest how the veil has been both instrumental in and a symbol of the struggle towards both national identity and the emancipation of women. The struggles for women's emancipation were an essential and integral part of national resistance movements that appeared during the early twentieth century.

Social and cultural change in the early twentieth century in Egypt – including the rise of anti-imperialist nationalist movements – centred on the debate of pro/anti-veiling.[3]

Historically, Egypt was amongst the first countries in Africa and the Middle East to witness the rise of both nationalism and feminism. While these issues have been linked, mainly due to male nationalists subsuming the demands of women into a larger political struggle, it is important here not to confuse the anti-colonial struggle with that of feminist discourses. As early as the 1870s, Egyptian women were publishing their writing and openly debating their position in society. Men, many of whom had been educated in the west, soon took up their argument in relation to the nationalist cause – and the veil was central in their discourse. Early feminists (and some nationalists) located veiling as a barrier to women's advancement (El Guindi, 1999: 178; Al-Ali, 1994).

The first stirrings of nationalism in Egypt were amongst the educated elite, who formulated an anti-colonialist movement. In the nineteenth century, the early expressions of nationalism grew out of dissatisfaction with the ruling Turkish overlords, when ideas of democracy, modernity and nation began to be incorporated from the west. Many factors also aided the spread of nationalism, such as the revival of Arabic as a language of communication (as opposed to Turkish) and the availability of print technology, a feature crucial to the rise of the national consciousness (Anderson, 1983: 36). Just as the west had created an image of the orient through literature, music and the arts, so now the poets, writers and musicians of the Arab world 'imagined' a new national identity.

The birth of the modern Egyptian state came about in the early 1900s as a reaction against Egypt's colonisation by the British. Nationalism in almost all instances favours an overtly homosocial form of male bonding, and is based on 'a deep, horizontal comradeship … a fraternity' (Anderson, 1983: 7). Nationalism is itself a concept fraught with ambiguities. Not all nationalist leaders see modernisation as a sign of progress. The Islamic world, especially, frequently sees nationalism as a return to pre-colonial traditions, or even harks further back to the early days of the Prophet, a golden era of purity and piety. (This is linked with the desire to resist what are seen as alien and oppressive 'western' ideas.) Edward Said, speaking in the Egyptian *Alif: Journal of Comparative Poetics*, argues that the search for national models

> is for us the battle – the battle over what the modern is, and what the interpretation of the past is. There is a school of writers, poets, essayists, and intellectuals who are fighting a battle to be modern,

because our history is governed by *turath*, or heritage. But the question is, who designates what the heritage is. That is the problem. For us the crisis of 'modernism' and 'modernity' is a crisis over authority, and the right of the individual, and the writer, the thinker, to express himself of herself, for it is also the battle over women's rights. (in Ghazoul and Harlow, 1994: 270)

His significant last comment here locates Arab nationalism as fundamentally an expression of patriarchy.[4]

In Egypt, women were encouraged to support the nationalists' movement, but mainly as wives and mothers. Colonial and indigenous patriarchies often collaborated to keep women in their place.[5] Women, even in countries where they have taken a leading role in liberating the nation from its colonial oppressors (such as Egypt and Algeria), invariably are ignored or even more oppressed following liberation than under colonisation. Women were (and are) reminded that their struggle is secondary to the larger fight for national independence and freedom against colonial rule. Promises that their freedom would come after liberation from the imperial yoke are almost universally forgotten.

Despite women's involvement in the nationalist struggle, since the establishment of independence in Egypt, few women's voices have been heard until recently. Throughout the twentieth century, Arab women sought a terminology suited to express their activism. Significantly, Leila Ahmed (an American-Egyptian historian) has distinguished between what she sees as two strands of feminism in the Middle East: one affiliating itself with western models, and the other seeking to define a path of female subjectivity within the terms of the indigenous culture (1992: 174).[6] The re-emerging public discourse has been divided between the newly-veiled Islamist and the secular 'western-influenced' feminist, both of whom arouse suspicion and controversy. The new generation of Islamic women is seen as more outspoken and confrontational in the way they view women's role in an Islamic state. Since women are also perceived as the bearers of the 'authentic values' of the culture, 'westernised' feminists (associated with the also despised *nouveau riche*) meet with increasingly fierce opposition and criticism. Nadje Al-Ali argues that the new feminism (*nassawiyya*) in Egypt focuses its debates on distinguishing between specificity and universality in an atmosphere of suspicion of western-based research and attitudes. Both Islamist and leftist groups regard western discourse and imperialism as alien and suspect, and feminists

4   *Veiled Egyptian Woman*, by Emile Prisse d'Avennes (1807–79). While the veil came to be regarded as 'definitive' of Islamic women's identity, in Egypt the veil became symbolic of both nationalism and class status. Here, an elaborately decorated face mask (one example of those worn by women across the desert stretching from North Africa to the Gulf) articulates beauty as well as giving protection from the harsh climate. (Victoria and Albert Museum, London, UK/Bridgeman Art Library)

fighting for women's civil rights constantly find themselves under attack. Yet women are now widely regarded as the main democratising force in contemporary Egypt (Al-Ali, 1997: 184–5).

In the dynamic rise of the Islamic movement in the past 30 years (an example of when religion and nationalism are indivisible), the veil has played a crucial symbolic, political, and ritual role. While unveiling was hitherto a symbol of Egyptian nationalism, the new re-veiling is now both the symbol and practical emblem of the new Islamic movement, a trope that denotes both activism and resistance.

EXPRESSIONS OF NATIONALISM AND FEMINISM

Claiming a historical past that included great queens and pharaohs, such as Nefertiti, Hatchepsut and Cleopatra, Egypt was a fertile ground for the early (that is, mid-nineteenth-century) support of women's emancipation alongside a growing national consciousness. At the turn of the twentieth century, Egypt was at the forefront of the fight for women's rights along with the movement for nationalism and resistance to imperialism. The champions of women's rights were first and foremost male reformers who pioneered ideas of female equality. Early pioneers such as Qasim Amin argued that the veil and arranged marriages were un-Islamic. Amin's books *The Liberation of Women* (1899) and *The New Woman* (1901), in which he attacked the inferior position of women in Arab societies, have led to his being hailed by many as being the founder of feminism in the Arab world. While he urged for the unveiling of women, his contemporary Tal'at Harb responded with another version of female emancipation, one in which women must remain veiled. Their debate has been regarded by recent feminists as being but 'muddled versions of domesticity' through which 'in appropriating a women's issue, men polarised discourse surrounding the veil' (El Guindi, 1999: 175). This early debate on women's rights and the veiling issue is 'fictionalised' in *The Map of Love*, by Ahdaf Soueif, and is discussed later in this chapter.

Despite the initial male interest in women's emancipation, when the new constitution was drafted in 1924, politicians ignored the question of women's rights – although women had taken an active part in the recent (1919) anti-colonial demonstrations (Jayawardena, 1986: 52). By the early twentieth century, women in Egypt had also joined in the dialogue. In 1923, under the leadership of Huda Sharawi (who is best remembered for throwing her veil into the sea on her return from a conference on women's rights in Rome), a group of middle-class women formed the Egyptian Feminist Union, which was one of the most radical ever feminist movements in the world. However, despite the early nationalist and feminist debate in Egypt giving rise to a powerful feminist consciousness, the early expectations were not fulfilled.

Suppressed by several generations of politicians, women have only begun to reclaim their voice in more recent years, most spectacularly in the writings of Nawal El Saadawi in the 1970s. Jailed under President Sadat, and repeatedly having her works either censored or banned, El Saadawi, now in her 70s, remains a forceful advocate of women's rights around the world and a tireless campaigner for human rights.[7] Her books, articles and lectures have been crucial in shaping ideas about women's oppression in Egypt, creating a feminist discourse that seeks to redefine patriarchal structures of history, culture, and identity. Her feminism is uncompromising in the forcefulness of expression, especially in her denouncement of veiling (and other 'non-Islamic' practices such as female – and male – circumcision):

> We Arab and Muslim women know that our authentic identity is based on unveiling our minds and not on veiling our faces. We are human beings and not just bodies to be covered (with religious slogans) or to be naked (for consumerism and Western commercial goods). We know that the veiling of women is the other side of the coin of nakedness ... Both consider women as sex objects ...
>
> Some Muslim women put on the veil as an anti-Western protest, or to assert their authentic, Islamic identity and indigenous culture. They do not know that the authentic identity of a Muslim woman is not to be veiled, and that the veil is not an Islamic dress. (1997: 96)

How the veil came to be regarded as definitive of Islamic women's moral and cultural status is best comprehended through a further analysis of literary voices.

EGYPT IN LITERATURE

In today's political climate, the veil has taken on a new symbolism as a nationalist emblem representing a rejection and suspicion of all things 'western'. While it may be problematic to unravel the cross-cultural processes that have occurred in the past century, neither can one examine the rise of nationalism (and feminism) without reference to the reciprocity between cultures in terms of literature.

Feminism and Islam: currents in Egyptian literature

Both historically and culturally, Egypt and its literature provide examples of the close and troubled connection between feminism, nationalism and veiling. As previously discussed, the 'woman issue' was first brought up in the late nineteenth century by reformers and nationalists, with the veil as the key symbol in the struggle for female emancipation. A century later, women – particularly university students in Cairo – began a new fight for women's rights to self-expression by taking up head coverings and veils more commonly associated with the styles in Saudi Arabia. These students were demonstrating their right to be identified as Islamic women believers. At the same time, their veils denoted their superior social status and education, to distinguish themselves from their rural, uneducated contemporaries (Abu-Lughod, 1998: 250).

An episode describing the resurgence of young women veiling takes place in Ahdaf Soueif's 1995 novel *In the Eye of the Sun*. In this novel, the protagonist, Asya, an Egyptian woman who has received her doctorate in England, returns to teach at a university in Cairo. The first task she sets her students is to write a short piece on why they have chosen to enter the Department of English. The answers are depressingly predictable, until Asya comes upon one answer, 'I want to learn the language of the enemy.' She finds this was written by a 'hooded figure whose face is hidden behind the narrow slit of a *tarha'* (Soueif, 1995: 753). Although anticipating the answer, Asya asks, 'Why is English the language of the enemy?' The young student, however, remains silent. Another student, who is unveiled, speaks up: 'She cannot speak, because the voice of a woman is "*'awra*".' (*'Awra* means immodest or imperfect – a blemish that must be concealed.)[8] In Islam both the face and voice of a woman are *'awra* and must be concealed since men are vulnerable to their corrupting influence.

Although Asya has always known about veiling and the related concept of *'awra*, she is stunned when confronted with the literal interpretation and manifestation of it in her classroom. She realises she herself is being judged and condemned by the eyes behind the veil as 'doing something shameful by merely being there – something worse than shameful; something for which the fires of hell were being stoked in readiness' (Soueif, 1995: 754).

Although part of her own culture, Asya finds the black-shrouded woman 'spooky' (755). With ambivalent feelings, she exposes her fears to her friend Deena:

'I know if they ever had their way we'd all be finished – but I do have a kind of sneaking admiration for them. I mean, they've sorted out some kind of answer to what's happening around us – all the manifestations of the West that they see as no good for them, for the way of life they want to hold on to, the values they feel comfortable with, even to the standard of living. And their answer is genuine, its not imported or borrowed from anywhere –'
'How genuine is it though?' Deena asked. (Soueif, 1995: 755)

How far can the desire of women to veil be regarded as a 'free choice' in terms of an Islamic tradition that defines identity? Can it not also be argued to be a supernaturally sanctioned means for patriarchy to exploit and suppress women? While the 'new' veiling has expanded to embrace all classes and age groups, secularists and feminists see this as a sign of backwardness, as well as one that embraces and makes visible new class distinction. In Cairo itself, ever-increasing numbers of women are now returning to wearing the veil (*hijab*) as part of what they see as a return to their traditional roles as 'women at home' and to signify their religious awakening.

In a recent interview, however, Ahdaf Soueif suggests that the assumption that the status of women 'was taking a backward step because the veil had become more widely used again', is not necessarily the correct interpretation. 'If by moving forwards what you mean is that you are free to make your own decisions and to implement them, then women are much better off than they were 100 years ago. Taking the veil is a decision.'[9] While in this article Soueif accepts that the reappearance of the veil is profoundly dispiriting for her mother and grandmother's generations, who saw it as a symbol of oppression, the veil is now indivisible from the rise of fundamentalism in the Arab world.

It is important to note, however, in today's atmosphere of Islamophobia, the difference between Islam as a religion (one that follows hundreds of years of tradition and learning) and Islam as a right-wing political movement. The 'new' veiling in Egypt, Turkey, Britain and the United States – as well as elsewhere in the world – is often a political identity-marker within the new wave of Islamism.

Islamic 'fundamentalism' itself is also a reaction to the economic and political changes that were introduced in Egypt with the rise of capitalism.[10] Ahdaf Soueif explains:

> Fundamentalism is a protest against being swept into the global market with a handicap, so that you end up being one of the poor of the world who really have no say. Fundamentalism says we don't want to be like that, and the veil is an expression of wanting to hold on to whatever it is that makes us who we are. (interview in *Guardian*, see note 9)

Just as in the early 1900s the veil was implicated in nationalist redefinition, so a century later the question of veiling/unveiling remains a potent indicator of individual and group 'identity'. These issues also inform Soueif's most recent novel, as I shall now discuss.

Ahdaf Soueif: realism and romance

The fictionalisation of historical events in Egypt's fight against British colonialism is the subject of *The Map of Love* by Ahdaf Soueif, a historical romance (published in 1999) which suggests a reconciliation of conflicts of both imperialism and gender. Intentionally creating an optimistic rhetoric in the light of the current political climate, in which peace processes are fraught with the tensions of state-sanctioned anti-western fervour, Soueif utilises the genre of historical romance in order to achieve a text that is able to elaborate the possibility of cultural reconciliation. The novel itself is a multilayered depiction of both English and Egyptian hegemonies, which offers a new postcolonial perspective on Egypt. The layered meanings of fact/fiction, past/present, personal/historical are presented in a narrative of different voices interwoven into a rich heteroglossia of meanings. Illustrating that 'the personal is always political', the novel is also underpinned with the Egyptian mythology of Isis and Osiris, used allegorically to mirror the novel's theme of the deconstruction and reconstruction of personal and historical identity.

Although not written explicitly as a feminist text, nor to challenge the validity of representing 'history', *The Map of Love* uses historiographic narratives to disrupt Eurocentric viewpoints of Egypt's past. Within this parameter, the novel is not free from the problems inherent within the acceptance of certain cultural representations; the non-differentiating stereotyping of 'the Arab' from a western perspective goes unchallenged, for example. Where Nawal El Saadawi uses fiction to challenge and undermine both history and history-as-myth (especially the myth of Adam and Eve), Soueif's novel asserts the repetitive patterns of human behaviour *through* history, breaking down cultural/national boundaries as well as those of space/time.

Ahdaf Soueif comments that she could see no forward progression in mankind. 'Morally and emotionally, mankind has not changed from 7000 years ago,' she argues, 'and it is naive and arrogant of man to think so. The end of the twentieth century looks very much like the end of the nineteenth in terms of politics and human nature.' She explains that she wrote a novel that held out a vision of reconciliation, since the alternatives were 'too horrible to contemplate'.[11]

The Map of Love interweaves narratives of past and contemporary stories of European women who reformulate their identities through their relationships with Egyptian men. These transformations involve repeating patterns of history and meaning: reconstruction and resurrection of fragmented personal identities and texts. The second, contemporary plot of *The Map of Love* reveals the current ramifications of Egypt's colonial past. Although one central episode in this latter plot relies on magic realism/mysticism for its signification, the novel overall maintains the conventions of historical romance.

The structure of the novel reflects a central concern of the narrative: how the past is re-structured through text. The discovery of the letters of Lady Anna Winterbourne from the turn of the twentieth century allows for a gradual re-construction of the narrator's family history and thus enables the (re)assessment of both her own identity and Egypt's. Together with the letters, the discovery of a fragment of tapestry suggests how both history and meaning (here indicated by the few embroidered words of an incomplete sentence) must be reassembled. The three panels of the tapestry must be reunited in order for the total reconstruction of family genealogy, history (and karma) to be assimilated and understood. Later in the novel, the 'objective reality' of the narrative is shattered by the mysterious reappearance of the final panel of the tapestry. Suggesting that all knowledge of the past cannot be 'found', here the book challenges the totalising mastery of realistic discourse. The challenge to the reader to bridge this 'gap' in realism parallels the 'leaps of faith' required by historiography, or the gaps in the veracity of history crossed by the imagination. The reader is thus involved as a reconstructor of fragmented history, just as the narrator herself orders and authenticates 'history' through the sequencing of Lady Anna's letters.

Taking as her starting point the romance between an Englishwoman (Lady Anna Winterbourne) and an Egyptian man (Sharif Basha al-Barudi) at the turn of the century, Soueif dramatises the turbulent political situation of the time. The story of Lady Anna's transformation from quiet but unconventional English widow to Egyptian wife and mother, where she finds 'peace of mind and peace of heart' (197) living a secluded but active life in her husband's house, is one which involves detailed representation of both cultures. When she marries to become a woman confined in the harem/women's quarters of her husband's home, she is immediately ostracised by European society in Cairo and must create a new identity for herself. Changes in her identity (both literal and metaphorical) are often described in terms of change of dress.

It is when she is dressed in male Arab clothing to explore the city incognito that she is mistaken for a man and kidnapped by nationalist freedom fighters hoping to demand a high ransom. When her kidnappers discover their mistake, she is 'rescued' by their aristocratic leader, Sharif Basha. Attracted by her courage and outspokenness, Sharif Basha offers to escort her on a journey into the desert. Once again disguised in order to start the journey, she negotiates the Cairo station, 'covered by the flowing black outer garment of an Egyptian woman of the city. My head and face were most thoroughly veiled' (195). She passes by her European acquaintances without being seen; she is not only unrecognised, but 'invisible' (195). She finds her anonymity a positive experience:

> Still, it is a most liberating thing, this veil. While I was wearing it, I could look wherever I wanted and nobody could look back at me. Nobody could find out who I was. I was one of many black-clad harem in the station and on the train and could have traded places with several of them and no one would have been the wiser. (195)

She changes into male Arab clothing again to travel with the party of men in the desert. Her various costume changes make her apparent identity fluid and undetermined. When they return to Cairo and Sharif Basha sees her for the first time in her female European clothes (after he has already proposed marriage to her) he is taken aback and appears not to recognise her (303). Once married, however, she insists on wearing appropriate Egyptian dress. Her transformation is symbolically completed as she learns Arabic and adopts the traditional lifestyle (which involves helping her husband and his family while observing the outside life of men from behind the latticed grill of the harem in the women's quarter of the house). Here, 'national identity' is appropriated by means of language and dress – a notion challenged by postcolonial writers such as Leila Ahmed, who has questioned the idea that Arab-ness is definable by a common language, culture or history (1999).

In addition to the fictional instances of veiling in the novel, the *The Map of Love* incorporates historical discussions about the politics of the veil. Lady Anna listens to the conversations of her husband and his nationalist friends (the historical figures of Qasim Amin, Mohammad Abdu, Tal'at Harb and Mustafa Kamal) in scenes where fact and fiction merge. The nationalist movement advocates removing the veil only to find, however, that the rival English imperialists also see unveiling as an important political weapon. To remove the veil, therefore, ironically became synonymous with siding with the English, and being anti-nationalist.

A further theme of Ahdaf Soueif's *The Map of Love* is the question of western culpability. Anna's first husband, Edward, suffers a mental breakdown as a result of the shame he feels when witnessing the ruthless and savage behaviour of the English in Egypt. (A sense of shame that Anna later shares, before her Egyptian husband urges her that individuals do not *by national identity alone* represent their national politics.) Yet *The Map of Love* does suggest that the Arab and English cultures are reconcilable and mutually understandable. The repeating patterns of transnational relationships also suggest some of the problems facing women that can be appraised as cross-cultural.

Naguib Mahfouz: women and nation

El Saadawi complains that in general the

> portrayal of Arab women in past and contemporary Arab literature does not reflect a genuine image of her. It is Arab woman as seen through the eyes of Arab men, and therefore tends to be incomplete, distorted and devoid of a clear understanding and consciousness. (1980: 166)

A writer who attempts, however, to portray this oppressed situation of women under the 'traditions' of patriarchy, is Naguib Mahfouz. Nobel Prize-winning author Mahfouz was born in Cairo in 1911 and was influenced by the great French and Russian realist writers. He has written over 30 novels, which include *The Cairo Trilogy* (one of which, *Palace Walk*, I discuss here). His work revolves around the axes of politics, sex and religion, although he has clarified that the latter two are subsidiary to his concern for politics (El-Enany in Hawley, 1998: 71). His later novels became increasingly symbolic and allegorical to achieve a heightened psychological dimension; *Palace Walk*, however, relies on the dramatic realism of events and characters to make a forceful social comment.

In *Palace Walk*, Mahfouz depicts the tyrannical rule of the patriarch of a Cairo family, Al-Sayyid Abd al-Jawad. While his wife and daughters are kept in strict purdah, never allowed to leave the house or be seen by men, the sons are free to lead a life of careless debauchery – as long as they bow to their father's authority in everything. The novel highlights the strict segregation of male and female space, the split between the quiet female world of home and the homosocial male world of commerce, politics, entertainment, and the fulfilment of sexual desire. A strict disciplinarian, the patriarch of the family bases his harsh regime on his understanding of the Qur'an. His own life is hypocritical: he drinks at parties every night, keeps mistresses and enjoys the wildest excesses of sex, music and dancing, while forbidding levity and entertainment of any kind to his family, even at his daughter's wedding. When, after many years of being shut up behind the latticed windows of the house, his wife, Amina, ventures out with her young son to visit a shrine, his punishment is to immediately banish her from the home.

Although eventually the sons discover their father's hypocrisy, instead of challenging him, they choose to emulate his lifestyle, thus perpetuating stereotypes of machismo male behaviour. In this way, Mahfouz suggests how the power of patriarchy and the oppression of women is reinforced and regenerated into the future. His depiction of his male protagonists exposes the emotional and social damage caused by such a regime of power. While not addressing issues of women's rights directly, Mahfouz's 'Cairo trilogy' exposes the foibles of the system without directly attacking it. El Saadawi has argued that 'his understanding of [women's] situation has not moved from a superficial analysis of their social conditions to a deep and sensitive realisation of the tragedy all women are made to live' (1980: 167). His depiction of women's exploitation, however, whether as honourable mother/wife or as prostitute (providing as she does nourishment, sex, adoration, entertainment), does reveal the hell of women's limited lives as servants to men. None of the women rebel (at least in *Palace Walk*) simply because of their fear of the father and their respect for the patriarchal world order. The South African novelist Nadine Gordimer has also defended Mahfouz from feminists who have attacked his depiction of women characters, claiming that his insight into the complex socio-sexual mores, the 'seraglio-prison that distorted the lives of women members of Abd al Jawad's family was a protest far more powerful than any of those who accused him of literary chauvinism' (1997: viii).

In the background of Mahfouz's novel *Palace Walk* is the nationalist struggle for independence. One of the sons is killed when taking part in a supposedly peaceful demonstration. At the same moment, the father forces himself on his neighbour, a widow, in an action depicted as parallel to the 'rape' of the nation by the British. This episode of the rape of a defenceless widow indicates that Mahfouz was aware of and sympathetic to the plight of women, yet it also reinforces the patriarchal identity of woman's body as symbol of the nation. The albeit unsubtle symbolism here suggests that while the British murder peaceful demonstrators, the commodity of woman's body is also vulnerable to rape from the same laws – those of patriarchal violence. Mahfouz suggests that woman, both literal and as symbol of the nation, is undefendable under the colonial mentality of ownership and enforced control. As El Saadawi again argues, while Mahfouz uses sexual aggression as a symbol of aggression against the nation, he nevertheless upholds traditional Arab values of judging women's honour, which depends on the type of sexual relations they have with men. His women are stereotyped in two categories of women institutionalised by the patriarchal system: 'the sacred pure mother or ... the prostitute and mistress' (El Saadawi, 1980: 166).

By the end of the trilogy, the state of 'modern Egypt' has been established and the conflicts within the family of Abd al-Jawad resolved. If one agrees with El Saadawi's analysis, however, despite Mahfouz's progressive views on social justice, which espouse a more humane socialist society, his attitudes and concepts in relation to women have not advanced from the traditional patterns of patriarchal thought, which deny women individual freedom. (For example, although *Palace Walk* describes the anti-British government demonstrations, Mahfouz does not mention the involvement of thousands of women, both veiled and unveiled – that is, from both upper and lower classes – who were killed or injured in the demonstrations.)

Even in works of social realism, such as those by Mahfouz, political implications of social events are not inscribed in the texts. Here, the writer convinces the reader of his humanitarian stance, while in fact the text itself can be accused of propagating a gendered perspective on patriarchy. In contrast to *The Map of Love*, women in Mahfouz's world are circumscribed within the veil, which becomes a prison just as restricting as the walls of the house. While wearing the veil allows the wife, Amina, in *Palace Walk* to break taboo by leaving the house and making a pilgrimage to the shrine of the local saint, the attempt ends in disaster – indicating perhaps that even such a limited degree of female freedom is to be discouraged and will result in both patriarchal and 'supernatural' retribution.

In this light, it is interesting here to consider Freud's notions of the uncanny. *Das Unheimlich* literally means 'un-homely' or perhaps 'not at home', 'not having at-home-ness', in other words: something not of this world. Freud claimed that the uncanny stood for everything that ought to have remained hidden but has come to light (Freud, 1919, 2000). To me this suggests that if women are displaced from their proper sphere, the home, they become 'not natural', 'weird'. Similarly, Julia Kristeva associates the uncanny with 'othering', with the process whereby the alienated become 'the Foreigner' (1991). Thus, being sent 'out of the home' (exile) can be used as a punishment as it places women beyond 'normal' gendered spatial positioning. Elaborating on Freud, Homi Bhabha sees 'the unhomely' as being 'a moment when something is beyond control' (1994: 6). *Unheimlich*, being 'out-of-the-home', again reflects patriarchal fear of woman beyond the control of male authority. Woman must be housed out of sight, or veiled, to avoid becoming 'the uncanny' as well as 'the forbidden'.

Nawal El Saadawi: challenging tradition

Despite her controversial reputation, El Saadawi remains one of the most influential and outspoken writers of both fiction and non-fiction in North Africa. Although her fictional works are arguably not 'refined' enough to rate as major works of literature, her themes are both revolutionary and provocative.[12] The very fact that her texts sometimes read as 'raw', also perhaps adds to the immediacy of the subject matter – dealing as she does with uncompromising descriptions of female genital mutilation, prostitution, madness, and women having to resort to murder in order to survive. As a writer through the 1960s and 1970s, she dared to put in print ideas and opinions that challenged both government institutions and public and private morality in Egypt. (Her writing has led to her being both imprisoned and forced to live in exile.) In this exploration of the representations of veiling, she is one of the most important writers to include, since she has taken the concept out of its restricted cultural bounds to a more metaphorical level as a means of attacking patriarchal norms of society. Her novels depict Egyptian women's fight for identity and female rights against patriarchy's fear of the 'goddess within' – the tradition of Egypt's past mythological and historical women of power.

Nawal El Saadawi's fiction often emerges from her concerns and experiences both as a doctor and a social activist. She writes realist stories (such as *Woman at Point Zero*, based on a true life-story of a woman in prison awaiting death) as well as allegorical fantasy (*The Innocence of the Devil*, which I discuss later in this section). In between these two extremes are several novels and short stories which deal with a variety of women's experiences in Egypt, highlighting problems as well as indicating women's varied means of negotiating new identities. Her fictional output is very much a 'parallel text', an interplay between concept and reality, to be read alongside her social criticism: harsh indictments of women's predicament within Arab patriarchy.

The analysis of her fiction starts with consideration of a story that uses the veil in both literal and metaphorical senses, and which lends itself to a feminist psychoanalytical interpretation. One reason it is valid to discuss some of El Saadawi's fiction in Freudian/Lacanian terms here is that she utilises ideas based on Freud's psychoanalytical theory in her written works. In fact, one of her essays 'The Impact of Fanatic Religious Thought: A Story of a Young Egyptian Muslim Woman' is based on her work as a doctor with women's neuroses and elaborates the psychological damage done to one woman through the social and mental isolation of being veiled (1999).

'The Veil': veiling and the male gaze

Nawal El Saadawi's broad range of fiction includes the story 'The Veil', a discussion of gender roles in Egyptian patriarchy, veiling and women's loss of self-hood (1987: 31). This short story reflects her own work as a medical doctor interested in psychoanalysis. 'The Veil' is El Saadawi's elaboration on a fascination with eyes and their role in phallocentric discourse. She reverses the scopic regime of man looking at women, subverting both the social and religious injunctions regarding the power of the gaze.[13] The story concerns the intimate relationship of a man and a woman from the woman narrator's point of view. Her opening statement, 'I open my surprised eyes to his face'

(31), sets the scene of two lovers negotiating sexual hierarchy. In an alienated situation of familiarity/strangeness, the female narrator's 'eyes fall on to his naked body' (32) in a reversal of the analytical male gaze that usually scrutinises a female body.[14]

By refusing to acknowledge the traditional locus of male power, the protagonist emphasises the mutual gratification of the mind, an intellectual relationship. El Saadawi also devalues patriarchal myths and reverses patriarchal hatred and fear of the innate spiritual power of women. The protagonist concludes, 'I do not kneel down and neither do I pray. I recognise no other deity other than the mind inside my head.' She rejects basing her life on fairy tales, especially that of Adam and Eve (cited elsewhere by El Saadawi as being the origin of slavery and veiling for women), believing them to be the main source of false illusions in life:

> All the fairy stories came to an end and the veil fell from each of them. Many veils fell from my mind as I grew up. Each time a veil fell, I would cry at night in sadness for the beautiful illusion which was lost. But in the morning I'd see my tired eyes shining, washed by tears ... I would leave the mirror, trample the fallen veil underfoot and stamp on it with new-found strength. (33–4)

Here, the veil symbolises illusions to be overcome and boundaries to be transcended, in a process of both growing up and liberating the mind. Unveiling for Arab feminists is both metaphor and reality: associated with empowerment and with finding their true identity.[15] While usurping the power of the gaze through her unwavering observation of the man, the protagonist does not associate woman with 'lack' or absence (a concept that is equally prevalent in both the Arab world and in the western thought via Freud and Lacan). She finally puts out her hand 'like a mother does to stroke the face of a child, and place a tender motherly kiss on his forehead' (35). This motherly kiss marks the change in her awareness, and the reader is left wondering at her next action:

> When I open my eyes the following day ... the veil has lifted from my eyes. I look in the mirror at my shining eyes washed with tears. I am about to walk away from the mirror, like every other time, to trample the fallen veil at my feet and stamp on it with new-found strength. But this time I do not leave my place. I bend

down, pick up the veil from the ground and replace it once more on my face. (35)

Her action of compassionate 'motherly' love corresponds to the mask, or illusion, of identity that she chooses to maintain.[16] Here, the protagonist gains ascendancy over her lover through an act of feminist empowerment that does not negate her ability to love. However, when the protagonist replaces the final veil and fails to discard the identity of mother/lover, we can question how far she accepts the 'Law of the Father' and has internalised the status quo of society. She creates her own reality within safe limits: she knows that her femininity has to be redefined by herself, and yet she ultimately upholds a traditional gender role.

In 'The Veil' an essential part of the woman's power lies in her unwavering gaze into the man's eyes – a look so shocking in the Arab world that El Saadawi uses it as the subject of another story 'The Death of His Excellency the Ex-Minister'. The female gaze is revolutionary in the sense that in Islamic thought the whole social order is threatened if a woman dares look into a man's eyes. This fear of the female gaze (also symbolised in Greco-Roman mythology by the gorgon Medusa) is of 'deep concern' even today in the Arab world. El-Saadawi's exploration of the gendered gaze incorporates the interacting dynamics of sexual with social and religious power as I now elaborate.

'The Death of His Excellency the Ex-Minister': the concept of 'awra

In the Arabo-Islamic world, the gaze is associated with the concept of 'awra. A word that literally refers to the female genitalia, it extends to mean anything shameful that must be covered and hidden from view. Women are considered to be 'awra: 'the most private of the private, to be governed by strict rites of concealment' (Arebi, 1994: 10). The word 'awra refers to that which cannot be looked at, specifically, the whole female body. In the Qur'an the words of the Prophet state: 'Woman is something shameful and impure ('awra). If she goes out the devil gazes at her.' A similar verse reads, 'And say unto women that believe that their eyes should look down, and that their genitals must be protected' (Qur'an Sura al-Nour, verse 31).

Malti-Douglas explains, 'The word 'awra is a sign whose signifieds expand outward in concentric circles from the physical reality ... to the dilemma of women' (1991: 121) who experience it in terms of social restrictions and feelings of moral inadequacy. As seen earlier, not only the body but also the voice of the Muslim woman is '*awra*. (In many countries, Iran for example, this is reflected in the style of *hijab*, where a woman must hold her head covering in place with her teeth: thus effectively being silenced.)

In El Saadawi's short story 'The Death of His Excellency the Ex-Minister', the eponymous protagonist confesses to his mother that he has been driven insane by a female employee's refusal to lower her gaze in his presence. This story illustrates the Islamic (as well as Freudian) notions of male ownership of the gaze and shame associated with women's 'lack'. Lying on his deathbed, he analyses his life, citing various instances of crisis in which his authority was challenged. He was furious with his small daughter, whose eyes can 'always see through me and expose my real self whom no one on this earth, not even myself can uncover ... The veil was transparent for a child ... when my daughter looked me in the face, I felt frightened' (14). The power of the female eye is at the basis of his deep-rooted fear of his loss of self. His life starts to disintegrate when a junior employee, a woman, dares to disagree with him, and above all because 'when she talked to me she dared to raise her eyes' (15). The minister relates to his mother his shocking experience:

> But I was angry, Mother, because when she talked to me she raised her eyes to mine in a way I'd never seen before. Such a gaze, such a strong and steady look, is daring in itself, even impudent when it comes from a man. So what if it comes from an employee, from a woman? I wasn't angry *because* she did it, but because I didn't know *how* she did it, how she dared do it ... Yes, Mother, any woman in her place would surely have died of shame. I wanted to kill her by any means, even by shame. But she wasn't overcome by shame, didn't even lower her eyes, didn't blink an eyelid. (15–16)

The emphasis here on shame is important since Freud claimed that civilisation was based upon the shame produced by the visibility of the genitalia. The sense of shame is also a cultural one, where women's behaviour is decreed to be based on accepting her inherent sin (that of Eve) and the consequent shame she is meant to feel. (Shame is an extremely important concept in Islam, and one that is deployed in Salman Rushdie's novel *Shame* – to be discussed in Chapter 5.) Veiling is also cited as being 'that which covers sexual shame' (Abu-Lughod, 1986: 159). Both Freud's society based on the Law of the Father and the 'laws' of Islam emphasise the fact woman should feel shame, and keep her place in the phallocentric social structure.[17]

The minister, unable to understand why his junior behaves in this way, attempts to ignore her, to make her feel that 'she doesn't exist'. But she responds by gazing on him again, reversing the power structure, at which point, 'I jumped as though all my clothes had dropped off me ... I felt ashamed' (15). In an attempt to restore the phallocentric order, the minister, sufficiently enraged to want to kill her, shouts, 'Don't you know that you're nothing but a junior employee and I am a minister and that no matter how far up the ladder you go, in the end you're a woman whose place is in bed underneath a man' (16). Even under this tirade, she does not avert her eyes, 'as though I were not a man, and she not a woman' (17). Distracted by his obsession, and intimidated by the authority of others, he loses his position as minister and falls ill. Ultimately, he loses both his control and his power, in a meeting where 'the full weight of [his superior's] eyes fell on me, like the fall of death' (24). His last moments are spent listening for the phone to ring, hoping that the sound will bring the re-establishment of his position as minister. But he has lost authority through another's power of *sight*, and cannot regain it through the sense of hearing.[18]

It is also relevant here to compare the minister's fear of loss of power and status through the loss of scopic superiority with Lacan's ideas about the importance of sight in the maintenance of self-identity. Lacan links lack of sight, the blind spot when something appears too threatening to be seen, with the male fear of castration. In his essay on 'The Uncanny', Freud proposed a relationship between castration, the fear of losing one's sight, and the fear of one's father's death. Commenting on Freud's obsession with the gaze, Luce Irigaray argues that 'castration' always involves the gaze for the 'woman supposedly has nothing you can see' (1985: 47). She continues: *'Nothing to be seen is equivalent to having no thing. No being and no truth'* (original italics, Irigaray, 1985: 48). Coming from a very different socio-historical context, Jacques Derrida nevertheless arrives at the same conclusion about women as Freud and Lacan. He also sees the woman castrated as 'Untruth' and insists on the indeterminacy of woman, believing that woman is not truth, 'nor is there a truth of woman' (Derrida, 1978).

A similar logic in Islam extends the 'non-being' of women to a social context, the consequence of which is again the validation that men must retain dominance and the sexes must remain segregated.

What is feared above all is *fitna*, social disorder. *Fitna* is the term used to describe civil strife or chaos; it is also used to mean a beautiful woman. Woman is the embodiment of destruction, the symbol of disorder. She is *fitna*, 'the polarisation of the uncontrollable, a living representative of the dangers of sexuality and its rampant disruptive potential' (Mernissi, 1975: 13). Mernissi argues that 'the whole Muslim social structure can be seen as an attack on, and a defence against, the disruptive power of female sexuality' (1975: 14). This fear of the overwhelming power of female sexuality – and spirituality – is linked to concepts of *'awra* and is responsible for the historic exclusion of women from mosques and religious space, and indeed the need to veil women, since their potential power is stronger than that of vulnerable, weak(?) and pious men.

The face as mask

It is interesting at this juncture to compare – despite problems inherent in cross-cultural analysis – the Islamic concepts of *'awra* and the identification of eye/genitals with the work of the American cultural analyst Michael Taussig. In his essay 'Crossing the Face', Taussig (basing his analysis mainly on African masks and rituals from the Tierra del Fuego) postulates the face as a fetish. In an anthropological context, the face as mask is a border: significantly, the '*mother* of all borderlands' (Taussig, 1993: 8, my italics). The face, he argues, acts as a mask that seems to initiate access to 'a beyond', but, like all fetishes, the face 'as it were, never arrives' (Taussig, 1993: 9). What is crucial, argues Taussig, is secrecy, which 'lies at the core of power' (1993: 225). He defines what he terms the public secret, 'that which is known but cannot be acknowledged', which he likens to the public secret of sex in Foucault, 'the secret about which we cannot stop talking' (1993: 226). Like *'awra* then, the face is necessary as a mask of the 'secret' of sexuality. Similarly, Taussig reasons that

> the face and the genitalia are not only poles apart, but intimately connected, the one covered, the other exposed, such that inappropriate exposure of the one leads to a thoroughly appropriate surge of shame, the blush, across the other. (1993: 227)

Such 'defacement', which leads to 'appropriate shame', is central to the power of *'awra* – and of the necessity to veil according to its logical ramifications.

Taussig's descriptions of the use of masks in the rite of passage into manhood can be useful here, since he concludes that it is the reality of *de-masking*, not the illusions of the mask, that are all-important. Veiling is also frequently an initiation into womanhood, first taking place in most countries at the onset of puberty. Yet for women, such a ritualised de-masking or un-veiling seems not to be available – unless undertaken as a form of rebellion against the hegemonic practices. Perhaps this is because, according to Taussig, the face occupies a dual role: the face as mask and the face as 'window to the soul' (Taussig, 1993: 227). This highlights man's fear of the beyond: his reluctance to acknowledge the existence of the window when he espies the mask. On a theoretical level, if, as Taussig argues, the face is harbinger of 'the always-beyond', men deny the fact that something lies beyond their power base by hiding the face of the 'other' – woman. Freud's metaphors of the uncanny also cast light on his conceptual-isation of the dark recesses of the mind as the 'dark continent' of female sexuality. According to Irigaray, safety for man lies in seeing his own reflection in the mirror, with woman safely positioned as the mirror's 'tain, imprisoned in a male ocular economy' (1985: 532). Here man defines his identity as 'all there is to see'. Looking at a female face directly (mythologised in the story of Medusa) represents a fallibility in his reflection, that it may not represent the totality of available knowledge. Taussig refers to 'defacement' as 'inappropriate exposure' (1993: 227), which can be compared to the shocking and shameful *'awra* of woman's exposed face, together with the threat it poses to man's security and identity (as revealed in El Saadawi's 'The Death of His Excellency the Ex-Minister').

Nawal El Saadawi significantly uses the trope of 'face as mask' in a similar context, in her novel *Woman at Point Zero*. Firdaus, a prostitute, is imprisoned for murdering her abusive pimp, an act which for her heralds a triumphant liberation in symbolically 'destroying all the men I had ever known' (98). Held in a windowless cell: 'I knew why they were afraid of me,' she narrates, 'I was the only woman who had torn the mask away, and exposed the face of their ugly reality' (El Saadawi, 1983: 100). Throughout this novel (similar to the short story 'The Veil') veils represent the 'illusions' (such as marriage, honour, and concepts of shame propagated and upheld by religious laws) that allow women to subject themselves to male abuse.

Returning to the present context, the relationship of the genitals and the eye is a particularly fascinating one in that it appears in both western and Islamic discourses. In the Muslim structure of reality, the eye is also an erogenous zone. 'When the Prophet was asking God to protect him from the most virulent social dangers, he asked Allah to help him control his penis and his eye from the dangers of fornication' (Mernissi, 1975: 83).

However, it is men who are most in danger of losing their self-control. According to Mernissi, Abu Hamid al-Ghazali's comment that 'The look is fornication of the eye' confirms that, 'A man can do as much damage to a woman's honour with his eyes as if he were to seize hold of her with his hands' (1975: 83). According to these texts, the gaze is equally powerful and potentially damaging whether male or female, although the destructive power of the gaze in man or woman is based on different reasons. The strength of the *woman's* gaze lies in its power to disrupt the social order, not to arouse her own sexual desire. (One theory behind the seclusion and veiling of women is that they serve as protection for the passive and weak male in the presence of the female. It is only old women, who are presumably no longer lust-inducing, who were traditionally allowed to go unveiled.) In El Saadawi's story, it is the minister who mentions sex to remind the woman of her inferior position (16), since many men equate sex *with* power. These Islamic representations of the danger of the female gaze, although from a vastly divergent theoretical (religious) framework, are reminiscent of Freud's essay 'Medusa's Head' where he argues that the eye of woman is the source of castration. Feminist writers critical of Freud such as Luce Irigaray (1985) have also linked ocularcentrism and phallocentrism as central in patriarchal domination.

Moreover, the link between sight, fornication, and honour is one that is used to political purposes today in conflicts where Muslims are targeted. Rape, the ultimate violation of women by both the eye and the penis, is used as a systematised weapon against whole societies. Kanan Makiya explains how violations of honour are aimed to destroy 'the core of one's identity':

The honour of a family is perceived in Arab-Islamic culture to be located in the bodies of the women of that family, in their virginity first and foremost, but also in the clothes that women wear ... The veil acquires its importance in the culture precisely because it acts symbolically to protect this honour from public view ... When [a man] rips off an Arab or a Kurdish woman's 'veil', and violates her sexually, he is in fact penetrating to the inner sanctum of an entire family's honour. (1993: 288)[19]

Nawal El Saadawi's novels and short stories link the invasive properties of the male gaze with violence and rape, especially her novel *The Innocence of the Devil*.

The Innocence of the Devil

Nawal El Saadawi's controversial writings condemn patriarchy and national politics as being responsible for the oppression of women. In *The Innocence of the Devil*, patriarchy is taken in its guise as organised religion. In this novel El Saadawi continues her angry indictment of Islamic jurisprudence that she began in her earlier text *The Fall of the Imam*. The novel can be seen to encompass all the major forms of violation of woman by man – physical (torture and rape), mental (the definition of women as 'insane'), social (the depiction of man as master, woman as servant), emotional (the denial of woman's past or future), spiritual (the cursing of woman as 'heretic' for hinting at a possible lesbian preference), religious (the suppression of the Arab goddesses by Islam) and even semantic (the erasure or the debasement of the female gender in the Arabic language). Rape is used in this novel as a symbol of male power over women – but here El Saadawi takes a daring stance since she depicts the rape of a woman by the Deity. Hence, in Egypt the novel could not be published with an equivalent of its English title, but was eventually published under the title *Gannat wa Iblis*. The name of the Devil (Iblis) could be linked with that of a woman (Gannat), but the devil could never be proclaimed as innocent. For, 'if the devil is innocent, then who is guilty?'[20]

The Innocence of the Devil is a novel that operates its own form of textual disguise, since it relies on playing with some of the most sacred writings of Islam (a level of textual complexity which may be lost in the process of translation for a reader unfamiliar with the Qur'an). The novel also refers to 'myths' common to all three monotheistic religions. The third person narrator remains external to the text, while the non-linear plot shifts between past and present, focusing on the different characters' experiences both internal and external, real and imagined. Setting the story inside a mental asylum, in which the rules of reality differ from those outside, allows for a plot that oscillates between political satire and Freudian fantasy. In her introduction to the novel, Fedwa Malti-Douglas describes the text as a dialectic interaction between the 'real' on the one hand and the world of dreams, fable, fantasy and illusion on the other.[21] Time, space, memory and history are distorted in the novel, so that identity is fluid and reality contorted. Malti-Douglas regards this 'complicated literary game of fantasy and reality' to be a subversive treatment of both theology and patriarchal rules. Its textual interaction between 'real' and 'unreal' is suggestive of a metaphorical veiling by simulacra (which represent and stand in for reality) in a Baudrillardian world where truth and falsehood are wholly indistinguishable. El Saadawi's text functions like Taussig's description of the masked face, which represents the 'always-beyond' of 'withinness', implying an infinite deferral of the signified.

Throwing further light on the metaphorical issue of veiling, El Saadawi returns to the myths of Adam and Eve, Isis and the power of the female, setting the story in what some critics have seen as a distopian Garden of Eden complete with serpent, God and the Devil. The high walls of the mental asylum confine three main female characters as well as Iblis (the Devil) and God. The three female characters, Gannat, Nafissa (a female patient) and the head nurse (who is also identified as Gannat's childhood friend Narguiss) are all used and abused by the male characters to their advantage.

Gannat, whose name means 'paradises' (plural), is regarded as dangerous, since she was born with her eyes wide open, in an unblinking stare.[22] El Saadawi has discussed how the ideal Arab woman remains the beautiful angelic obedient housewife whose main role in life is to look after her husband and children. A woman with courage or ambition, who shows strength 'with eyes wide open' is considered ugly, repulsive and vulgar. 'In other words she symbolises the prostitute, the fallen and degraded woman' (El Saadawi, 1980: 166). Gannat's eyes being open at birth literalises the metaphor (as well as suggesting a defiance of 'awra). She also has total recall, and can remember back five thousand years to the serpent whispering in the Garden of Eden (El Saadawi, 1998a: 32). Since her eyes change colour, black at night and clear blue during the day, people question if she is human or a devil. Her extraordinary and threatening memory is considered a disease, and she is institutionalised. When she first sees the patient God, she easily recognises him as all the violent men who had subjected her to rape or incest. For Fedwa Malti-Douglas, 'Gannat embodies the eternal woman, doomed to destruction' (1995: 137).

The head nurse is first portrayed as a grim figure wielding a syringe and wearing a grey veil. All the figures of authority in the asylum wear veils, either grey or white, perhaps intended to define their anonymity. Since El Saadawi has discussed how veils remove rather than define identity, their lack of features may be intended to designate them as Every-woman.

No woman in this novel avoids being exploited or abused by patriarchy. The head nurse, in her turn, is used by the director of the institute for sex. She has gained a 'Medal of Honour' for exemplary fulfilment of duty and for 'bringing happiness to others' (110). This is chillingly ironic, since the 'happiness' she brings is either through giving in to enforced sex, or, through giving patients such as Gannat compulsory electric shock therapy. However, the veil she wears masks her dual nature. Her identity shifts. When the Devil calls to her from the garden, her mind goes back to remember her childhood as Narguiss. (A confusing shift for the reader – but feminists often argue that women have to negotiate between several 'identities'.) The head nurse/Narguiss herself distinguishes her 'hidden mind' (her unconscious, which remains vigilant) from her visible mind (the conscious mind, which becomes separated from her body) (112). She remembers that as a girl, 'Between her self and her body was a barrier, like a sheet of glass ... the surface of her eyes was covered with a film of water and the world seemed to waver behind it as though in a dream.' In this dual state of consciousness, which witnesses the world as an illusion, 'She carried a body which was unreal, and she tried to hide it from people's eyes ... but the eyes were incapable of penetrating through the glass' (113). Here, the barrier that protects her inner identity from the eyes of the world is like *hijab*. She cannot see the world clearly through it, and the world cannot see her.

Her flesh is also described to be like *hijab*: 'it permitted light to pass through it, but not air ... In fact, she was suffocating.' The artificial identity she has constructed is destroying her. However, her false self has been maintained because like Faust, 'she wanted to walk, to be able to see others without being seen herself. She wanted to fly up to the Heavens, to be able to see God and yet be invisible to Him.' Through the years of enforcing this false self, she has only gained the reverse of the freedom she wanted: 'She wanted to hear a voice other than that of the Devil. He kept whispering to her at night ... nothing could save her from the Devil except sleep' (114): sleep here being a negation of conscious awareness.

Her release from the nightmare comes when she admits the truth to the director. Asserting her true identity, she says that she is Narguiss, and that she 'hate[s] all men'. The director responds by telling her she will go to hellfire for 'To be a lesbian is a sin, don't you know that?' She retorts, 'No sir, it is not mentioned in God's Book' (172).

Fedwa Malti-Douglas discusses how 'the intensity of female–female relationships' is one force that can effectively battle the universal power of the patriarchy (1995: 207). Narguiss's declaration of her homosexual preference is empowering, especially since she is aware that, although taboo, there are no religious statements against it. However, 'this female force, powerful though it may be, cannot destroy patriarchy', for 'woman in the Saadawian feminist literary construct is doomed to fight a battle she rarely wins' (Malti-Douglas in El Saadawi, 1998a: 208).

When Narguiss/the head nurse tries to flee the asylum, 'the veil around her head came undone ... it twirled around her neck and started to choke her. She undid the veil from around her neck, slipped it off her head and threw it into the air.' She continues to shed all her clothes, and a new veil forms: 'over her eyes formed a film of unshed tears. Thirty years of sadness. But under the surface was another woman, happy to be free.' The veil has been symbolically strangling her (and by implication, all women) for so long, but it is only as she tries to remove it that she feels it choking her. Narguiss miraculously turns into a white butterfly, which hovers in the air before being shot down in drops of red blood (174).

Here, El Saadawi emphasises that all women must remove the veils that hold them captive, even though it may be difficult, or painful, to do so. When questioned as to why her heroines are usually damaged or beaten by the system at the end of her novels, El Saadawi refused to agree that this was so. Although in several short stories and in *The Innocence of the Devil*, the female protagonist(s) are imprisoned ('In Camera') or dead (*Woman at Point Zero*), El Saadawi proclaimed forcefully that they 'have triumphed'.[23] Neither her heroines, nor by extension real women in Arab society, are passive victims. For El Saadawi, the women triumph by finding true freedom through their defiance of patriarchy. Also, in terms of the heroines having lasting impact in Egyptian society through El Saadawi's millions of readers, we can say that the women *have* triumphed by becoming archetypes of female resistance. When asked if she may write a book that might give a more positive vision of the future (as in the genre of feminist utopian fiction, for example) Nawal replied that it was the responsibility of fiction to reveal life *as it is*, not create a picture of how it might be. The importance of 'raw' experience translated into literature explains perhaps the appeal of El Saadawi's novels for Egyptian readers and the success of her unrefined, often brutal, writing style.

The other female characters in this novel also share an ostensibly dismal fate: Nafissa, another patient, while trying to placate and obey the demands of the patriarchal order, is raped by the Deity. The veiled staff rush to stifle her screams (84). Malti-Douglas views this rape as referring to 'normal' male–female power relations. The episode links the theological with the sexual, and once again brings into play the association of the Devil with woman. El Saadawi explains elsewhere that 'men see women as the other. This may explain why women and the devil (Satan, Iblis) are often related to each other, why God speaks in his holy books only to men' and why women in all three monotheistic religions 'have an inferior position to men' (1998a: 137). While God is associated here with the abuse of power and violence, Iblis (the Devil) is a source of strength (he tries, for example, to protect Gannat from the enforced shock treatments). At the end of the novel, God declares Iblis innocent, 'thus destroying his own identity by becoming dissident to himself' (Cooke, 2001: 77). God is depicted as a tyrant to be resisted, and against whom women must protect themselves.

Once she forgets the past and her identity, Gannat is declared cured: 'Loss of memory indicating complete cure' (172). She is to be released, but then she rebels, remembering her theological arguments as a girl with the arch exponent of religio-patriarchal values, Sheikh Bassiouni, in which he refutes the female. She proclaims, in defiance of two basic tenets of patriarchal Islam, 'I do not hide my face. I am not ashamed of my body' (204). Gannat defies the right of any man to impose rules in God's name, as well as challenging Islamic concepts of women's inherent evil.

El Saadawi's narrative next focuses on a linguistic slip made by Gannat, in which the name of Allah becomes 'Allat' by two stray ink drops falling on the page. Alluding to the three female goddesses in Mecca who were worshipped by the Arabs before Islam, it is interesting to note that this novel has three female protagonists perhaps intended to parallel the three goddesses. The three goddesses: Al-Lat ('the goddess'), al-Uzza (the 'mighty one') and Manat (the 'fateful one'), were worshipped by certain Arab tribes and were often called *banat al-Lah* – the daughters of God. The so-called Satanic Verses were first mentioned in the work of a tenth-century historian who related how some 'rogue' verses were spoken by Mohammed, which allowed the *banat al-Lah* to be venerated as intercessors. These verses were later declared to be inspired by Satan and were withdrawn by Mohammed and replaced with verses (Qur'an, 53: 20) that condemned the goddesses as 'nothing but empty names which you have invented' (Armstrong, 1993: 172). El Saadawi has written that the important position of the goddesses was 'symbolic of the relatively higher prestige enjoyed by women in Arab tribal society ... a vestige of the matriarchal society' (1998a: 74).

The connection between the veiling of women and the repression of the three goddesses based on fear of the primeval power of women is a topic that has not been addressed in cultural criticism.[24] While El Saadawi mainly links the origins of veiling with slavery, inherent within all three monotheistic religions, Fatima Mernissi discusses how men associate women with the violence of the goddess. She reveals that the construct of sexual inequality in the west, which is based on the belief of women's biological inferiority, is absent in Islam; on the contrary, laws and social practices such as polygamy, segregation and veiling 'can be perceived as a strategy for containing her power'. As she points out, however, 'Women never let themselves be tamed. Men believed that a person could become accustomed to confinement, but women are just waiting for the right moment' (Mernissi, 1993: 150). The covering up of women's bodies and women's power seems a logical extension of the destruction of ancient desert statues to the Arab goddesses. Once women's 'control' of the realm of the sacred was destroyed and even access henceforward prohibited (as women were to be prohibited from worship in mosques), the mythical rights of women to the spiritual also had to be destroyed. This was most easily achieved by associating women and their bodies with indecency, pollution, and sickness/insanity. The original concepts of God as a woman, or the Great Goddess (whether Al-lat, Isis, Demeter, or the Divine Mother) had to be rendered as 'myth', as 'nothing but empty names that you have invented'.

El Saadawi's harsh exposure of the victimisation of women in Arab society highlights the veil as symptomatic of the abuses of women by patriarchy. However, she confirms that Mohammed was 'more emancipated with respect to women than most men of his time, and even most Muslim men today. He gave his women the right to stand up to him' (1998a: 75). Those who came after Mohammed did not follow his example. History, as El Saadawi explains, 'was to plunge the Arab woman into a long night of feudal oppression and foreign domination in which women were condemned to toil, to hide behind the veil, to quiver in the prison of a harem fenced by high walls, iron bars, and windowless rooms' (1988a: 79): a situation that is comparable to that of the asylum in *The Innocence of the Devil*.

CONCLUSION

In terms of both feminist and nationalist experiences, the novels discussed in this chapter demonstrate the multiple discourses and inscriptions of the veil. *The Map of Love* illustrates how the veil is both a site of manipulation and a symbol of nationalism and how it may enable a woman to travel unrecognised, transgress social and sexual codes of conduct and achieve an unexpected mode of agency. Lady Anna uses the veil to transgress geographical and social boundaries, and ultimately to redefine her identity. She utilises the anonymity of the veil for her personal advantage. *The Map of Love*, however, 'romanticises' the female protagonist's experiences of the veil and the secluded world of the women's harem, possibly distancing the reader from social realities outside the text. While the novel incorporates the contemporary discussions of veiling amongst the male educated elite, it does not elaborate an 'indigenous' female stance towards veiling, nor include points of view other than those of an upper-middle class. Lady Anna challenges the authority of the British patriarchs (who wish to prevent her cross-cultural marriage), yet she unquestioningly submits to the authority of her husband. (This type of submission is responsible for the perpetuation of men's abuse of women in a master/slave relationship according to El Saadawi.)[25] The text, however, creates its own 'class of truth' through the interplay between fiction and reality. The reader cannot expect a historical romance to deal with value-laden oppositions to the extent that texts such as El Saadawi's, which are written with the intention of being weapons to fight injustice, do.

Historically in Egypt, women's liberation was sacrificed for national liberation, women's rights forgotten in the emergence of the 'right' for rule of a powerful male elite. The patriarchal system is based on the exploitation of women's labour alongside the positioning of woman as threatening 'other', whose intelligence, sexuality and strength pose a lasting threat to patriarchy's questionable power base. The fact that writers such as El Saadawi (and her husband Sherif Hetata) are continuing to be victimised for their liberal views (perceived as threatening to past and present governments) is confirmation of the fragility and paranoia of fear-based regimes, whether their power be based on masculinist, secular or religious principles.

For a female writer such as Nawal El Saadawi, the veil is both a metaphorical indicator of the disempowerment of women, and a literal example of patriarchal, religious and misogynist cruelty. While not attacking the tradition of veiling as such in her fiction, she implicates the veil as symbol of confinement, oppression, as well as physical and mental torture (for example, within the enclosure of the mental asylum). She uses the terminology of veiling in a variety of situations, speaking of the veil of tears, of breath, of cloth, of the veiled staff stifling screams, or the eyes acting as veil to reality. In the short story 'The Veil', it is a metaphor of ignorance as well as the social roles women don as 'masks' of identity in order to be socially and spiritually accepted, despite a latent desire to rebel.

Ultimately, the veil denies female difference and any sense of 'female unity' through the apparent homogeneity of the veil, since any definition of 'Islamic' or national identity associated with the veil as an 'Islamic uniform' is argued by El Saadawi to be based on a misinformed, if not fraudulent, notion. As she comments:

> our authentic identity is based on unveiling our minds and not on veiling our faces ... The authentic identity of the Arab woman is not a straight jacket or dress or veil. It is an active, living, changing process, which demands a rereading of our history, and a reshaping of ourselves and our societies in the light of present challenges and future goals. (El Saadawi, 1998a: 97)

We have seen from the differences between the situations of the women in these different novels that we cannot generalise the veiled woman as the 'other', which is to put woman within brackets of a finite set. Women, especially women writers, are in the process of constantly reconfiguring and renegotiating their identity. The veil may be part of the negotiation process, a process that is mainly internal and personal but yet also involves external and public signifiers of change. The contradictions and paradoxes of the image of the 'veiled woman' confirm the feminist discussion in which, as Hélène Cixous remarks, 'her-story is not one story' (1986: 160).

However, the discussion of these texts exposes the problems inherent within any discussion of the veil. Representations of veiling depend largely upon class positioning rather than geographical location. Analysing works of literature here in the context of their specific geographic and national contexts, obfuscates possible wider issues of variations according to class, education, economic status, and so on. (Similarly, the authors here, although all Egyptian, come from very different social backgrounds.) Soueif's novel *The Map of Love* excludes any women characters from a disadvantaged social background: all the characters in both generations are well-educated, middle- or upper-class women who are able to travel and explore issues of identity, politics and history from their advantaged positions. In distinct contrast, El Saadawi's protagonists are women who are often poorly educated, from rural backgrounds, for whom cities are often the location for rape, poverty, exploitation, and every sort of social disadvantage. Her protagonists are women who struggle and fight against legal, economic, and religious, as well as patriarchal gender bias. Issues raised in her stories are perhaps better compared with some of the narratives from Saudi Arabia (or Iran), where problems of similarly disadvantaged and victimised women are exposed.

4
Piety and Patriarchy:
The Arabian Peninsula and
the Eastern Mediterranean

In the dynamic of locating the veil within diverse contexts it becomes clear that one of the central concerns here must be the religious site of veiling. This chapter analyses the claim that, throughout the Middle East, regimes, whether socialist, conservative, monarchic or not seem to aim to disempower and subjugate women in the name of Islam – although, 'there is an increasing trend within the region, from Morocco to Iran, of women challenging the so-called authenticity of male-imposed Islamic prohibitions' (Milton-Edwards, 2000: 188). Just as western feminists have argued that the very concept of nationalism amounts to the 'sanctioned institutionalisation of gender difference' (McClintock et al., 1997: 89) granting men unequal access to the rights and resources of the nation-state, so Arab feminists highlight the hegemony of religion as sanctioning a gendered discourse of inequality. Leading Arab feminists have asked the agonised question, 'Why is there so little outrage in the academic literature against crimes targeting women in the name of religion?' (Moghissi, 1999: 7).[1]

Although religion is widely implicated as the sole reference point to conceive veiling, as I will discuss in this chapter, the perpetuation of veiling occurs through a combination of socio-economic factors: religion, politics, state laws, and the desire of state rulers to keep power firmly in the hands of patriarchy. Established on logic conflating religion and Arabic cultural traditions, the institution of veiling is seen as one method of secluding and restricting women both in private and public spheres of life. Elaborating the controversial site of the veil in recent feminist discussion, my choice of literature in this chapter will expose the trauma associated with the problematic situation of women within state-sanctioned religious patriarchies.

Since the 1970s the veil has been adopted as a 'universal' feminist cause, and associated, misleadingly, with the 'Islamic' practices of polygamy and female genital mutilation. It is as if the figure of 'veiled

Islamic woman' herself has pulled a veil across the eyes of western feminists and journalists, so that they have been unable to perceive anything in Islamic culture beyond or beneath the veil. Rana Kabbani recalls a female American journalist who interviewed both herself and Fatima Mernissi for hours, yet her article in *Vanity Fair* 'was a catalogue of horrors about Islam ... illustrated with a huge blow-up photograph of ghost-like women, veiled from head to foot. It ignored any of the important debate within Islam about the rights of women' (Kabbani, 1994: ix)

Conflicting ideas abound as to whether or not the veil can in fact be empowering. If some Islamic feminists argue that the veil acts to bestow agency, a very different picture is depicted by Haideh Moghissi, who refutes the validity of arguments such as 'protected space' or the *hijab* as a way of women gaining empowerment, condemning any such notion as inaccurate if not downright dangerous.[2] Moghissi also suggests that other indigenous customs and patriarchal cultural practices that sanction gender violence and should be condemned as violating human rights are tolerated in western academics and politics since they symbolise Muslim 'cultural authenticity' (1999: 7–12).

Where academic feminists have singled out the veil as being symbolic of Arab women's victimisation by patriarchal laws, many Arab women writers cite veiling as only one of the social ills afflicting women in the area and locate more fundamental issues of rights to mobility, agency, and choice in marriage as taking precedence. While western eyes may regard women as powerless within restrictive theocratic societies, women are in fact actively seeking empowerment. Women in several countries such as Iran, Sudan and Pakistan are fighting back to reclaim 'their humanity' and change structures of gendered power. Deniz Kandiyoti suggests the extremes of possible avenues of agency for women:

> If some women's response to their vulnerability is a retreat into the protective certainties of religious conservatism, others may be motivated to struggle for a social order in which they no longer need to veil to legitimise their public presence and to fend off male aggression. (1991: 18)

In many Islamic societies, women are met with an equally fierce and often violent opposition to change.

If change in the Arab world does come about, its most important indicator is the treatment of women. Muslim women are, as Jan

Goodwin expresses it, the 'wind sock showing which way the wind is blowing in the Islamic world' or, more graphically, they are 'the canaries in the mines' (1994: 28). Yet women may be instigators as well as indicators of change. Bernard Lewis suggests that women

> will, if permitted, play a major role in bringing the Middle East into a new era of material development, scientific advancement and socio-political liberation. Of all the people in the Middle East, women have the strongest vested interest in social and political freedom. They are already among its most valiant and effective defenders; they may yet be its salvation. (1997: 47)

Similarly, Hisham Sharebi in the book *Neopatriarchy* writes enthusiastically that

> The women's movement ... is the detonator which will explode the neopatriarchal society from within. If allowed to grow and come into its own, it will become the permanent shield against patriarchal repression, the cornerstone of future modernity. (1988: 154)

The words 'permitted' and 'allowed' seem to destabilise this tenuous possibility of change. We must ask by whom are these women to be 'allowed' to be empowered? Is it local religious sanctions or neo-colonialism that is disallowing such progress (Jihad or McDonaldisation)? In light of these comments, which expose the central location of women within both social order and change, before examining how women themselves express some of their experiences, it is necessary to understand how the predicament described arose, and how women are perceived and positioned in the patriarchal hegemonic and social structures of the Arab world.

WOMEN AND IDENTITY IN THE ARAB WORLD

Within the Arab world, 'woman' as a concept is based on hundreds of years of religious definition and interpretation, and is one which in recent years women writers have fought to redefine. Some Arab feminist writers observe the process whereby women negotiate change:

> the notion of 'the woman' sprang from society's system of concealing women as real human beings and revealing them only as symbols ... Women writers, in writing about women's experiences,

not only politicise women's lives but redefine women and transform their status from that of 'symbol' to that of a 'real' being. This idea is not only a revelation but also revolutionary. (Arebi, 1994: 269)

Within this process, the veil and 'woman' as symbols are so closely intertwined in the closed Islamic kingdoms as to almost be inseparable.

In the literature I will discuss from this region, the veil becomes variously the means of retaining social status, defining modesty and piety, and maintaining a strictly gendered social space, while simultaneously emphasising a rejection of gender stereotypes and mores of the west. Veiling in this cultural context is associated with the reclamation of female modesty and male honour: concepts that resonate throughout the Islamic world. In many countries (such as Saudi Arabia) the wearing of the veil currently provides the sole means of a woman's access to public (male) space.

In the discussion surrounding the problems inherent within conceptualising 'universal human rights' the question of 'whether woman has a real choice' is fundamental to her freedom (Arebi, 1994: 269). Many women in the Muslim world do not have the privilege of choice since their identity (as inherently inferior to man) is defined by religious and national law. Many now turn towards embracing Islam as a cultural identity in response to spiritual needs as well as to socioeconomic crisis and the weakening traditional structures of the patriarchal family. From a European feminist perspective, it would be argued that such women are manipulated by patriarchal hegemony. Muslim feminists struggling against western stereotypes of oppression stress that the original doctrines of their religion are favourable to women's equality. The conclusion to Cherry Mosteshar's autobiographical account of life in Iran under the Ayatollahs, for example, indicates this dual positioning:

Before I left Oxford in 1991 I had a pang of comradeship as I saw the growing number of women wearing the Islamic *hejab* on the streets of England. Now it raises my blood pressure; I want to drag their scarves off their heads and shake them till they see what a disservice their choice is doing, not only to their fellow women but also ultimately to their faith. The very religion they wish to glorify is dying under the weight of hypocrisy and ignorance. It is withering in the thirteenth century and if we don't help drag it into the twenty-first it could die. (1995: 456)

While advocating change, Mosteshar also implicates the extent of religious and social indoctrination. Living exiled in England, she hopes that, 'one day I will be able to go out bareheaded in the street without feeling ... that I am wicked' (Mosteshar, 1995: 456). Here, Mosteshar constructs her own image of the veiled woman, who, like the subaltern discussed by Gayatri Spivak, becomes a palimpsest or symbol used by others upon which to write their own political, religious or social agendas. Mosteshar's own positioning is caught between tradition and modernisation.

In an area of the world where religion dominates every aspect of social life, and every moment of the daily routine, the veil is an article of clothing that symbolises women's role in personal and professional contexts. Yet the veil cannot be discussed as aesthetically or politically signifying only one state of being: it can be a signifier either of oppression or of emancipation/rebellion. The following discussion of women writers aims to clarify this dichotomy.

ARAB WOMEN WRITERS

Writing remains for Arab women a key means of subverting dominant hegemonies and reasserting agency, a means of voicing their 'silenced' narrative beneath the veil. Women write to negotiate a 'textual, sexual, and linguistic space' for themselves, while writing itself remains for many secret and subversive (Faqir, 1998: 9).[3] Risking censorship, slander, or possible imprisonment, the woman writer is a dissident, crossing into the traditionally male space of language. Such violations of sacred sexual/textual space impinge on a woman's honour (*sharaf*) which is contingent upon her silence and invisibility, and challenge both cultural concepts of women and the 'master narratives' that always assume the speaker to be male.

It is perhaps difficult for a western reader to appreciate the danger for Arab women inherent in writing. The great international outcry in the wake of Salman Rushdie's *fatwa* did little to draw attention to the plight of many female authors across the Islamic world under similar threat, or the women writers who routinely are imprisoned by religious theocracies. Women's task in writing is therefore doubly subversive of patriarchal structures of language and society. Creating new traditions of both self-representation and language, they must 'carry out a multiple translation of the darkness, espoused with a search for a new language free of the religious and the dominant' (Faqir, 1998: 22). When Saudi writers, either male or female, commit their inner thoughts or experiences to paper, they violate a culture that is based on concealment, the repression of emotions and feelings, a culture where expressions of love are taboo. In this light, the veil is but the outward manifestation of a ubiquitous concept underpinning social and religious mores.

SAUDI ARABIA

The kingdom of Saudi Arabia established itself in the early twentieth century based on a reformist religious movement, the Wahhabiyya. This Sunni Muslim government upholds the shariah (Islamic canonical law) and a belief in the literal interpretation of the Qur'an, strictly adhering to the way of Mohammed (the Sunna). It idealises the past and early Islam's simplicity and strict orthodoxy. With a conservative Muslim monarchy, the kingdom's stability is based on balancing tribal traditions, religious influence, family power and oil wealth. While the impact of the west has made Arab leaders realise the need for new political identity and the need to reform authoritarian systems, Saudi Arabia remains punitive in its treatment of those who do not conform to its way of life (Satloff, 1993: 119–24).

Women have less freedom in Saudi than in any other Islamic country. Even so, the religious leaders, the *ulema*, constantly demand that more restrictions be put on them. It is illegal, for instance, for women to drive, to go out or travel without an official male escort (*mahram*), and strict codes of sexual segregation and covering up apply. As Jan Goodwin comments, 'the kingdom of Saudi Arabia never forgets for a moment the Prophet's statement "if a man and a woman are alone in one place, the third person present is the devil"' (1994: 222). In Saudi society, the veil, as well as having spiritual meaning, has become associated with social and cultural traditions. Religious doctrines and traditional norms have become inextricably linked. Many women are aware that the veil is an inherited social custom and not from Islam, yet accept that to go without it might invoke both divine retribution and a social stigma. In Saudi Arabia, the dilemma of whether or not a woman should veil remains a critical and ambivalent subject.

The whole of Saudi society is structured in such a way as to keep a woman within strictly defined social and spatial limits. Separation of the sexes is maintained physically, socially and psychologically. Segregation means that women's activities outside the house are restricted. Even western women married to Saudi men must conform to the strict norms of veiling. Most women are prevented from working by their male relatives; to work without a husband's consent would lead to divorce.

Education remains one possible avenue for women's personal development and self-expression. Fatima Mernissi describes how, despite women in Saudi Arabia being the targets of intimidation and violence, and despite the strengthening of surveillance in their prison-like environment, many are hiding university diplomas and degrees beneath their veils. The rise of qualified women and their insistence on employment have to some extent liberated women. Trends are changing within Saudi Arabia as authorities try to maintain a sensible balance between their strong centuries-old traditions and way of life and introducing positive elements of a western lifestyle.[4]

Highlighting the discrepancies and variations within the Islamic world, critics have questioned the relative merits of female liberation where millions of women in Egypt enjoy the right to vote but women in Saudi Arabia remain disenfranchised according to a strict interpretation of Islam under Wahhabi rule. Even the creation of wealth in the oil-rich Gulf States has not empowered women. Mernissi, in fact, insists on the crucial connection between the veiling of women and economics, especially oil wealth. She contends that 'a better term for fundamentalism in Saudi Arabia would be petro-Wahhabism, whose pillar is the veiled woman' (Mernissi, 1993: 166). As long as the elite patriarchy holds a firm grip on power and wealth by restricting opportunities for women to work, the 'anachronistic regime' and its attitude towards women is the ethical responsibility of 'whoever consumes Arab oil'. Like El Saadawi, Mernissi implicates neo-colonialism and western economic exploitation of Africa and the Middle East in the perpetuation of the 'indigenous' suppression of women.

An analysis of the representations of veiling in women's writing focusing on the multiple significations of veiling – religious, educational, status and national – must ask how far veiling itself supports or subverts traditional patriarchal control of women. An exploration of women's fiction considers how far this public symbol of honour and religious piety can provide possible avenues for female agency, bearing in mind that the very act of writing, although fraught with social and legal dangers, is itself a means to negotiate new identity and of achieving independence.

Fictions of Saudi Arabia and the Gulf

How far can the predicament in which Frances Shore finds herself in *Eight Months on Ghazzah Street* (discussed in Chapter 2) be compared to the traditional position of Arab women in Saudi Arabia?[5] If, as Foucault claims, knowledge and truth are products of power (1978: 93) then it follows that in a position of powerlessness, women are also deprived access to the truth. Yet how far is a Foucauldian model of knowledge/power demonstrated in the daily lives of Arab women? Saddeka Arebi discusses how Saudi women writers 'reflect an understanding of what Foucault has dubbed "the regime of power/ knowledge" and "instances of discursive production," of power that is based on silence, prohibition and the circulation of systematic misconceptions' (1994: 8). She argues that the history of the Arabian peninsula reflects a 'unique interconnection between the poetic and the political', both women and words are wrapped in ambiguities such as 'strong/weak, good/bad, sacred/profane' (1994: 10).

If, however, we can argue that the veiled Arab woman is the 'seer' rather than the 'seen', as such she can be argued to have more complete knowledge than the English woman (in a novel such as *Ghazzah Street*) who is 'the seen', but as such remains very much *in the dark*. In a nonfictional example, Arebi (a scholar based in the US) describes her own experience of having to wear the full *hijab* while in Saudi Arabia. She writes, 'I can attest to the sense of power and control a woman feels in having the advantage of being the seer, not the seen' (1994: 281).

Homi Bhabha also sees the migrant woman as occupying a similar position. He asks, 'What is the secret art of Invisibleness that enables the woman migrant to look without being seen?' (Bhabha, 1987: 5). He locates the 'I' of the other as a challenge to 'see what is invisible', a redefinition of the gaze that previously demanded an object referent and is now forced to look at the missing person (woman). Such interpretations possibly demand a rethinking of the concept of identity, as Bhabha posits a repositioning of identity as 'contradictory places that co-exist', a phrase that could be applied to the position of veiled woman. He continues with a theme that is applicable to the positioning within discourse (and society) of the veiled woman, since he sees orientalist stereotypes as being erased and evoked at the same time. Yet he argues that this reinscription of the self must be outside metaphysical philosophies of self-doubt, 'where the "otherness" of identity is the anguished presence within the Self of an existential agony that emerges when you look perilously through a glass darkly' (Bhabha, 1987: 6).

Veiled woman could be argued to have an advantage, in that being restricted access to an outer world, she must turn within, with the resulting heightening of prescience or awareness. It is this inner knowledge that Frances (in *Ghazzah Street*) denies. She intuitively knows that it is only inner consciousness that will transcend the boundaries; but lacking this, she falls prey to her 'willed annihilation', to the existential agony of looking 'through the glass darkly'. In rejecting this transcendental dimension – or being forced to do so – she is left only with the meaningless outer vision in her room without a view.

Having discussed a western view of Arab culture, it is interesting to query how far Arab women are themselves discerning enough (or brave enough) to construct an alternative to the prison of patriarchal order. Fatima Mernissi claims that

> women are the only ones who publicly assert their right to self-affirmation as individuals, and not just through their words but also through their actions (e.g. in unveiling and going out). Today they constitute the most dynamic components of developing civil society. (1993: 157)

She explains how often, the more feminist books are banned, the more they are written, leading to the concept of the 'tireless pen', reaffirming the status of fiction and literature as both perspicacious documentary and deconstructive weapon. Saudi women writers continue this tradition. Perhaps, as Arebi argues, women place themselves outside the Foucauldian discourse of power. She proposes their writing as

> a peaceful and almost feminine weapon – used for the purpose of preserving blood, not shedding it ... contemporary Saudi women writers have in fact opted for more than having a 'voice'; they are concerned about transforming or at least affecting the entire cultural discourse. (Arebi, 1994: 11)

Voices of change

In the collection of short stories by Arab women *Voices of Change* (Bagader et al., 1998), the narrators scarcely remark upon the fact they are veiled, or merely mention it *en passant*. One could speculate why this is. One reason could be the incredibly tight censorship of the written media and television – any articles critical of Saudi Arabia or Islam are forbidden, as are articles suggestive of sex. Men do not take women seriously, yet they are more heavily censored and penalised than male writers. [6] Perhaps for this reason, women find alternative realities hard to envision. Another reason might be that the veil is ubiquitous and normalised: the reader does not need to be alerted to the fact that women are wearing it.

While Hilary Mantel in *Eight Months on Ghazzah Street* takes the image of the veiled woman to an extreme, dwelling on the secrecy of 'veiled truths' and the eventual terror of the 'unknown because not seen', these short stories by Saudi women dwell mainly on concerns of the inner emotional life. Two themes are particularly prevalent; one is the desperate need for a free choice in marriage (and the misery that arranged marriages can bring) and the other is the need for a society which upholds justice for both women *and* men equally.

The Saudi writer Sharifah Ash-Shamlan, for example, vividly portrays the latter theme involving the prevailing attitudes of her society. In the story 'Nawal', Ash-Shamlan uses the veil (here the full body cover of the *abaya*) both as dramatic narrative device and as symbol. A woman has been thrown out of the house (presumably by her husband) into the midday July sun. Exposed and shamed by being 'on the street', she tries to escape the heat and to protect her small daughter within the folds of her thick *abaya*, but she is in a state of mind that 'allowed me neither to think nor to remember' (130). In this state of bewilderment, she does not understand why later she is being taken by the police through huge doors, which 'make me shiver just imagining my having to pass through'. In prison, she is victimised both by the male police and by the other women in the cell:

> I was still in my *abeya* when one of those [women] in their slips screamed at me, 'Take off your *abeya*!' And then she added bitterly, 'It is safe here, there are no men.' Two of them suddenly pulled off my *abeya* ... I felt exposed ... fearful, I resumed a foetal position. (131)

The reader appreciates the irony of the fact that it is certainly not safe even without men being present: patriarchal laws seemingly assimilated and replicated by these women. The mother tries to explain to the other inmates that she only ever takes off her *abaya* at home, to which one on them replies with laughter, 'This is your home until you go back to the other one' (131). This apparent power of the *abaya* to protect the mother from harm is significant. Once she is exposed, she appears both humiliated and powerless. She is taken away for questioning, and finally she is told she has killed her daughter. She screams in disbelief, 'Impossible ... I could not have killed Nawal ... I was embracing her, protecting her from the blazing sun' (133).

In much writing by women, the *abaya* emerges as 'being good in reality but bad in its symbolic meaning' (Arebi, 1994: 280). In this short story, the *abaya*, the total covering of the Arab woman, is ostensibly protection against the harsh heat of the sun and against the gaze of other people. Yet, as Arebi discusses, the *abaya* can also be, as in this story, a symbol of darkness and claustrophobia (Arebi, 1994: 162). The very fact that in trying to protect her daughter, the mother suffocates her is also symbolic of the author's attitude towards society. It is society, in the form of the husband, which has thrown the mother out into the blazing sun – exposure from which, as from the women's gaze in prison, there is no protection. (The sun also represents the omnipresent and malevolent 'eye' of patriarchal power.) The mother faces death. It is the individual woman who is punished for her infanticide – not society. This story provides a dark vision of powerlessness and lack of female agency within the Arab world.

Further indictment of society appears in Ash-Shamlan's stories 'Zainab' and 'Secret and Death'. Both stories illustrate the importance of women's role as 'communal symbols' within Muslim society. This role is at the basis of the restrictions placed both on women's mobility and on their separation in physical space – 'symbolic' forms of veiling, which are no less real than the piece of black cloth or white muslin. Anita M. Weiss writes, 'Muslim social order revolves around the concepts and values associated with *izzat* (respect) and *sharafat* (honour)' (Ahmed and Donnan, 1994: 127) and argues that women's actions are pivotal for both the family honour, and for the larger society.

The short story 'Secret and Death' also portrays a woman's destruction by her society. The local village washerwoman, Zahra, is allowed to go about her work outside and – since the villagers consider her to be mad – unveiled. Only one man seems to understand her, realising that, 'No, Zahra, you are not crazy. You are a good-hearted person at a time when goodness is considered sheer madness' (128). Following their affair that ensues from his kindness, she becomes pregnant. Ostracised and condemned by her community, she remains silent to protect the man, even when interrogated by the authorities. The unnamed man does nothing to save her, or her reputation. Ironically, the narrator now questions where sanity lies. 'She is the most sane of the sane, she had protected his name ... She had protected

him, the sane, while he let her down and left her to face the unknown'
(129). Zahra is trapped and punished by the gender bias of misogynist
moral and religious law.[7] She dies, not in childbirth, but from the
poisoned foot that everyone has overlooked in their obsession with
her swollen belly: 'the baby had died with her, and so did a secret
she would never reveal' (130). Here again, both society and men are
indicted: man, both individual and symbolic, appears as the agent
of the forces that crush women. Even if unintentionally, men are the
agents of victimisation.

This story is a strong critique of society's obsession with woman
as a symbol of honour, rather than a human being needing care and
understanding. Such a sensitive issue can only be voiced through the
device of having a 'mad' character that puts the message across.
Despite their madness, or because of it, such women act as models
for resistance. Madness as literary device effectively critiques the
spurious 'sanity' of the world. In this story, it is probably only because
the outspoken Zahra has been branded as mad that she has survived
unharmed for so long. As her sanity is hidden from society by a social
stigma of 'being crazy', madness could also be argued to be another
type of 'veiling'. Other characters who speak their minds (as too in
life) soon find themselves arrested, tortured, and in the courtroom,
as in the story 'The Appeal' by Ruqayya Ash-Shabib.[8]

In these stories of 'victimisation', the writers expose the problems
but remain silent as to any solution for women's lack of agency. In
general the institution of physical concealment, as manifested in
veiling, receives little criticism. Similarly, women writers, while
creating characters that portray the oppression of women throughout
the Arab world, present no feminist alternative to replace the existing
regime. Another story by Ash-Shamlam, 'Complete Calm', offers the
only apparent means of escape available to women: leaving Saudi
Arabia (with an official male escort) to study overseas. As mentioned
earlier, education is not seen as a luxury for a woman but as a chance
for survival.

While 'escape' to study abroad seems a solution for individuals, it
is certainly not a solution for the society as a whole. Ultimately both
men and women are 'inmates in a big prison called society' (Arebi,
1994: 176). Victimisation in many Arab stories, Arebi argues, is not
at the hands of men in general but by particular men as individuals.
While a solution may be madness or death,

it is never the switching of gender roles to acquire power. It seems that man may stand as a victim of society or as the victimising agent to women but he does not stand as a *model* for women. Women's lack of desire to trade positions with men is a function of ... contempt for the qualities of oppression which may present themselves in some men. (Arebi, 1994: 177)

Thus for Arab women, the western concept of equality between men and women holds little validity: it has been met with ridicule and viewed as a 'lie'.

Mirage

In his novel *Mirage* (1999), Bandula Chandraratana presents life in the closed and restrictive world of an Arab kingdom from a 'male perspective'. (The author is a Sri Lankan doctor who spent many years working in a hospital in Saudi Arabia.) Published in 1999, the book tells the story of an impoverished Saudi hospital porter, Sayeed, who is unwillingly persuaded by his family to take a wife. In a xenophobic nation which seems to blame all its problems on the presence of the many foreign workers, and yet one in which the characters are portrayed drinking only Pepsi and 7-Up, the local workers struggle to make a living. Unfamiliar with women, their world, and their needs, Sayeed takes on a huge debt in order to pay for the wedding and improve the shack of wooden boxes that is his home in an urban shantytown. His new wife, Latifa, as all the women in the novel, is heavily veiled. He only sees her face after the wedding (151), and although we are not told his reaction, elsewhere she is referred to as beautiful.

The crisis of the story occurs when Latifa removes her veil and another man, not her husband, sees her face. When Latifa's herd of goats escape into the desert, she falls and injures her leg in trying to follow them. She removes her *abaya* to use it to bandage her wounded ankle, and eventually her calls for help are heard by her husband's friend, Hussain. But the temptation of beauty in a face unveiled – considered sexually provocative in the Islamic world – leads Hussain to rape Latifa. 'She wanted to scream, resist, run away... She could not push him away, she did not push him away' (208). For Latifa it is an ambiguous moment, of pain and sorrow as well as of great freedom and exhilaration: 'She felt no fear of anyone, and she felt as if she were the happiest person on earth at that moment. She screamed and she laughed and her voice came out unhindered' (208).

In a moment of true freedom, having sex with a young, handsome, and kind friend, Latifa is both unveiled and unsilenced – we see her face as well as hear her voice (both considered *'awra* in Islam).

   The hypocrisy and intolerance rife in society is demonstrated in the behaviour of the friends and neighbours who witness the incident: they betray Latifa and delight in actively assaulting her. Poverty and sexual repression lead to a fatal ending. Latifa is accused of adultery and stoned to death. Her 'lover', Hussain, is beheaded in public.[9] This pivotal episode, in which a young woman is seen without her veil, could be interpreted as showing how a woman's sexuality is *fitna*, a corrupting influence on man, and by extension, on society as a whole.[10] From an Islamic viewpoint, it is entirely understandable, if not inevitable, that a man seeing an unveiled woman would be unable to restrain his own sexual desires. In a society where veiling is synonymous with virtue, an unveiled woman is considered to be loose, one who incites lust and is without shame.[11] The author of *Mirage*, however, writing from outside an Arab culture, is able to depict the event in more tragic terms. Sexual and social repression due to the severe laws of society seem to be blamed here: judgement is equally meted out to both the male and female 'sinners' (although stoning is debatably a much 'worse' death).

   The inhumanity of the political and social regime is reflected in the barrenness of the desert. The 'mirage' of the novel's title denotes the facade of human society covering over its stillness and silence. Chandraratana sympathetically portrays both sides of the gender divide: the unhappiness of the wife having to leave her parents and marry a poor and much older man; and the desperation of a man knowing nothing of women due to the strict segregation of the sexes. This example suggests that the pro-veiling stance, which argues the veil protects women from sexual harassment by men, is highly debatable. Veiling may in fact make men *more* prone to violence against women, since the 'obsession with sex, women, and the human body [amongst frustrated Arab men] ... borders on the pathological ... the larger the veil, the greater the desire to recognise what it hides' (Moghissi, 1999: 46).

   In this society both sexes suffer: the women in their restricted world within the veil, and the men in the restricted world outside the veil. In a rigid patriarchal system, men oppress other men not only women. Thus ending such a system is better for all humanity. Sayeed is left a broken man, impotent against the forces of religion and law: 'He lay there wailing loudly and slapping the Earth with both hands' (214) – as if the earth itself could feel his suffering and it too might one day respond against human injustice, the illusion of man's power – the mirage.[12]

THE ARABIAN GULF AND EASTERN MEDITERRANEAN

Hanan al-Shaykh's 1988 novel *Women of Sand and Myrrh* takes place in an undisclosed country, which bears similarities to Saudi Arabia or one of the Gulf States. The 1980s were a period of great upheaval in the Arab world, with Lebanon becoming the focus of world attention with the detention of western hostages and the violence of the Hizbullah. Iran's 'export of revolution' supported the Hizbullah as well as the worldwide Islamic Jihad and the Islamic revival, which forced women back into the veil in several countries – a process that continues today in countries as culturally diverse as Jordan, the Sudan, and Palestine. Ethnographically, Lebanon is a widely diverse culture, comprising 18 different sects, with over 40 per cent of the population being Christian, and the other five main Muslim sects being dominated by the Sunnis, Druze, Shi'i, and Isma'ilis. Individual political identity is very much defined by sectarian attachment. Although recently described as being 'widely condemned for its corruption, inequity, and instability' Lebanon is nevertheless a 'microcosm of the Arab world' and 'a fascinating experiment in managing cultural and religious diversity' (Esposito, 1995b: 475).

The writer Hanan al-Shaykh takes a refreshingly different view of women in the Arab world. Born in Lebanon, educated in Cairo and now living in London, al-Shaykh's writing reflects her 'between-worlds' experience and the women who reside in it. Her two novels set in Lebanon, *Beirut Blues* and *The Story of Zahra* (a powerful narrative about the Lebanese civil war), tackle religious and social taboos, and vividly depict the liminal 'Third Space' experience of the heroines as they live in war-time border zones of the divided city. Due to the outspoken and controversial portrayal of women and gender relations these novels, originally written in Arabic, were initially banned across the Arab world. Al-Shaykh's novel *Women of Sand and Myrrh* provides a viewpoint of Arab women that encompasses both 'eastern' and 'western' perspectives. It is also a novel that addresses the notion of women renegotiating their identity despite, or even through, the veil.

In *Women of Sand and Myrrh* al-Shaykh takes the lives of four women and exposes the multifaceted dimensions of life under a strict patriarchal regime (similar to that of Saudi Arabia). The novel exposes

5   Iranian tourists, outside Topkapi Palace, Istanbul, May 2001. A party of women wearing the black *chador* emerge from a visit to the Topkapi Palace harem. A variety of veils are still seen in Turkey (as in England and elsewhere), although in Turkey itself, especially in universities, wearing the veil remains an issue of political controversy. (Photo: author)

a collage within the culture: a society in which women wear expensive jewellery and designer dresses beneath their black *abayas*, and yet may not either choose their own husbands or see them before marriage. It is these kinds of contradictions in society that ultimately limit both men and women's ability to comprehend the other, since any sharing of social spaces is prohibited in the belief that women are dangerous to society (i.e. men) and need to be controlled.

To explicate uses of the veil within the novel: the first story is that of Suha, a Lebanese wife, bored and lonely in a society that enforces her separation from the outside world. Similar to Frances Shore in *Ghazzah Street*, living in the foreigners' compound makes her imagine she is 'somewhere in space' (8). As a college graduate, and desperate to resist the torpor that envelopes the place, she throws herself into various activities (4–5). While teaching in the local women's institute, she meets other wives (the other three women in the novel) all of whom are desperate to find a reason for existence. She is soon drawn into a close friendship with Nur, a Saudi wife who lives in the luxurious and hedonistic, yet cloistered world of her house and pool. Nur reawakens Suha's interest and curiosity, mainly because of the contradictions of Arab life she personifies. While Nur must live beneath the *abaya* when she goes outside, her home incorporates a wealth of imported luxuries 'the latest of everything, including the furniture and the chocolates, the video machines, animals, and birds' (40). Suha enjoys the visits from Nur's relatives, who, further portraying this clash of traditional and modern, are 'enveloped in *abeyas* and veils and had henna patterns on their hands, while others wore clothes in the latest styles and colours, [and] jewellery ... in modern international designer styles' (40).

Women's ability to manipulate and subvert the dominant male discourse is often expressed through the use of the female body. The four women in *Sand and Myrrh* – three Arab women from different countries and one American – develop different strategies of survival in their isolated life segregated from the male outer world.[13] Suha's search for agency within the limited cultural possibilities of her circumstances involves a lesbian relationship with Nur, which offers her fulfilment in a way she had never imagined (despite her feelings of guilt and disbelief when she returns home to her husband and son). Suha uses her 'secret relationship' as her means of protest against the patriarchal constructs of society.[14]

Her insights into the contradictions inherent in society are confirmed at a women's party. At the gathering of women, many remove their *abayas*, which were 'bundled up on their laps and it looked as if their dresses had big black stains in the middle' (61). Dressed in evening dresses by Valentino, and wearing thick gold chains and seed pearls, the women begin to sing together:

> some of them were unveiled and stared at me, chewing gum and sipping tea ... They were passing a narghile round. One of them took a long drag as if it was the elixir of life; ... another older than the rest, drew on it ... as if it would give her youth back. (62)

Suha questions how the women could sing and dance and enjoy 'hearing words that were so much at odds with reality' (63). One woman 'lifted her veil a little so she could let out a wild trill of joy and appreciation' (63). Suha gains a clear perception of how these women are trying to escape their realities, their hopeless situation in the world outside this decadent party: 'They were like old women trying to darn enormous holes in socks' (63). Sick with embarrassment at the 'primitive ... lust-crazed' dancing of the women, Suha nevertheless appreciates that such behaviour is aroused by the feeling of freedom away from the house and children. Yet although 'their emotions that night were out of keeping with their veils' (65), she appreciates the irony that these women are trying to escape the world outside and feel free, they 'knew that they were prisoners even in this hall because they couldn't leave it until their drivers or their husbands came to pick them up' (65).

Disillusioned, Suha realises that her lesbian relationship does not provide the escape she thought. Finally, she leaves her husband to return to her mother's home in Lebanon. 'I'm an Arab', she reasons, 'I'm supposed to feel that I have some connection with the culture here, but I feel none at all. I'm completely detached from it' (77). Suha's dilemma in lacking a sense of belonging is pertinent in the east/west binary of my discussion here.[15] If feminism is the 'permanent shield against patriarchal oppression' (Moghadam, 1993: 170), then it is woman's right of self-determination that is all-important. Ultimately, only Suha's ability to leave ensures her self-respect – suggesting perhaps that alternatives to heterosexuality do not provide a lasting escape from patriarchy.

Having lost her cultural identity, feeling uncomfortable amongst the other veiled more traditional women, Suha is rootless. Homi Bhabha writes that in the 'beyond', we find ourselves 'in a moment of transit where space and time cross to produce complex figures of difference and identity, past and present' (1994: 1). Thus, Suha could be compared to Homi Bhabha's 'hybrid' living a 'border life' and permanently 'in transit'. She measures her own identity *against* those of the veiled Arab women and ultimately locates herself outside their sphere of reality.

Subjectivity, as Bhabha argues, can be remade and remodelled in new and innovative ways. The indeterminacy of women's identity while living on the symbolic if not the physical borderline of a nation, demonstrates how women inhabit an 'in-between' site, characterised as 'both inside and outside, inclusion and exclusion ... These in-between spaces provide the terrain of elaborating strategies of selfhood – singular or communal – that initiate new signs of identity' (Bhabha,

1994: 1–2). For Bhabha this space is also one where traditional patterns of thought are disturbed. Likewise, the veil or *hijab* places women in a position where traditional means of gaining knowledge are invalidated and they must rely on an alternate means of gaining knowledge, an *inner* experience of self or an 'inner gaze'. Women's struggle for freedom from prescribed identities through recourse to an 'inner gaze' does not imply any uniformity of experience, however, but an expansion of possibilities.

The other women characters in the novel provide further insight into the dislocation of cultural and gendered subjectivities. Tamr, brought up to be a modest and obedient Saudi daughter, and now a widow beholden to her older brother, rebels against her upbringing in order to find fulfilment in an independent career. She lives behind the veil (the *abaya*) yet knows how to use the symbols of her culture to ultimately gain her goals. She goes on a hunger strike to protest against her brother's refusal to let her study at the local Institute. Using the *abaya* as her cover, she manages to penetrate the male domain of the bank to arrange a loan to start her own women's tailoring and hairdressing business. Her beauty shop also becomes a refuge for women to be together unveiled, a sanctum away from men rather like the traditional *hammam* (public bath). In contrast, the story of Tamr's mother (narrated to explain her own psychological stance in the battle for agency) is a life-time's silent endurance of suffering through marriage. It serves to remind the reader of the traditional foundation of women's plight in the Arabo-Islamic world. Sold as a young girl into a Sultan's harem, and then sold again when she fails to become pregnant, many years pass before she has a chance to gain a divorce from her brutal husband. Now old, she dreams of returning to her lost homeland of Turkey. When she eventually does make the pilgrimage to her village, all has changed and she recognises nothing. She loses both her present dreams and her past memories, which suggests support for critics who claim that both women and the colonial subject must have access to reclaim historical identity in order to be able to move forward.

In the next section of *Women of Sand and Myrrh*, the American wife Suzanne contorts the rules of Arab society to suit her own version of fulfilment. She discovers that Arab men constantly look out for accessible foreign wives, and she revels in her new 'desirable' identity. One of her affairs with a married Arab man, Maaz, soon develops into an obsession, so much so that she even wants to become his second wife (something despised by Arab women themselves).[16]

Disillusioned with her American identity of small-town suburban wife and mother, she wants to become more 'Arab'. For Suzanne this choice of a new identity is defined by veiling:

> I draped the bed cover over my head, and let it hang down around me just like an *abeya*. I smiled, wishing I could get used to an abeya and cover my face with a black handkerchief and become like the others, wrapped up because I was precious and easily damaged. (186)

When ultimately Suzanne's relationship with Maaz ends, she does not want to abandon her new life. Men pursue her night and day and, 'more than Maaz, they made the fantasy of *A Thousand and One Nights* come true for me' (231). Although her husband's company is closed down, she is determined to find a way to stay in the country: 'I found that I loved this reality ... I vowed not to leave here whatever happened ... I could say I'd converted to Islam and ask to stay on' (236).

All four women in *Sand and Myrrh* are able to claim elements of agency, however limited, within the Arab world. While men attempt to protect the symbolic value of women by keeping them secluded and veiled, the 'real' women are finding ways within that system to either rebel (Nur and Tamr) or to subvert the system to their own purposes (Suha and Suzanne). In addition, *Women of Sand and Myrrh* demonstrates how women are able to negotiate 'new' identities within prescriptive religious and social rules. The veil is implicated in all these renegotiations of identity. Suha redefines her identity as an Arab woman in juxtaposing her own values with those of the veiled women whom she finds emotionally repressed and socially trapped in inept behaviours. Suzanne isolates the veil as a symbol of her desired new sexual identity within Arab culture, while Tamr escapes from traditional patriarchal positioning of the veil by utilising it to access male space to further her education and independent career.

In the Arab world, women are struggling to claim any individual identity, other than the stereotypical one of daughter, wife, and producer of sons for the nation. The novel suggests the possibility that other women too may be playing with these possibilities: redefining and negotiating agency within the limitations of their social space. Hanan al-Shaykh's characters (for whom the veil does not preclude redefinitions of identity) would contest the stereotyped western viewpoint in which the identity of Arab woman is all too often negated by the veil, remaining a blank, black sheet, face-less, and voice-less. Her novel reminds us that the veiled woman (especially in Saudi Arabia) may be enjoying enormous wealth, as well as utilising the strategies available to her for personal fulfilment.

Woman's identity is argued to be in a constant state of flux (particularly when caught in the 'in-between space' of hybridity).[17] The female characters in this novel reformulate their fragmented identities, seeking self-definition beyond masculinist designation, to form a new sense of the self, one that can always be open to redefinition. I would suggest that women must and can manipulate the dominant male discourse through language, and through their inner experience, in order to find a *modus vivendi*.

PALESTINE

The theme of woman's power to use her 'inner gaze' or her inner spirituality as a means of agency is elaborated by Zeina B. Ghandour in her novel *The Honey* (1999). It is also a novel set in a state which could itself be seen as being on the borderline or 'in-between': Palestine.

Set in Palestine under Israeli occupation, the novel takes a fresh perspective on the themes of politics and war, suicide and liberation. The story is played out against the political background of violence which began when Palestine lost the territories of the Gaza Strip, West Bank and East Jerusalem (which were all conquered by the Israelis) and the PLO took an independent course of action based on both diplomacy and on guerrilla warfare.

Since the 1967 war, and the escalating violence of both Hamas and the Israeli incursions, Palestinian women have lived under a double burden, that of Israeli aggression *and* the cultural patriarchy which has become increasingly Islamicist. Women have traditionally participated in the nationalist movement, and encouraged their children to do so, and yet after abandoning the *hijab* in the 1940s they have recently been forced to return to it. As Valentine Moghadam claims in relation to Palestine, 'People resort to cultural references like the veil, especially when they perceive their whole national existence is threatened' (1993: 163).

The relative freedom that women enjoyed in previous decades in several countries such as Palestine has in recent years been increasingly and dramatically curtailed as veiling has been enforced and leaving the home prohibited. The example of Palestine shows how the enforcement of the veil sometimes has unforeseen effects. When Hamas, the Islamic Resistance Movement supported by the mainstream government, organised campaigns in the 1990s to compel women to stay at home and adopt the Islamic dress, it simultaneously brought the women's movement in Palestine to a new feminist awareness – although the battle for equality ultimately has fared badly. Hamas first encouraged and then insisted that women return to the full-length *abaya* and to wearing face veils and gloves. They then carried out a violent campaign to force women to veil, to the extent that non-Islamist women were threatened, harassed and assaulted.[18] Some Hamas graffiti read: 'Hamas considers the unveiled as collaborators of a kind. It is our religious duty to execute collaborators' (Brooks, 1996).

With *hijab* and gender being politicised, the female body becomes a preoccupation and focal point of the political and economic crisis, the locus of cultural interpretation, while patriarchy in making and controlling such interpretation seeks to safeguard its own powerful status. Women in Palestine have not been docile in the face of Islamist male aggression, however, and many resent the imposition of *hijab*. Many women also stress the irrelevance of *hijab* to intifada. At the foundation of the women's movement in 1991, its founder, Maria Hassan claimed, 'The existing political parties refuse to confront the patriarchal traditions which oppress women' (Moghadam, 1993: 163). The blurring of the lines of religion and politics leads to feminists walking a 'difficult tightrope' between reclaiming national identity and rejecting oppressive traditions – yet, as Valentine Moghadam conjectures, 'One possible outcome ... of Islamist movements, of the politicisation of gender, and of women's activism for and against these movements could very well be the subversion of the patriarchal order and its rapid demise' (1993: 169).

However, as one Palestinian woman commented, 'Once you put on the veil, you accept everything it symbolises, your life changes completely and it is hard to take it off again' (Goodwin, 1994: 300). The revolution from 'beneath the veil' is one fraught with physical as well as political dangers.

It is refreshing therefore to find a novel that tackles this cultural situation from a different perspective: that of the spiritual or 'mystical' tradition of Islam – the tradition of Sufism. In her essay 'Beirut Fragments, a War Memoir', Palestinian writer Jean Said Makdisi claims 'the question of women lies at the bottom of things and cannot be touched without upsetting the whole order' (qt. Moghadam, 1993: 250). If women are at the centre of change and discourse about change in the Middle East, *The Honey* provides an example of how the actions of one woman can subvert the whole social order.

The first novel of the Palestinian writer Zeina B. Ghandour, *The Honey*, is set against the violence of the PLO/Israeli conflict and the hardships in the lives of the Palestinian people. The poetic style of the text renders the violent background remote, while enhancing the spiritual connotations underlying the plot. In the novel, the female protagonist, Ruhiya, is the daughter of the village muezzin. When he falls ill, the village despairs as to how the call to morning prayer will be made. Breaking tradition and taboo, Ruhiya climbs the minaret and gives the call. For this act of defiance, she removes her *abaya* and ties it around her waist, ascending the steps of the minaret unveiled: a liberating experience in more ways than one, since 'it had been years since she felt the coolness of the wind at the base of her neck' (23).

The village is divided in shock: the men because she has violated the most sacred of sex roles, and they felt her song 'pierce through their hearts like a burning spear' (28); the women because, 'she was like some exotic bird that had come down to rest from her flight' (28). For both, her song was 'unbearable. Like pure sugar ... like golden, liquid sugar' (64). For Ruhiya herself, her call has another purpose. She knows that her lover, a recent convert to militant Islamism, is to be a suicide bomber in Jerusalem that morning. Prepared to die along with his friend, her lover hears her dawn call:

> But my seagull is upon me, drowning me in song, ripping my insides with her beak until I drop my weights and fly ... The sky is pouring its honey along the Old City Walls and I am ... still alive, still weak, still striving. (42–3)

Brought back to a sense of reality by this experience, he avoids the lure to death and runs away from the walled city. He withdraws to a monastery in the desert, where the monks give him shelter and tend his shattered spirit. Turning within to discover the truth, he is also nourished by Ruhiya's presence, both physical and spiritual.

Ruhiya and her lover, Yehya (meaning 'life', 'the will to live'), both escape from the war-torn reality of Palestine into a reality of their own. The novel suggests the need for a spiritual (as opposed to religious) answer to the social problems as well as a need for spiritual healing. The author explains that the title *The Honey* refers to the metaphor of a life-enhancing balm that can pervade society to heal the land. The plot of *The Honey* gradually unfolds in a sequence of 'unlayering' of compacted truths. The past of the characters is unpacked as the reader learns of a disastrous love affair which resulted in Ruhiya's mother committing suicide, aided by her lover, who is eventually revealed to be Yehya's father. In the village, a strange young girl, Asrar (whose name means 'secrets'), sees all and seems to understand everything. She is able to see behind the illusion of appearances that hides reality. She witnesses Ruhiya's dawn call from the minaret, knowing the purpose of it and knowing also the unspeakable secret that Ruhiya and Yehya are half-brother and sister. 'I saw everything. I saw what the Honeyman [Yehya's father] did to Hurra, how he had unveiled her, and what she did to herself, and I kept their secret' (76). Here, the term 'unveiling' implies more than the mere removal of a piece of clothing: the girl has seen how the man stripped Hurra (Ruhiya's mother) of her inner strength, peace of mind, and her self-respect: 'The amulets she [Hurra] made and the one she carried with her couldn't protect her, because no charm can keep you from dying inside ... from the witchcraft, once it's in your blood' (76). In Arabic, the word 'hijab' also means an amulet to protect against harm. Thus, the mother, Hurra, is unveiled both of her physical and psychological protection; she has 'died inside' even before her lover places the rope around her neck.

Mernissi explains that,

> In Sufism, one calls Muhjab (veiled) the person whose consciousness is determined by sensual or mental passion and who as a result does not perceive the divine light in his soul. In this usage it is man who is covered by a veil, or a curtain, and not God. (1991: 93)

In the Sufi tradition, 'unveiling' (*kashf*) is a metaphor of sight, when we see not only with the eyes but with the heart, when the veils are lifted 'between the creation and the Real' (Chittick, 1998: 95).[19] In this novel, Zeina Ghandour uses the concept of *kashf*, defining it as: 'the uncovery; the removal of the veil; revealing the reality beneath' (71). This spiritual dimension is associated with Asrar and her penetrating perception, with which she sees into the heart of nature, even able to hear across the desert 'Yehya calling out her [Ruhiya's] name, straight into my dreams, where I kept his secret' (73).

The novel concludes with Yehya wandering the desert in search of inner truth, an exploration in which he is joined by Ruhiya. Through her spiritual power, she ultimately gives him the key to inner peace, as Yehya realises: 'Ruhiya, I will always love you, my lioness. I leant against the date palm and closed my dry eyes. I sense God everywhere. I can't tell him from another' (107). To elaborate upon this experience, in the Sufi texts, *kashf* is described as the revelation that 'existence remains eternally as it truly is, without cover, without secret ... When the curtain of illusion fell there was only One, no one but God' (Angha, 1991: 10). In this novel, escape from the realities and hardships of both war and of living in occupied Palestine is presented in both spiritual and ethical terms. The characters of Ruhiya and Yehya seek to redefine their identities by defying both cultural expectations and sexual taboos. While Ruyiha breaks the religious taboo of a woman calling the dawn prayer, Yehya also defies the political identity of 'fundamentalist' that has been thrust on him by his friends. They both transgress the cultural and religious laws and the concept of what is *haram* (forbidden) in their incestuous relationship. Since the community is unaware of the con-sanguinity between Ruhiya and Yehya, their 'unveiled' friendship would be *haram* – as would their sexual relationship were the con-sanguinity known.[20] The spiritual and telepathic nature of their relationship enables a transcendence of cultural or religious boundaries, allowing them a further sense of freedom from the constraints of a society defined by patriarchal aggression.

The Honey, with its portrayal of the intuitive, spiritual power of women, makes use of concepts of the veil in Sufism. As already mentioned, in Sufism the veil holds special significance as being the cover that hides man from his real nature. This notion that veils prevent a person from perceiving his/her inner consciousness is likened in a Persian Sufi poem to the relation of the wave with the ocean:

> The veil of thinking becomes an obstacle on the path to Unity
> When the bubble shatters its shell, it becomes the sea.[21]

The gradual unveiling of reality reveals that at the basis of creation all existence is Being, is-ness. As Yehya declares at the end of *The Honey*, 'I sense God everywhere. I can't tell him from another' (107).

Fatima Mernissi uses the example of the twelfth-century Sufi poem *The Conference of Birds* (Attar, 1954, 1974). Written in 1177 by the Persian poet Farid ud-Din Attar, the allegorical poem tells the story of a group of birds that set out on a pilgrimage to find the Simurgh – the city of God.[22] Although a thousand birds start the epic journey, only 30 eventually reach the court of the Simurgh. There, 'the Chamberlain, having tested them, opened the door; and as he drew aside a hundred curtains, one after the other, a new world beyond the veil was revealed'. As a new life begins for them, they realise that, 'They were the Simurgh and the Simurgh was the thirty birds ... And perceiving both at once, themselves and Him, they realised that they and the Simurgh were one and the same being' (Attar, 1954, 1974: 132).

Mernissi shares the Sufi poet's dream for the establishment of the Simurgh: a world where every individual recognises themselves for what they truly are (just as the 30 birds see themselves in the Simurgh's mirror, which reflects not only themselves but the whole planet 'soul and body ... completely'). Mernissi claims this message provides a vision, from *within* Islam, that 'will probably be the only successful challenger to the electronic agenda, for it offers something the latter can never threaten or replace: the spirituality that gives wings'. She hopes that with present-day communications and technology, we should be able to 'create that global mirror in which all cultures can shine in their uniqueness' (1993: 174). However idealistic Mernissi's vision, it does suggest the multidimensional nature of Islam, and that – as many Arab feminists hope – a solution to the oppression of women can come from within Islam itself.[23]

CONCLUSION

Such representations from Islamic women living both inside the Arab world and in the diaspora, highlight that improvements in the quality of gender relations will only come about when women secure the space they need to articulate oppositional discourses. Haideh Moghissi cites what Nancy Fraser has called a 'subaltern counterpublic' which would permit women to 'formulate oppositional interpretations of their identities, interests and needs' (1999: 147).

Feminists within the Arab world are moving forward, but not necessarily in parallel with western concerns. These are seen to be inherently fraught with problems and often irrelevant to their cultures and situations. Wearing the veil may be an informed choice for many women, or an expression of a desire to maintain the traditional – and spiritual – values of the culture. The availability of choice, often determined by the freedoms associated with socio-economic privilege, also allows for a shifting between cultural frames of reference.

Yet the restrictions placed on women by the veil and social segregation can be harsh, even life threatening (as illustrated in Chandraratana's *Mirage* and in the short stories by Ash-Shamlan).

This analysis in fact exposes and highlights these polarised images of the veil, which create an unresolved tension both in society and in literature. Yet, from the works I have discussed, women cannot be seen simply as passive victims. While Islamic rule from outside may be viewed as cruel and archaic, the women and their writing raise public awareness so that change – albeit slow – is possible.

While the viewpoint of 'orientalist' Europe may consider the veiling of women as a sinister phenomenon or as a social evil in itself (as in Hilary Mantel's *Ghazzah Street* and Kate Millet's account of visiting Iran) texts from many Arab writers themselves regard veiling as an inherent part of the Qur'anic requirements for strict gender segregation and for modesty and piety. Moreover, the imposed veil is only a part of an extensive cultural and patriarchal system of the domination of women through the restriction of women's roles and mobility in society. Dawn Chatty, for example, claims veiling is only a part of the total structure of personal appearance which is 'consciously manipulated to assert and demarcate differences in status, identity and commitment as part of a much wider social reality'. She concludes, 'As elsewhere in the rapidly changing and confused social world of the Middle East, the significance of face covering can only be understood in the context of the totality of society' (Chatty and Rabo, 1997: 147).[24]

Religion is only one factor in the veiling of women: as discussed in previous chapters, veiling goes beyond misogynist religious sanctions to indigenous patriarchal values that have long retarded Islamic society. To cite religion as the sole cause of this seeming oppression of women is therefore reductive. Many other influences contribute to the current status experienced by women in the Middle East today. Other issues relating to national and international conflict, the nation-state system, economic conditions, and identity are all interconnected with issues of gender and women's rights. The fictional texts in this chapter confirm that socio-economic status is also important in determining the degree of oppression associated with veiling. Gender and class together construct the connotations of the veil and how far control through religious extremism suppresses individual identity. The Arab women in *Sand and Myrrh* who occupy an upper socio-economic bracket (such as Nur or Suha) escape the restrictive oppression of the veil. Money allows them not only material comfort, but also the freedom to act without their husbands' control in a women's world of their own. In *Mirage*, poverty gives women no alternative but to be victimised by a retributive legal system and the unenlightened attitudes of an ignorant population. (This sense of individual powerlessness obviously extends to men.) This same social disadvantaging is demonstrated in the stories by Saudi women writers. For the poor and uneducated women characters, society offers no choices. They quickly discover their lack of control over their own lives. The veil and its social counterparts engulf their identities.

The 'strict' adherence to the religious laws of Islam dominates all aspects of life in Saudi and the Gulf States, yet the history of North Africa and its colonial past has forged different interpretations of Islam – along with different struggles for women. While women in the Saudi literature may attempt to rebel, there is little sense of individual liberation implicating larger political goals. As the feminist and political activist Latifa al-Zayyat comments, in the making of literature into art: 'what matters is whether the specific personal experience is confined to the level of the subjective and the particular, or transformed to the level of the general, the impersonal and aesthetic [whereby] a meaning to this experience is discovered' (Ghazoul and Harlow, 1994: 248). The need of fiction to suggest a larger social and political meaning is most successfully achieved by *The Honey*, where the drama of the couple's emotional and spiritual relationship is connected to the wider drama of the battle for autonomy in Palestine. It also suggests an avenue for agency and autonomy *within* an Islamic spiritual tradition of unity-in-diversity.

5
Violence, Liberation and Resistance: North Africa

In relation to the North African context of the Maghrebian countries, it is relevant to ascertain how the veil can be a sign of not only religious piety, but also political protest. This chapter will explore the political and colonial associations of veiling in literature from the North African Maghreb: the countries of Algeria, Morocco and Tunisia. I discuss literature that examines political issues, especially with regard to women's resistance to the imposed 'identity of Arab women' imported from the west. In order to examine these problematic images in the light of literature, this chapter presents an overview of the historical events that have lead to the use of the veil as a trope of both colonial resistance and political identity. Imbricated within the arguments surrounding the suppression of female identity is the use of the veil as a symbol of rebellion during the colonial period, its practical use as cover, and its use by national independence movements as a symbol of both emerging nationhood and traditional values. Events in the area over the last 50 years have left a legacy of imagery that has resulted in the *hijab* today representing notions of respectability, morality, identity and resistance.

As already discussed, the sense of the western male's innate superiority was used to perpetuate and legitimate colonial power and the imperialist ethic. The imagery of Muslim women as 'slaves to be liberated' by western men focused on unveiling women as the primary task for the liberating colonialist. The similar latter-day attitude of western feminists has perpetuated and repeated the notion that the unveiling of women is fundamental to their independence and self-determination.

The practices of veiling traverse distinctions between 'colonial oppression' and 'traditional' religious and cultural practices, which can often be interpreted as oppressive. However, women themselves are constantly redefining *hijab*, generating new cultural meanings. Re-veiling can be a way of women 'actively and skilfully renegotiat-ing ways to affirm their own religious and cultural values' (Woodhull, 1993: 5). Many Islamist women who wear the veil, for example, are attempting to discover 'an appropriate identity which fits their tradition as it redefines their future' (Duval in Ask and Tjomsland, 1998: 68). While veiling for women may denote attachment to Islam as a religion, many women seek to avoid identification with Islamism as a militant political movement. Yet today it is the potential identification with Islamism that makes the *hijab* a highly charged political symbol (Charrad, 1998: 66). While a return to veiling is depicted in the west as a form of fundamentalist oppression, or reactionary rule, many women are voluntarily – if not ardently – embracing the veil as a means of expressing their gender identity and even (paradoxically to a western viewpoint) of demonstrating their protest against their more liberalised husbands (Ask and Tjomsland, 1998: 11).

To recapitulate within a Maghrebian context, the following can be seen as the major reasons for wearing *hijab*: as a way of women participating in a defined cultural legacy within a sphere of Muslim solidarity; as a means of rejecting western 'morally corrupt' ways; as a way of finding a safe place within male space by tracing clear sexual boundaries that men may not cross and indicating that women are not sexually available; and finally as a way of acceding to male family pressure to respect norms of modesty (Charrad, 1998: 67).

This chapter aims to uncover what lies behind the emergence of the *hijab* as a potent political symbol. It analyses the novels of writers from the Maghreb, whose texts encompass a vast range of experience across several decades of political turbulence and repressive patriarchal regimes in Algeria. However, before discussing the contributions of writers to the controversy of the veil as a political signifier in the latter half of the twentieth century, it is essential to locate these texts within the background of historical events and postcolonial theory, as well as in orientalist art.

HISTORICAL AND GEOGRAPHICAL BACKGROUND TO THE MAGHREB

The countries of the Maghreb encompass a diversity of cultures and a vast geographical area that are nevertheless often subsumed under the general heading of 'the Middle East', although the word *Maghreb* itself denotes 'western' or 'The West' in Arabic – the land of the setting sun.[1] This ambiguous geopolitical position, 'west' from the standpoint of the Arabs and 'oriental' from that of Europe, as well as being part of Africa, allows the Maghreb to be a potential site for dismantling the opposition between occident and orient. Although part of the

Islamic world, these countries are culturally distinct from other Arab nations in many ways. Algeria for example is a country of mixed Arab and Berber population, with 85 per cent speaking Berber as their mother tongue. Once part of the vast Roman Empire, the countries of North Africa were amongst the first to be converted to Islam. Long influenced by Arab traders and settlers, the area experienced upheaval when in the mid nineteenth century it became the site for the scramble by Britain and France to claim territory in the African continent. While Britain focused its attention on the 'Dark Continent' and the thrilling achievements of explorers such as Burton, Stanley and Speak, the French slowly gained North Africa.

Algeria was conquered after a long and bloody campaign in 1830, with Tunisia and Morocco becoming French protectorates in 1881 and 1912, respectively. Later, Algeria again became the battleground for protracted violence from 1954 to 1962 in a war of liberation from France, after which Algeria was left in a volatile state, in which violence has dominated. It was during this time that the veiling of women became a focus of political activism. As Fadwa El Guindi explains, 'The role of the veil in liberating Algeria from French colonial occupation is popularly known, idealised, romanticised, ideologised, and fictionalised, but nonetheless real' (1999: 169).

Historically, Morocco, Algeria and Tunisia have been the object of desire, the *phantasm* of the French since the first invasion of Algeria in 1830.[2] The French conquest of the area has had lasting repercussions up to and continuing today, both on the social order and on the literature produced in these countries. Culturally Tunisia shares much with Algeria, although in recent years as Algeria has become an increasingly Islamist state, its neighbour to the east is perceived by western powers as an island of stability in an unstable region. Tunisia has been spared the violent divisions that have torn apart Algeria. In terms of different attitudes to veiling: while in Algeria the Islamic party (FIS) now insist on women wearing the veil in order to stop 'looking like cheap merchandise that can be bought and sold'; in Tunisia the black *hijab* is rare and only older women are to be seen wearing the traditional white *haik* (Charrad, 1998: 67).

MAGHREBIAN IMAGES OF THE VEIL

Much of the work discussed here comes under the category of Francophone literature, although for the most part the writers maintain an ambivalent relationship with their French colonial past.

(Many texts I access here in their English translations were originally written in French, which until quite recently remained the national language of Algeria and Tunisia.) By the end of the Second World War, Maghrebian literature had emerged as a voice of anticolonialism. From the 1960s onwards, it expressed the widespread disillusionment with the aftermath of independence, especially that felt by women. Having fought, been imprisoned and tortured alongside the men, women had hoped for governmental recognition of their rights. This was not granted, since the new government decreed that they should return to their traditional domestic role as wives and mothers.[3]

For many of the writers, the issue of veiling is a practical one, while for others such as Assia Djebar it also takes on a more metaphorical meaning as a fundamental concept in the Islamic – and patriarchal – mind. The Moroccan author Tahar Ben Jelloun also expands the discussion of the role of veils and clothing in the masking of gender identity. (His novels are analysed later in this chapter, to provide an alternative 'gendered' reading of the veil and to expand the discussion of clothing in social and self-identity.) Evelyne Accad argues that women writers of the area, while describing 'the unfulfilled and circumscribed lives' that women lead, nevertheless fail to depict the most brutal and violent aspects of this experience (1978: 17). Since she wrote this, the later novels of Assia Djebar have responded to this lack, reflecting her culture's oscillating attitudes towards women and towards veiling. Both an outspoken author and film director, Djebar is principally concerned with women's voice, memory and language, and the role that women have played in the history of Algeria. Djebar, along with other women writers, such as Leïla Sebbar, have brought the issues of women's identity and freedom into a contemporary context, in which women seek to define themselves as more than a colonial or patriarchal 'other'. 'Plurilingual' societies, such as Algeria, allow for the emergence of an 'alternative' poetics or 'other-literature' as Winifred Woodhull (1993) has suggested. Assia Djebar for instance, while writing in French, draws upon her Berber-Arab background.

Before discussing the contributions of these writers to the controversy of the veil as a political signifier in the latter half of the twentieth century, it is essential to locate these texts within the background of postcolonial theory. The works of Frantz Fanon are central to any discussion of veiling in Algeria: indeed for Fanon, veiling was at the very heart of national identity and the cause of independence. Although Fanon died in 1961, his works and ideas are still fundamental to the postcolonial debate.

Frantz Fanon: the revolutionary veil

Writing in the late 1950s and early 1960s, Fanon drew together aspects of psychology, sociology and politics to develop one of the first discussions of the impact and consequences of colonialisation. His groundbreaking works, such as *Black Skin, White Masks*, discussed the apparent willingness of colonised peoples to don the mask of 'white' culture with its cultural privileges. From his insights as a psychiatrist, Fanon was able to perceive discourse as a form of power that allows people both to disarm opposition and to reclaim their past and structure a future. Written in the political context of opposition, his revolutionary ideas were to form the basis of nationalist movements in the Maghreb and other colonised countries. A recent reappraisal of Fanon claims that his work is as relevant today as it was when written since, 'as Fanon proposes, today's struggle is not to resurrect the past, but to change the unbearable present and the potentially (now a fact) bewildering future' (Abdi, 1999: 53).[4]

Recognising and challenging characteristics at the heart of colonial oppression, Fanon (originally from Martinique) emphasised how African countries must differentiate themselves from European culture. For Fanon, the issue of women and veiling became the symbol of national liberation.[5] For the revolutionary struggle, the veil remained emblematic both of women's role in resistance and of the symbolic identification of woman with nation. In Fanon's analysis, the veil and woman become interchangeable signifiers of colonised Algeria, both oppressed, inscrutable, and dispossessed.

Fanon's essay 'Algeria Unveiled' in his first book, *The Wretched of the Earth*, focuses on the role of women in the war of independence from France. While woman's body has long been used as synecdoche for a nation, in Algeria particularly, the metaphor appears more literal in the identity of 'veiled women'. During the years of the war for independence, Fanon summarised the doctrine of colonial oppression as 'If we want to destroy the structure of Algeria, its capacity for resistance, we must first of all conquer the women' (Fanon, 1965: 14). The colonial battle was fought on the level of the displaced female, with unveiling being a part of breaking women's and hence national resistance. Making women accessible to the eye is part of male colonial ownership and control. For Fanon, women who were 'saved from slavery' and unveiled by the west, were 'accepting the rape of the coloniser'. Fanon emphasises an 'aura' of rape surrounding the veiled Algerian woman and insists on the link between territorial and sexual possession (1967: 47).

By extension, the forced exposure of women represents the abuse and oppression of not only women, but of the nation. Fanon saw the colonial project as the 'unveiling' of Algeria, and appealed to the loyalty of women to join the nationalist cause. While a symbol of women and of national honour and identity, during the war the veil also took on more practical purposes, for the hiding of weapons. The veil also became women's refuge, acquiring new significance 'not only as a symbol of cultural difference but also protection from and resistance to the colonial-qua-Christian gaze' (Lazreg, 1994: 53).[6] As Bhabha points out, as the veil becomes the means of liberating women into public space, it becomes 'the object of paranoid surveillance and observation' (1994: 63).

Fanon's essay 'The Algerian Family' (in Fanon, 1965) discusses how traditional social structures and relationships changed as women became centrally involved in the war. Algerian women were liberated from their traditional roles as they joined the war by carrying concealed weapons, as well as fighting in the maquis alongside their 'brothers', and running the field hospitals. The fact that girls started to veil earlier (before rather than at the onset of puberty), that the veils themselves became longer, and that women veiled voluntarily, showed how the Algerians viewed colonisation as both morally and physically destabilising.

Meanwhile, the French encouraged women out of the veil to give them the status of 'Europeans' then consequently reviled the unveiled women as evil and depraved. In a famous incident on 16 May 1958, a deputation of French women (accompanied by the Marseillaise) publicly unveiled several Algerian women. According to Marnia Lazreg, this event did lasting harm to Algerian women, since it 'brought into the limelight the politicisation of women's bodies and their appropriation by colonial authorities' (1994: 135). Henceforward, veiling became an instrument for political action. However, this enforced unveiling of women had the opposite effect of the one hoped for by the French, since the veil quickly became a national and patriotic symbol. The harsh reality of the unveiling for the women themselves can be understood through Assia Djebar's linguistic analysis: the moment of unveiling is spoken of in colloquial Arabic as 'I no longer go out protected (that is to say, covered up), the woman

who casts off her sheet will say "I go out undressed, or even denuded"'
(1980: 138).

Despite Fanon's emphasis on the importance of women in both
the struggle for liberation and the remaking of the nation, Fanon has
been the target of much feminist criticism. Some of his most
contentious arguments include a stereotyping of the neurotic
psychology of white women, his emphasis on sexual violence, and
his use of the masculine as normative with its resulting erasure of
the black female subject. His description of woman's way of walking
with or without veils (the *haik*) has brought accusations of sexism:

> Without the veil [Algerian woman] has the impression of her body
> being cut up into bits, put adrift, the limbs seem to lengthen
> indefinitely ... The unveiled body seems to escape, to dissolve. She
> has the impression of being improperly dressed, even of being
> naked ... She has to invent new dimensions for her body, new
> means of muscular control ... The Algerian woman who walks stark
> naked into the European city relearns her body. (1965: 37)[7]

Many Arab feminists now realise that nationalism remains one of
the main oppressive factors *against* women. Writers have pointed out
that the secular nationalism of the FLN (the National Liberation
Front) in Algeria has reclaimed many of the most patriarchal values
of Islamic traditionalism (Accad, 1990: 14). While the veil was used
by Fanon and the FLN to symbolise the revolution, since the 1990
victory of the FIS (the Islamic Salvation Front) the veil has been used
to 'turn back the clock on the socially transformative potential the
revolution offered' (Sharpley-Whiting, 1998: 61). The veil is currently
used in Algeria as a tool of repression and violence against women,
since, in today's Maghreb (particularly Algeria), the Islamists 'embrace
the female body as the symbolic representation of communal dignity'.
Yet while drawing on the Qur'an to gain religious endorsement for
subjugation of women, they in fact recycle the colonial conception
of women's rights. Ironically, as Moghissi explains, 'As with other
forms of extremism, the two opposing poles end up on the same side'
(1999: 30). Women in a country such as Algeria find their space of
agency limited rather than expanded, despite active and valiant work
on the part of Arab feminist writers. Valerie Orlando, for example,
discusses the case of violence against Algerian women since the rise
of the FIS where women in Algiers are being forcibly enveloped in

the *haik* (veil), and where going 'bare-faced' is a justification for murder (1995).

I will now use as an introduction to the central role of woman in the colonisation of North Africa a brief foray into the relevant visual representations, especially those within orientalist art of the late nineteenth century – a time of intense colonial fascination and imagination.

The colonial background: visual representations

The forced unveiling of Arab women by the French, in life and in representation, demonstrates the concept of erotic voyeurism as well as the inherent violence of coloniser against colonised. In painting as well as literature, the European colonial gaze longed to see into the forbidden realms of the lives, and bodies, of women. As Malek Alloula elucidates in *The Colonial Harem*, the representation of veiled and unveiled women in the hundreds of French colonial postcards in circulation at the turn of the century shows the intense preoccupation of the colonisers with the veiled female body. 'More than an analogy links the imperialist project of colonising other lands and peoples with the phantasm of appropriation of the veiled exotic woman' (Alloula, 1986: xvi). The penetration of woman was a clear parallel to the penetration of the harem, and indeed the core of the Arab world – an object of imperial desire ever since Richard Burton infiltrated the haj (in disguise) and violated the sacred space of Mecca.[8]

One of the most famous and widely discussed paintings of the early colonial period, Delacroix's *The Women of Algiers in their Apartment* (1834), epitomises for many the male, imperialist voyeuristic desire to violate cultural taboo.[9] Delacroix paints for the western voyeur so that he can gaze at 'oriental woman'. According to Delacroix's diary, during his visit to the recently captured Algiers, he was allowed a few moments' glimpse inside the harem. He took a hasty sketch, from which he later reconstructed the scene. For Delacroix writing in his diary, the harem was 'that borderline in motion where dream and reality converge' (Djebar, 1980: 134). The harem is traditionally a space that both protects and imprisons, an extension of the veil, the enforcement of literally 'forbidden' (*haram*) space. A more emotive picture is given in Fatima Mernissi's description of the harem as:

> a power structure, a system in which oppression and violence work together in the lives of women to turn their daily lives into a prison

6 *The Women of Algiers in their Apartment*, by Eugène Delacroix (1798–1863). Delacroix entered the harem in order to create an orientalist 'imaginary Algeria'. Confronted by the intruding male gaze, the women in the picture avert their eyes, becoming 'the object of fixation and fascination'. (Louvre, Paris, France/Bridgeman Art Library)

universe ... But although the harem is a prison, it crushes the aspirations of young girls in different ways, according to the class to which they belong ... It is the reflection and mirror of the vice of colonialism which held the master of the harem in its grip. (1988: 21)

The visual representation of the women in the harem, while transgressing prohibitions, can in itself be regarded as a process of unveiling, stripping away reality to produce an imaginary realm. Conversely, the imperialist imagination had to simultaneously superimpose its own meaning onto what was regarded as an otherwise inert and vacant land – in a similar process to what Gayatri Spivak discusses in terms of the palimpsest: the writing over of the history-less 'blank' of female subaltern experience (1988). For the imperialist project to be successful, it had to assume that the world was uninscribed – blank – for the required text to be written on it. Similarly, the veiled woman as representative of the nation was a blank face, a *non*-entity, which had to be unveiled and given a new – colonialised and Christianised – identity. While a painting such as *Women of Algiers* produces a visualisation of an 'imaginary Algeria' in the imagination of Europeans, it also fills a void by creating an interpretation of what it *should* look like, even if it does not.

Throughout orientalist art in general, Arab women appear languid, satiated, voluptuous, and indolent, in an environment that is pampered, opulent and charged with eroticism. Alternately, images of the 'slave market' present women as veiled, delicate, beautiful, and extremely white-skinned, as illustrated, for example, in paintings such as *The White Slave* (1888) by Jean-Jules Lecomte du Noüy; *The Odalisque with a Slave* and *The Turkish Bath* by Jean Auguste Ingres (1863). Later, both Renoir and Henri Matisse continue the fascination of orientalist painters with harem women, both painting a series of odalisques: such as *Odalisque in Red Culottes* (Matisse, 1922) and *Seated Odalisque* (Renoir, 1918). (Picasso also painted a dramatic version of Delacroix's *Women of Algiers in their Apartment*.)

The painting *The Gate to the Desert* by Frederick Goodall (1864) exemplifies the discrepancy between the reality and the coloniser's imagery of the Arab world. It shows the romanticised encounter between an Arab camel rider and a young woman, associating her unveiled face and breasts with the life-giving water she offers in her hand. While denying the reality of desert life, the picture also essentialises woman as breast/mother/nurturer and feeder of man.

Oscillating between binaries of seclusion/availability, sacred/secular, forbidden/permitted, and concealed/visible to the male (and colonial) gaze the (un)veiled female, as in this painting, is located as the symbol of fulfilment of basic masculine drives of sexual desire and survival.

The stripping away of the veil could be constructed as the colonialist's desire to find 'the face of the orient' – another means of essentialising woman. In removing the veils, man could find either the 'essence' of the orient, or vacancy. In pictorial terms, this intense male fascination with unveiling is seen in, for example, *The Babylonian Marriage Market* by Edwin Long (1828–1891). This type of colonial 'rape' of the oriental woman by forcing her to remove her veils goes back in fiction at least as far as the episode involving Ayesha in Rider Haggard's *She* – an unveiling motivated by insatiable curiosity to understand woman's 'secret'.

Similarly, for Malek Alloula, the veil stood as a mask, acting as a 'refusal' of the scopic desire of the artist/photographer. The veil 'signifies the injunction of no trespassing' he argues, also remembering that representations of the human body in any form are taboo in Islam (Alloula, 1986: 13). The French photographer unveils his model and in so doing, gives representation to the twice forbidden. Not only does he force the woman to reveal her face, but also breasts, so that she becomes, as Alloula puts it, 'the embodiment of the site of fulfilment of desire' (1986: 14). The model is the symbol of the appropriation of the female body, as well as the appropriation of forbidden space (a combination Alloula compares to a synthesis of Delacroix's *Women of Algiers* and Ingres' *Turkish Bath*). He concludes that the photographs are 'an imaginary revenge' on behalf of the coloniser upon the inaccessible world of Algerian women (Alloula, 1986: 120).[10]

I will now discuss works of fiction that illustrate these representations of the veil and colonial unveiling, focusing on the novels of Assia Djebar.

Women's fiction of the Maghreb: Assia Djebar

Assia Djebar uses fiction as means of expressing her concerns for the vicissitudes of her native country, and her novels have become part of her country's revolutionary discourse for women. She deals primarily with the struggle of Arab women to find an identity and with the importance of language and memory in this process. Djebar (a pseudonym concocted for her anonymity) is a writer who is above all concerned with writing as a means of liberation and of celebrating a shared experience among women. Identifying with her Arab and

Berber ethnicity, she writes with the intent of becoming a voice of the silenced women of her country, who have been suppressed by the combined oppression of religion, colonialism and patriarchy. Her novels *Women of Algiers in their Apartment* and *Fantasia, An Algerian Cavalcade* are attempts to reconstruct these voices lost from Algerian history.

Born in 1936, Djebar was educated in France (with a degree from the Sorbonne) and in the late 1950s, while in exile in Tunis, she wrote pieces for Frantz Fanon's revolutionary newspaper *El-Moudjahid*. In the 1970s she stopped writing, saying that her writing had become uncomfortably close to her own life, and for many years concentrated on filmmaking. Djebar has lived exiled from Algeria for many years, first in France, now – due to the controversial nature of her writing (since even France proved too dangerous) – in the US. She is one of the writers for whom exile is empowering, since it gives her insight into different cultures. As Valerie Orlando comments, 'Within her space of exile [Djebar] negotiates new feminist parameters for all women of the Maghreb' (1999: 32). From a feminist perspective, Djebar's novels validate woman's presence and experience. The silencing of women has been argued to extend across the whole colonial world and to be indicative of both patriarchal and colonial morality. For women to free themselves from the patriarchal space that enforces their silence, they must 'retrieve a voice that has been driven into silence' (Spivak, 1988: 122). According to Djebar, women have been silenced due to Islam, patriarchy, and French colonisation. Anticipating Spivak, Djebar does not claim to 'speak for' the women of Algeria, but to 'speak next to' the words that would be spoken by 'incarcerated bodies' as they first gained their freedom. She writes from a liminal position, struggling as a colonised subject to find the language for the expression of freedom and protest.

Djebar seeks to define how far veils take on a metaphorical significance in women's lives, symbolising this inner world of silent experience. Djebar emphasises in her works that woman must remove her veils in order to become a 'full' human being and to be able to express both her inner and outer worlds. Women's narratives, such as that in *Fantasia, An Algerian Cavalcade* (originally titled *L'Amour, La Fantasia*), express not only events but also emotions. (Hence the importance of *L'Amour* in the French title of the novel, omitted in the English translation.) Djebar's focus is on the experience and narration of compassion and care between women, of the need for women to overcome the sense of rivalry that has been instilled by patriarchy. Djebar also proposes an escape from 'male space' into a space in which women can be free from the male gaze and communicate without boundaries – a place out of time and space. Djebar's descriptions of the *hammam*, the traditional Turkish bath, (for example in *Women of Algiers in their Apartment* and in *A Sister to Scheherazade*) propose an alternate women's space comparable to Bhabha's 'between spaces' of negotiation that are beyond the politics of polarity.

The first volume in Assia Djebar's quartet of novels, *Fantasia, An Algerian Cavalcade*, encompasses both historical and autobiographical themes. History is rewritten to include the women's role in the war of the 1830s and the war of independence (1954–62). The second novel, *Ombre Sultane (A Sister to Scheherazade)*, juxtaposes the lives of two women in Algeria, both wives of the same husband, and deals with the themes of seclusion, freedom and unveiling. Written in the 1980s these novels depict a very different 'contemporary' Algeria to the one that has emerged since the cancellation of the result of the 1990 elections. Djebar's latest novel to be translated into English, *So Vast the Prison*, (originally published in 1995) consolidates many of her previous concerns, while also bringing them into a more contemporary situation, that of the Algeria of the 1990s.

Djebar's collection of short stories written between 1959 and 1978, brought together under the title of *Women of Algiers in their Apartment* (a title inspired by the painting by Delacroix), provides a fascinating and explicit discussion of veils, initiating a theme that will be taken up again in her later novels. Djebar aims to reconstruct the voices of not only the silent women in Delacroix's painting, but some of the mute women trapped and struggling to be free in the narrow patriarchal confines of their traditional lives. Language itself demands a political choice, and, according to Djebar, creates veils in terms of layers of interpretation and meaning. In the 'overture' to *Women of Algiers*, she comments that the language a woman uses is almost arbitrary, and yet all-important:

I could say: 'stories translated from ...' but from which language? From the Arabic? From the colloquial Arabic or from feminine Arabic; one might as well call it underground Arabic. I could have listened to these voices in no matter what language, nonwritten, nonrecorded, transmitted only by chains of echoes and sighs. Arabic sounds – Iranian, Afghan, Berber, or Bengali ... but always in feminine tones, uttered from lips beneath a mask. (1)

For Djebar, this female language transcends national and linguistic boundaries, since whatever the words, they always belong to an 'excoriated language' that has never appeared in the daylight. They have been 'intoned, declaimed, howled ... always in the dark'. Significantly she explains this is so because they are 'words of the veiled body, language that in turn has taken the veil for so long' (1).[11]

In the section of the novel entitled 'Forbidden Gaze, Severed Sound' Djebar recalls the women seated around a hookah in the portrait of harem women by Delacroix, and 'reconstructs' the voices of these women and the drama that we observe in Delacroix's painting. From Djebar's viewpoint, the whole meaning of the painting is 'played out in the relationship these three [women] have with their bodies, as well as their place of enclosure' (1).[12] She discusses that the women have no relationship with the gaze of the artist or the viewer; they 'neither abandon nor refuse themselves to our gaze' (136). Between the women and the spectators 'there has been the instant of unveiling', she writes, 'the step that crossed the vestibule of intimacy' (137) – the intrusion of both artist and colonial voyeur. The gaze itself is a male prerogative. The women in the picture, comparable to the women in Alloula's colonial photographs, avert their eyes from returning the artist's gaze.

As already mentioned, Delacroix's painting represents both colonial aggression (he was in Algiers only two years after the fall of the city to the French) and the violence of gender violation of prohibited space – both a metaphorical and literal violation of female space. The image of Delacroix's harem women sets the theme that recurs throughout the novel: women are portrayed as secluded in their own world by oppression.[13] Djebar suggests, as she does elsewhere, that true emotional communication is only possible between women (even though it is across the lines of nationality). Through the friendship across borders of nationality and politics, of Sarah (an Algerian) and Anne (a French woman), Djebar outlines a means of agency through such communication: 'I see no other way out for us,' says Sarah to Anne, 'except through an encounter like this: a woman speaking in front of another who's watching ... it is by means of listening and remembering that she ends up seeing herself, with her own eyes, unveiled at last' (47).

Djebar expands the theme of women's communication in her elaboration of feminist notions of patriarchy's treatment of women. Comparing Sarah's brutal treatment by the French to that of the Algerian regimes to their own women, she relates the story of Leila, a former fighter in the war, who is now in hospital addicted to drugs, and neglected by the new government for whom she fought. Historically, women in Algeria were 'used by the revolution as tools, as cheap labour, cheap fighters – to die first and be liberated last!' (El Saadawi, 1980: 89). Sarah communicates her compassion for Leila by silently opening her own blouse to reveal a long scar – the legacy of her torture in the French prison. After this encounter with the destitute Leila, Sarah finds that she is able to break through her silence to speak about her own prison experience for the first time. She compares this to the removal of a veil:

> I was a voiceless prisoner. A little like certain women of Algiers today, you see them going around outside without the ancestral veil, and yet, out of fear of the new and unexpected situations, they become entangled in other veils, invisible, but very noticeable ones. Me too, for years after ... I was still carrying my own prison around inside me. (48)

Here, Djebar stresses that it is not visible veils alone that confine women. Veils equate with the 'invisible' chains of continuing, more subtle forms of oppression. Yet being denied facilities in the 'outside' world encourages a female bonding, in which agency can be based on the intimacy of a shared 'female gaze' as well as language.[14] One sanctuary for women, suggested in Djebar's novels, is the communal bath, the *hammam*. It is in this 'female space' of cleansing and purification – where women can be free from the male gaze – that intimacies are exchanged and stories told. It is both a place of escape from the outside world and the chance women have to create for themselves a space for agency. In *Women of Algiers*, it is where Anne and Sarah attempt to lay aside their clothes *and* their national differences. Yet for Anne, as a foreigner, the intimate experience she shares with the women in the *hammam* makes her want to weep, 'For nothing, for all of them' (149). She sees Sarah's long scar running down her abdomen and asks if it is a burn. Sarah, however, ponders about admitting it was 'a war injury' but is reticent to reveal it was caused by her torture at the hands of the French. (This situation exposes how war negates subtle avenues of agency for women.) This reticence could be compared to a veil of secrecy between hostile cultures, necessary to maintain their individual friendship and yet denying Anne and Sarah the freedom of open communications that is their prerogative in the *hammam*.

In several of her other novels, Djebar emphasises that the *hammam*, rather than the traditional female space of the harem, is a refuge conducive to female bonding.[15] Djebar describes the bath as a place of respite, a place where women can communicate by signs, thus removed from the linguistic field dominated by patriarchy, and in a timeless 'twilight realm' of secret collusion (1985: 149). It is only in this space, when women are physically naked and unadorned (that is to say, stripped of class and pretension), that the voice 'speaks true', for it speaks the 'heart's truth' (Djebar, 1985: 149).[16]

Marjo Buitellar also highlights that the inaccessibility to outsiders makes the *hammam* the most private of female domains, and also a place where women can extend their social network beyond their immediate surroundings. The atmosphere of shared intimacy provides an escape from family obligations as well as a sanctuary of 'temporary immunity'. As in the story discussed here, the *hammam* is a place of revelation, a private space where 'the scars and tattoos on the nearly naked bodies of the bathing women tell details of their personal histories without words' (Buitellar in Ask and Tjomsland, 1998: 112). Similarly, (in Morocco) Fatima Mernissi locates women's places of refuge and renewal in the *hammam* and the shrines of saints: these sanctuaries are the locus of anti-establishment, anti-patriarchal values, and

> provide women with a space where compliant and verbal vituper-ations against the system's injustices are allowed ... [giving] women the opportunity to develop critical views of their condition, to identify problems and to try to find their solution. (1977: 67)[17]

While delineating also an inside/outside, private and public dichotomy, which in itself creates a problematic of gendered space, the veil also represents a temporal dimension of tradition/modernity for Djebar.

As we have seen, the theme of veiling occurs, as in much of Djebar's work, on three levels of discourse: historical, linguistic and metaphorical. She associates the problematic of writing in French with the freedom of the unveiled body.[18] For Djebar, the gap between cultures, between languages and between worlds is a central preoc-cupation, and her novels are an attempt to bridge, or at least come to terms with, that gap. The veil represents the gap, the theoretical and yet all-too-real conflict between the worlds of France and Algeria, between French and Arabic, the 'modern world' and traditional patterns of behaviour. Rafika Merini locates the veil as primary signifier in Djebar's narratives of love–hate between the peoples of Algeria, a love–hate relationship that is at once shameful, destructive and gruesome – and concealed by history until exposed like a wound by Djebar (Merini, 1999: 100).

As in the example of Sarah and Anne successfully crossing political and language barriers to communicate, in *Fantasia* (the novel I discuss next), the friendship of women cuts across national boundaries. Djebar's narrator recalls her childhood friends, a household of women secluded in their harem, who would receive visits from their friends outside – a French woman, the wife of the police chief, and her daughter (20–7). Although the Arabo-Berber women spoke little French and the French woman little Arabic, they remained close friends, even though the French still remained 'the other'. When criticised by her Arab neighbours, the Arabo-Berber mother would exclaim, 'She's my friend! She's French but she's my friend' (21).[19]

Similarly, for Djebar, the 'other' is both the colonial other, the French male enemy, and the traditionally name-less Arab lover (just as French is the language both of love and war): 'To write confronting love', she explains, is to 'help lift the taboo, to lift the veil ... To lift the veil and at the same time keep secret that which must remain secret ... The word is a torch; to be held up in front of the wall of separation or withdrawal ... To describe "The Other's" face, to fix his image ... Armed only with the written word' (1980: 62).

Fantasia, An Algerian Cavalcade

In *Fantasia, An Algerian Cavalcade* (1985), Djebar's fascination with the written word leads her to examine several eye-witness accounts of the historical events of the French occupation and war. These documents gradually expose the limitations and banality of the French version of 'history', which subverts their authenticity as well as revealing the need to revive the 'lost' history of Algerian women. Djebar reappropriates the French documents and then – in a reversal of the colonial rewriting of the palimpsest – reinscribes them with her own version of female history. Alternating between centuries with dramatic effect, her historiography compares the women's plight in the 1830s Algerian conquest with the 1950s War of Independence. Djebar asks 'but who will write of it?' stressing the unreliability of 'history', since such texts are presented from a male, and French, perspective (1985: 7). Orlando sees the novel *Fantasia* as 'constructing a hybrid narrative of culture, language, and historicity, [in which]

Djebar reconsiders and re-narrates the legacy of French colonialism, which has altered the identity of Algeria' (1999: 111).

Thousands of silent 'watchful eyes' were spectators of the siege of Algiers and of the ensuing conflict. Djebar imagines the lives of the women witnesses and how they would have been affected by the conflict. She wishes to extricate women from the orientalist stereotype, and emphasises the important role of historiography. While compacting space/time and personal undocumented and documented history (as well as male/female history), she creates a new dynamic of analysing the past. Just as Fanon emphasises memory in its role to reconstruct a people's past history, Djebar meditates upon how silenced memory becomes transmuted into words (75, 78). Yet 'do not memories fetter us as well as forming our roots?' she asks (178).

Djebar uses the veil as symbol to distinguish between the binaries of imprisonment/freedom, silence/speech, subservience/rebellion, the 'condemned and the fortunate' (205) when she describes the veiled traditional women who are free to roam the city. In contrast she presents the women with their 'cries of rebellion piercing the very heavens': the women who are brave enough to run the gravest risk of refusing to veil their voices (204). Djebar's attempt to reconstruct women's voices from Algerian history is linked throughout the novel with the purifying memory of her own childhood experiences. *Fantasia* opens with the image of a young girl holding her father's hand as he takes her to school.[20] This is the start of her education in French, which will be, in part, responsible for her cultural alienation from her homeland, a conflict between two worlds and an 'incipient vertigo' (185). For the neighbours who watch her as she leaves, the fact that she is going to learn to write is a dangerous omen. Writing is associated with love and with freedom – a theme that will be taken up repeatedly by Djebar in this novel. Veiling represents the antithesis of this freedom of expression, 'so wrap the nubile girl in veils. Make her invisible. Make her more unseeing than the sightless, destroy in her the memory of the world without' (3). In one episode, in which she recalls when she/the narrator reached adolescence and had to leave the village school for an education abroad, the split in destinies between herself and other girls is reduced to the fate of being veiled or unveiled.

Later in the novel, the narrator's mother is challenged as to why her young teenage daughter is not yet veiled. Her mother replies in her defence, 'She reads!' (179). Reading and studying are linked in the narrator's young mind to the mobility of her body, while later knowledge of the French script in contrast becomes for her a degrading 'public unveiling in front of sniggering onlookers' (181). The written word is a way of speaking from the enforced silence, of exposing 'a space filled with desperate voiceless cries, frozen long ago in a prehistory of love. Once I had discovered the meaning of the words – those same words that are revealed to the unveiled body – I cut myself adrift' (4–5).

This novel juxtaposes elements of love and war, friendship and rape, woman, with her characteristics of nurturing and honour, and man, intent on cruelty and the destruction of both woman and nation. The contrasts between personal narrative (autobiography) and the historical accounts retold by women interviewed by Djebar set up a dynamic of opposition that both stuns and informs. The historical accounts of war with their unflinching documentation of atrocities are paralleled with the narrator's search for expressions of love within the constraints of Arab society, and the unresolved tensions in her discussion of language.[21]

This oscillation between emotions and events across the borders of time (Djebar takes her stories from the wars of both the 1830s and 1950s) is analogous in theory to Gayatri Spivak's explication of the 'worlding of a territory' and is reminiscent of the 'violent shuttling' of third world woman herself, caught between tradition and modernity. The 'worlding' of a text in some ways is similar to the reinscription of a palimpsest, although the crucial factor here is the process of conflict out of which a text, or a work of art, emerges. Here, the conflict is in the real terms of colonial struggle, and the slate to be rewor(l)ded is the territory itself. This is particularly relevant in terms of the recent history of Algeria and the role of women within it. Spivak discusses the conflict between two societies ('between the thrusting world and the settling earth') – causing a rift, a schism or breach (*Riss* in German) – and how a work of art comes out of the violent collision.[22] This fracture, both cartographic and social, physical and political, suggests the possible opening up of a space of freedom and expression, or the creation of a new ground for self-definition.

In her description of the process involved in writing *Fantasia*, Assia Djebar writes of her experience in similar terms to Spivak's violent artistic and cultural rifts:

Even where I am composing the most commonplace of sentences, my writing is immediately caught in the snare of the old war between two peoples. So I swing like a pendulum from images of war (war of conquest or of liberation, but always in the past) to the expression of a contradictory, ambiguous love ... While I thought I was undertaking a 'journey through myself', I find I am simply choosing another veil. (216–17)

This is the same dynamic that creates *das Riss* – a violent striation in time/space that forges a new state of understanding, a new work of art. Since Djebar likens the process of writing to the wearing of veils (217 *inter alia*) it is possible to draw parallels between unveiling and 'the violent implications of fracture' in Gayatri Spivak's discussion of 'worlding', which, to me, also describes the situation of unveiling. *Das Aufreissen*, the act of creating the rift, in German also means to tear, to rip or gash open. Violence is integral in *das Riss*, as is a rending apart – like the rending of the veil. Fanon provides an example of violent rift in his claim, which equates unveiling and rape, that 'the rape of the Algerian woman in the dream of the European is always preceded by a rending of the veil'. In colonial conquest, he writes, there is no 'progressive conquest' but 'with the maximum of violence, there is possession, rape, near-murder ... The woman-victim screams ... is penetrated, martyrised [sic], ripped apart' (Fanon, 1965: 24).

It is in this way that the violence of unveiling women has become such an explosive image, and one that is used in conflicting contexts and appropriated in different arguments – representing both/either the world (unveiled/modern) and the earth (veiled/traditional). Using a similar image in the debate on human rights in Islam, for example, Fatima Mernissi claims that all such argument 'is an obscene debate that can only be formulated in terms of veils, of *hijab*, that is, of thresholds that prohibit and boundaries that protect' (1993: 184). Extending the range of paradoxes surrounding the veil, she comments that what is veiled is both the obscene (the unmentionable) and the sacred. It seems that much of 'the violence of the rift' that occurs in the colonial world, as in Islam itself, is between these two poles of existence. Women are caught in the violence of the 'worlding', the reinterpretation or violent appropriation of a landscape or territory: here, the violence of the colonial encounter and the ensuing conflicts. As states and governments try through the political upheavals to destroy nomadic space, women are the victims – no matter what or whom the regimes involved in creating the violence.[23]

To discuss Djebar in these terms, in forging a 'new' narrative from the violence of the past, Djebar's writing could be placed as an example of creativity born of the 'tearing apart' of a culture. Since Djebar's own life was spent growing up between two cultures, two languages and two traditions, she is able to depict both the French and the Algerian cultures as 'other' through the eyes of the other. She likens this alternating of cultural identity to being alternatively veiled and unveiled. It allows her to oscillate between two worlds, to experience the swing of awareness between the opposite poles of alterity. This is both a liberating and an agonising process. She describes the responsibility that is inherent in her vision:

> My fiction is this attempt at autobiography, weighed down under the oppressive burden of my heritage. Language ... crouches in this dark night like a woman begging in the streets ... I shelter again in the green shade of my cloistered companions' whispers. How shall I find the strength to tear off my veil, unless I have to use it to bandage the running sores nearby from which words exude? (219)

Here again we find an experience of *das Riss* – creativity being forced out of the violent rupture, the ripping off of the veil, words being thrust up out of the gap. Freedom for Djebar is in part created by this forging of an intellectual and emotional space by writing, which helps to 'lift the taboo, to lift the veil. To lift the veil and at the same time keep secret that which must remain secret' (219). The symbol of the 'wound', for example, that occurs vividly in various contexts throughout her narratives is also indicative of a painful splitting apart – not only of flesh but of human communication. As we shall see in the novel *Sister to Scheherazade*, a wound is also the name for a co-wife, and is associated with the pain, and necessity, of culturally-enforced secrecy.

The veil, as a visible symbol of woman's oppression, also acts to cover the reality of what she is enduring. Rafika Merini interestingly notes that Djebar in one instance uses the word '*suaire*' when referring to the veil, a garment associated with death. Why, she asks, should women hide behind veils when they maintain both women's silence and when 'they are the destroyers of women's vitality, and the stiflers of love in all its forms'? (1999: 100). Similarly, feminist leaders throughout the Arab world have voiced questions about the veil and regarded unveiling as a necessary prerequisite to the achievement of women's civil and political rights:

> It can never be repeated too often that the veil is no mere fashion, it is a wall which materially and spiritually is debarring its bearer

from developing intercourse and opportunity for co-operation with the men in a world crying out for co-operation. (Rydh, 1947: 167)

In the third section of the book, entitled 'Voices from the Past', episodes are related by different women recalling the violence of the wars of the 1830s and 1950s. They tell of the suffering of women: victims of the extermination of whole tribes; nomadic women and children slaughtered in their tents; women endangering their lives and homes by sheltering their menfolk, and others who join their 'Brothers' in the mountains or who spend their lives fighting or imprisoned. One story in the novel relates how a bridal procession in 1830 is ambushed and once the men have been killed, the bride and her sister are captured. Ordered to remove their jewellery and ornaments, the veiled women are threatened that if they do not comply their clothes will also be torn off them. The bride, Badra, removes her heavy jewels one by one, including her slippers embroidered with gold. The women watching are horrified; the bride's actions being tantamount to stripping herself naked (99). As a maid rushes to cover her, Badra cries out in an act of defiance, 'I am naked! Praise be to God, I am naked!' From the social perspective, the aggression of war and conquest decimates traditional structures and negates social custom. In the scene above, the woman is stripped of her identity as bride as well as of her future (she disappears from history as one of a group of prisoners). The traditional rites of passage of girl to woman-hood change to become terrifying ordeals of leaving home and family, rape, imprisonment and torture.

To be a woman is, as Assia Djebar suggests, 'to refuse to veil one's voice and to start shouting' for this is real dissidence. Those who do not cry out in protest are in 'a prison without reprieve' (Djebar, 1985: 204). Once women have spoken out, they move away from being 'generalised woman' to being woman as an individual.

A Sister to Scheherazade

The second novel in the quartet, *A Sister to Scheherazade*, is Assia Djebar's most explicit – and exciting – polemic of veiling. She leaves her previous theme of reconstructing the historical voices of women, and tells the story of two women, both married to the same man, in order to explore the polarities of tradition and modernisation. Isma, the narrator, a modernised, veil-free, and French-educated woman breaks free from the boundaries that marriage has placed upon her. Hajila, the subservient second wife, is 'veiled in despair' after six months of marriage. Forbidden to leave the apartment, she dares to find a reason for life by escaping the apartment and venturing out onto the street. The veil allows Hajila the freedom to go out, but soon she longs 'to be able to throw back [her] head and look up at the sky as she did as a child' (19). She suddenly decides to take off her veil. 'As if you wished to disappear ... or explode!' comments the narrator/Isma (30). Intoxicated by the experience of life and nature without the 'shroud of wool', Hajila is 'transformed into another woman ... out in the real world' (31).

In the chapter entitled 'Veils', Djebar explores the various associations attributed to clothing, focusing on its use as disguise or cover. 'We clothe ourselves in covering of flannel, crepe or wool: we veil ourselves to face the world! Otherwise would the secret – what secret? – be destroyed?' (36). That the veil is to hide women's 'secret' is a common theme in Islam, although what the secret is remains undisclosed. Later in this novel, Djebar/Isma describes how, in Arabic dialect, over and above her beauty a woman is praised for her 'secret', or some 'elusive trace' of her grace as a woman (153). Once Hajila has 'dropped her veil' she is a stranger whom no one knows and she can walk about with 'open eyes' (41). Ironically, it has been the veil that gave her an identity: when she drops her veil, she becomes anonymous, a 'stranger whom no one knows' (41). It is this sense of invisibility once she is *unveiled* that gives her the sense of liberation.

The French philosophers Deleuze and Guattari discuss that the process of 'becoming-woman' is a phase in a journey of diminishment, a step on the road to becoming-*imperceptible*: 'imperceptibility is the immanent end of becoming' (1987). Undergoing her own process of 'diminishment', Hajila not only feels she cannot be seen when she is unveiled, she also believes she cannot be heard. When a man stops her in the park to ask her a question, she is seized with panic, for not only does she not hear what he said, but she has also lost the power of speech. Isma comments

> As if you were able to speak! Don't people realise that you are out of doors? ... when you throw off the woollen veil, when you roam around, your voice seems to have left you behind. It catches up with you again at the very last minute, when you have wrapped the cloak around you again. (42)

This passage details a reversal of the Islamic understanding of woman's voice as *'awra* ('shameful') and is another instance in which Djebar subverts the use of the veil. While women are famously 'silenced' by Islamic patriarchy – and by the 'religious' tenet of veiling – here Hajila is mute since she is caught in the gap between identities, veiled and unveiled, while in the process of negotiating a new identity. The gap, for Hajila, is a gap in space/time; in terms of patriarchy, it is a gap of morality.

One could propose here that the veil and physical seclusion are not used to protect women, but to protect men. If women remain inside and unable to see men, they cannot judge them. The husband's violence when he discovers that Hajila has been leaving the house unveiled, exposes that the 'real wound ... cannot be healed ... By staring into the void you hope to find out why, why the exile? As if the exile were something visible!' (89). Exile, pain, and the real 'veiling', Djebar suggests, are all invisible, and internal. Exile, both physical and mental, is a recurring theme in postcolonial writing and one that especially epitomises the location of veiled, secluded woman (a theme I elaborate in my next chapter in the context of India).

The narrator comments on how fear is transmitted from generation to generation: 'the seraglio has been emptied but its noxious emanations have invaded everything' (145). Hajila, physically weakened, is unable to continue to fight for herself. Djebar here launches her strongest attack on patriarchy, one that appeals for an end to the rivalry between women that undermines women's solidarity. What if, Djebar suggests, the two rival women create bonds of friendship and protect one another as sisters? (Mortimer, 1988: 38).[24] When Isma and Hajila meet for the first time, Isma refers to Hajila as 'my daughter and my mother, my half-sister, my reopened wound' (147). (Significantly, the Arab word for co-wife, *durra*, is the same as for 'wound'.) Their identities converge and to some extent they exchange destinies – Hajila may become a freer and more outspoken woman and wife; Isma will return to the home of her ancestors and retreat into the past. As the novel concludes, 'The second wife stands on the threshold, devouring the space: and now the first one can put on the veil, or go into hiding ... At the end of the long night, the odalisque is in flight' (159).

This ending raises a series of questions: most importantly, once women have freed themselves from the past, then where can they go? Does Isma flee from her apparently fulfilling marriage because she has lost herself, or because she is hoping for an alternative homoerotic relationship that is hinted at in the narrative? The answer possibly lies in the last section of the novel: the only hope for salvation being through 'the flight of the imagination' (160).

While freedom from the veil may suggest a modernisation of the oriental woman (and for the colonial a modernisation of the orient itself) (Yegenoglu, 1998) and while liberation from the veil does allow the 'traditional' wife both subjectivity and agency, ultimately Djebar leaves the situation unresolved. Hajila's new-found liberty ends in tragedy when, unfamiliar with the 'outside world', she is knocked down by a passing car. Paradoxically, Isma finds her modern, unveiled lifestyle unfulfilling (even though her marriage is based on love) and decides to withdraw from life to return to her mother's village. The situation for women veiled or unveiled is presented as not dissimilar: women in patriarchal Islamic societies are subjected to both visible and invisible methods of control. The ultimate ambiguity in the situating of the veil in this novel reflects its multifaceted and paradoxical symbolism in today's Islamic society: gendered power and subjection takes many forms, with modernity ushering in many new forms of gendered subjection (Abu-Lughod, 1998: 283).

Assia Djebar's recent novel *So Vast the Prison* (1999) is Djebar's most angry book, written at a time when to be a woman writer in Algeria is punishable by death. She places herself in a clear position of antagonism to the fratricidal conflict of the present Islamic regime in Algeria. The last section of the novel, entitled 'The Blood of Writing', dares to delineate some of the recent atrocities in Algeria. The progression of the text between the years 1988 and 1994 demonstrates the shifting position of woman in society, in a world increasingly unsympathetic to, if not intolerant of, women. The protagonists evolve from protected wife/mother/lover to their later stance as victim and target of violence (as the chapter 'Yasmina' dramatically portrays). The central character is again identified as Isma, but even this identity is deconstructed, when at the end of the novel, Djebar asks, 'Shall I call the narrator Isma once again? "Isma": "the name"' (341) – an identity that is, after all, no identity. Her non-identity endorses the argument that in patriarchy 'the ideology of gender makes woman's life script a non-story, a silent space, a gap in patriarchal culture' (Smith, 1987: 50).

Djebar's recent non-fiction work *Algerian White* (*Blanc de L'Algérie*) also documents the horrors of recent decades (2000). Concerned with the lost compatriot voices of journalists, intellectuals, playwrights, and poets (from Frantz Fanon and Albert Camus to more recent Algerian writers) who have died as a result of suicide, illness or assassination, Djebar movingly recreates conversations and events to honour the bravery of their lives and writing. She catalogues the atrocities in the contemporary 'Algeria of blood', serial murders wrought by the 'madmen of God' (2000: 127): a religious fundamentalism that 'has decided to take power at any cost' (226).

To conclude this section: Djebar's novels expose 'the wound' of pain and abuse of women in the Islamic countries of North Africa, highlighting the veil in many contexts. Although Djebar addresses the debate on the veil and women's agency in terms of distinguishing between tradition and modernity, the veil is not emphasised in a political or revolutionary context (as she might have done following Fanon) but is manipulated and described as an emotional and linguistic symbol.[25]

Male veiling and masquerade

In concluding the analysis of gendered representations of veiling in the Maghreb (especially the renegotiating of gender in terms of clothing) it is important to establish that the veil itself is not an exclusively female garment. Fadwa El Guindi cites various instances of pre-Islamic male veiling, and argues that to analyse veiling as a 'woman-only phenomenon' misdirects analysis (1999).[26]

The issue of veiling also necessitates a short discussion of the veil as masquerade. Homi Bhabha (in writing about Frantz Fanon) emphasises the 'crucial engagement between mask and identity, image and identification ... from which comes the lasting impression of ourselves as others' (1994: 64). Significantly, Luce Irigaray discusses masquerade from her psychoanalytic viewpoint in terms of gender definition. She examines the potential of the masquerade in terms similar to those of my previous discussion:

> What do I mean by masquerade? In particular, what Freud calls 'femininity'. The belief that, for example, it is necessary to become a woman, whereas a man is a man from the outset. He has only to effect his being-a-man, whereas a woman has to become a normal woman, that is has to enter the *masquerade of femininity*. (1977)

The masquerade of cross-dressing has been used in order to explore this realm of self as other. In *The Sand Child* and *The Sacred Night*, both by Moroccan writer Tahar Ben Jalloun, the veil is a device in the gender switch of the protagonist – a woman who must disguise herself as a man, only later returning to her 'true' female identity –

as well as a metaphor for the covering up of gender identity. Ben Jalloun focuses on the need for woman to masquerade as man in order to gain an identity in the strictly patriarchal Arab world.

The Sand Child

In *The Sand Child*, Hajji Ahmed is in an intolerable, and shameful, position since he has produced only daughters and no son. (Under Islamic law a daughter can only inherit one third of a father's wealth.) He decides therefore that his next child will be a son regardless of its sex. The novel explores the theme of dual identity, as 'Ahmed' struggles to discover her identity, her sexuality, and a code of behaviour. Underneath her mask of male clothing, she is never a man, nor can she ever express herself as a woman. She is forced to repress any female emotion and becomes a distorted figure, mimicking an authoritarian Arab male. (S)he is an aggressive and uncaring son to the family, oppressing his sisters and ignoring his mother. The author, writing as a woman, shares this role reversal to some extent, so that he is able to empathise with her predicament – and the predicament of all women in their restricted social role in his society. The author frames his narrative within the shifting authority of oral narrative, with various characters taking up Ahmed's story, and providing different versions of her 'history'. The structure of Ben Jalloun's novel can be compared to its theme, elaborating parallels between the veiling of women and the veiling of text (Erickson, 1993: 47–64).

Presenting his novel as oral narrative, the author appropriates what is often referred to as 'female narrative' thereby further blurring his own gender and subverting his own and his characters' voices. Like 'feminine' space, oral narrative has been described as 'an inhabited, dynamic space where characters interact with one another, the storyteller interacts with the tale, the performer with her audience ... This is the space where continuity and change interweave' (Lazreg, 1994: x). By utilising this genre, Ben Jalloun accesses areas of narrative experience that undermine the structures of Islamic society.

The veil in this novel is not so much a physical covering of cloth as a symbol, such as the metaphor of 'the veil of flesh' that separates Ahmed as man from the real Ahmed as woman. Without this veil, this 'protecting distance, he would be thrown naked and defenceless into the hands of those who had constantly pursued him with their curiosity, mistrust, even hatred' (1). His strategies for survival in this hostile environment of entrenched patriarchal practices are, ironically, concealment through clothing (including binding up her breasts) and confinement to his room – ironic, since these are the two forms of *hijab*/seclusion forced upon women; but Ahmed is supposedly a man.

As Orlando argues, Ahmed is a 'site of confusion because she is neither totally man nor woman, but a body where genders overlap, yet are never individually defined' (1999: 79). Protected by 'that layer of mist that served me as a veil', her female identity is repressed to such an extent she dares not look in the mirror (83). The narrator points out that not only the hidden character of Ahmed is 'veiled' from the world; what is veiled is 'the inner face of truth' (61). Gradually, Ahmed seeks to hide him/herself behind mask upon mask of pretence and fabrication of an adopted social and sexual role. She seeks to answer the question, 'Who am I, myself or the other?' Crossing the line of sexuality, both character and author explore the other within the self. In this process of locating the other in the self, as Gilles Deleuze puts it, 'the actual is not what we are, but rather what we become, what we are in the midst of becoming, in other words, it is the Other, our becoming Other' (1990: 190). Ahmed's fight for self-expression is continued in the sequel, *The Sacred Night*, in which Ahmed, now Zahra, does accomplish an 'unveiling' of her female identity, but with disastrous consequences.

Critics of Ben Jalloun, such as Evelyne Accad, regard the author himself as an impostor, superficially claiming to advocate women's liberation, while 'deeply perpetuating all the stereotypes that feed the male fantasy of women, thus reinforcing their oppression' (Accad, 1990: 157). Accad corroborates one of the central theories put forward here, that one of the main reasons behind man's oppression of woman is his fear of her power. She argues that the essentialisation of woman into 'madonna/whore' within Arab literature such as Ben Jalloun's (as well as European texts) is due to man's connection between the fear of death and the fear of woman, and the sublimation of his violent sexuality (Accad, 1990: 163).

The Sheltering Sky

In the light of discussing the veil as a masquerade of gender identity, it is interesting to contrast Ben Jalloun's work with the novel *The Sheltering Sky* (1949) by Paul Bowles, which is also set in Morocco. This novel, although written by an American,[27] is included here as it portrays a situation comparable to that in *The Sand Child*. The heroine, Kit, transforms herself into a male identity, disguised in the *masculine* veil of the Tuareg nomad. Here, paradoxically, Kit's gender-change disguise enables her to experience her *female* sexuality. She changes into male Arab dress and is taken to the tribal village disguised as a tribesman but is kept in seclusion as a fourth wife (252).

Kit moves into a liminal zone, in which she 'loses' both language and gender. This process of loss is also one of unveiling: once she is 'rescued' by Europeans, Kit finds that 'the words were coming back, and inside the wrappings of the words there would be thoughts lying there' (271). After her husband dies, she defies the French colonial 'civilisation' and ventures off alone into the desert. After weeks of travel with Tuareg tribesman (one of whom becomes her lover), she undergoes a process of losing her identity and finding another, Arab *male*, identity.

While Bowles relates this episode of 'desert romance' in totally uncompromising terms of bleakness and alienation, the Bertolucci film version of the story depicts the new Kit as emerging like a chrysalis from behind veils. In a dramatic and silent scene, she escapes from the room where she has been living as wife and sexual slave, and walks out through the Arab village. Temporarily transformed from the object of the male gaze to the subject, it is *her* gaze that transfixes the local population and makes possible her freedom. A stronger, wiser, and more enigmatic woman emerges from the desert at the end of the novel (and film), only to disappear again out of the 'civilisation' of the colonial cities to return to the desert. While, for the western men, the desert symbolises the horror of the unknown, alien, and untameable (just as the west African jungle did for Conrad's Marlowe),[28] for Kit the desert is a place of transformation, a liberatory nomadic space (discussed by Deleuze and Guattari as 'rhizomatic').

Although in the novel the Tuareg Arabs are stereotypically depicted with 'kohl-farded eyes ... fierce above the draped indigo veils that hid their faces' (165), in reality the veil is worn as a symbol of power, virility and prestige. One Tuareg man explains that 'We warriors veil our faces so the enemy may not know what is in our minds, peace or war, but women have nothing to hide' – an interesting reversal of what is generally assumed to be a universal ethos within Islam (Brooks, 1996: 22). Although Muslims, the Tuareg allow their women considerable sexual freedom and permit Platonic friendships between the sexes. (Other Muslims consider the Tuareg close to heretics for these customs.) Kit's veiling as a Tuareg male in *The Sheltering Sky*, while ironic here in the light of the claim that 'women have nothing to hide', also raises questions of her sexual preferences: a topic discussed by critics who identify the character of Kit with the author's wife, Jane Bowles.[29]

Here, we have seen that veils may allow access to transgressing gender boundaries and heteronormative subjectivity. They may represent the prestige and power of the Tuareg male or the oppression and silencing of Maghrebian women. It is possible, in this light, to discuss the veil in a more expanded gendered context, in terms of a complex series of meanings: opportunity, privacy, and respect versus repression and anonymity.

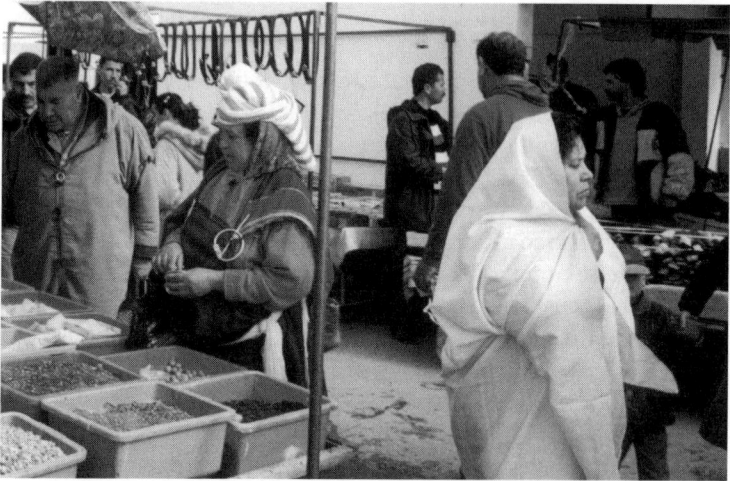

7   Tunisian women in the market, Al Qayrawan, March 2000. A Berber woman shops alongside an older woman wearing the traditional white *haik*. Changing social trends have meant that the silk or wool *haik* is frequently becoming replaced by the black *chador*, the 'uniform' of political Islamism. (Photo: author)

CONCLUSION

Even within Islam, the veil has a variety of nuanced meanings and connotations beyond stereotyped cultural/political tropes, while also implicated within other religious traditions.[30] The US-Vietnamese cultural critic Trinh T. Minh-ha concludes that veiling, like the use of silence, 'has many faces' and can be either subversive or oppressive, depending on the context.[31] If, as she claims, identity is related to its enactment of power relations, then woman can take the step of undercutting the inside/outside opposition, so that otherness and difference become a means of empowerment.

The feminist sociologist Fatima Mernissi, like Assia Djebar in her novels, argues that veiling and the institution of harems (veiled space) are both 'visible and invisible' (Mernissi, 1994: 58). A continuing debate of the positive and negative aspects of the veil again raises the question of women's identity and the problem of oppression versus freedom of choice for women in an Islamic world. The veil remains a highly contentious symbol, especially in Algeria. Marnia Lazreg concludes that in Algeria the colonial legacy has effectively prevented the emergence of a sense of self 'that could transcend the boundaries of Islam'. As the rising religious movements use women to embody the specificity of Islamic culture (just as the colonial powers had equated 'the orient' with woman), so both the state government and other religious parties use women for the furtherance of their own political interests. At the same time, women themselves are being forced to veil, a process of 'violent silencing' (Lazreg, 1994: 225–6).

The multifaceted meanings of the veil are evident in Assia Djebar's novels, whose complexity and ambivalence expose conflicting views on the veil. Djebar's own attitude towards the veil remains unresolved – as does her relationship to Algeria itself. In *So Vast the Prison*, she refers to Algeria as a monster, 'do not call it woman any more ... not even a madwoman' (Djebar, 1999: 356). She sees Algeria now as a land of tears – and blood. Despite her own work and success (albeit in exile) she argues that women are once again forgotten 'because they have no writing' and no voice (Djebar, 1999: 348). Djebar in fact predicted such a return to oppression in 1979 when she wrote,

> Then the heavy silence returns that puts an end to the momentary restoration of sound. As if the fathers, brothers, or cousins were saying: 'We have paid plenty for that unveiling of words!' Sound severed once again, the gaze once again forbidden, these are what reconstruct the ancestral barriers ... There is no seraglio [palace] anymore. But the structure of the seraglio attempts to impose its laws in the new wasteland: the law of invisibility, the law of silence. (1980: 151)

The violence of the colonial encounter, discussed here in terms of the 'worlding' of a territory, can equally well be seen in terms of the violent rift between the sexes within much Islamic culture. In the postcolonial strife in Algeria, women have been thrown back into traditional roles, back into wearing the veil, 'redoubling the immobility that makes women a prisoner' (Djebar, 1980: 141).

No political system has truly liberated women nor freed them from the fears (that is to say, the fear generated *by* men) and excesses of patriarchy. Even democracy in the Euro-American nations emphasises the female body as commodity, cheapening women's role and women's integrity in a way that appals many Islamic feminists and Middle Eastern (and western) women. Muslim women see their 'western sisters' as oppressed and cheapened through the emphasis on women's bodies in advertising, the media, careers and relationships. For them, the veil offers a sanctuary of respect, protection and pride. As Nawal El Saadawi argues, veiling and nudity (where women are expected to be fashionable and feminine in order to conform to media and global culture) are two sides of the same coin: 'Both mean that women are bodies without a mind and should be covered or uncovered to suit national or international capital interests' (1997: 138). While previously-colonised countries in North Africa are now threatened by neo-colonial forces, on both sides of the divide women have 'become their own jailers': because in order to resist, in order to force change, women must first appreciate the cultural indoctrination that takes place through both religious propaganda *and* western acculturation. Meanwhile, in late capitalist societies such as the United States, 'sexism instead of receding with the triumph of modernity, has probably become more general and more difficult to locate in a single institution' (Fox-Genovese, 1991).

Having analysed the positioning of the veil within Islamic Middle Eastern and African contexts, it is important to expand the discussion to another cultural location: veiling on the Indian subcontinent. The discussion in the next chapter highlights that veiling is not only found within Islamic, but also Hindu 'traditions' – also that such traditions are endorsed through indigenous class as well as colonial hegemonies.

6
Subversion, Seduction and Shame: India

Having explored the multifaceted contexts and meanings of the veil in the Arab world of the Middle East and North Africa, I will now analyse the role of the veil in another cultural context, that of the Indian subcontinent. Evidence from previous chapters demonstrates that veiling is not a phenomenon restricted within cultural or religious limits: it is a widespread and dominant feature of many societies that seek to maintain a rigid enforcement of obedience to male authority. Within the varying contexts to be discussed in this chapter, the veil can be described as bearing meanings ranging from statements of class status to debatably outmoded religious dogma. Yet the continuing significance of the veil (and the veiled world of purdah), no matter how ambiguously configured, collides with the apparent progress of 'modernity' and seems to be antagonistic to it.

In the context of India, negotiations of identity, agency and even daily safety for women revolve around conflicts between tradition and modernity. Indian women from Muslim and Hindu backgrounds continue to be positioned as both mother/maintainer icon of home and nation, and locus of erotic danger. Traditions of purdah exist within both religions – based on the concepts of *fitna* (social disruption) and a woman's *dharma* (sacred duty) respectively. (One can question whether within these contexts a woman's 'home' means a haven or a prison.) Traditions of modesty and piety are prevalent within both Hindu and Muslim cultures, and codes of dress are similarly powerful in displaying both class and caste status. The Hindu–Muslim divide in India is often cited as being both recent and contrived (Lewis, 1992; Dalrymple, 1999); an argument for the relatively 'recent' split between religions would explain the commonality of many cultural practices. Strict behavioural codes are found within both Muslim and Hindu contexts, as the literary texts discussed here reveal.

In order to investigate the meanings of the veil within an Indian context, this chapter discusses how gendered representations reveal the changing role of Indian women in terms of the 'traditional' place of woman behind the screen of purdah, within the confines of the *haveli* (women's quarters). It also elaborates further meanings and connotations of veiling within the debate of the veil and sexuality, questioning understandings of the veil as suppressing female sexuality, the veil as a 'fortress' to protect women against being the focus of male sexual desire, and the exotic/erotic mystique of unveiling. The discussion on colonial India elaborates on the orientalist fantasy of the veiled woman as sexual object of desire, previously seen within the context of the Maghreb. The Indian/Pakistani context extends the previous hypothesis of repression/liberation to include political, religious and national aspects of the veil: drawing as it does on centuries of cultural and spiritual tradition.

The veil is also associated with a 'mythologising' of the past and the stereotyping of the role and attributes of a 'good' woman.[1] These powerful hegemonies, still disseminated throughout India and Pakistan, in fact become increasingly virulent in the face of modernisation and social change. While women are given a 'religious' status, they are simultaneously denied any access to religious space or agency. Just as in Islam, where women were barred from the sphere of sacred power, so women in Indian culture are silenced and distanced from power by having their 'sacred' role defined as to wait in silence at home.

In recent decades India's world importance has increased – with India now, for example, one of the leading exporters of expertise in computer technology. Yet while educated women are more visible as a part of the business working class, women outside this 'democratic, western' mode of development may be more disadvantaged than ever.[2] Sunder Rajan describes the 'new woman' of India, the educated woman who 'has been drawn out of the privacy and invisibility of the home' and describes her new visibility as being 'a measure of her reality' (1993: 137). The freedom these 'westernised' women enjoy from the traditionally prescribed modes of marriage and relationships is entirely dependent on wealth and high-class status, however. In cities such as Mombai, rich young women defy their elders by having relationships based on cohabitation rather than marriage.[3] While women still may be encouraged, if not actively pressurised, to conform to traditions such as arranged marriages, paradoxically the trope of a woman hidden behind her clothing or the walls of her home is one that corroborates her lacking a corporeal, intellectual or emotional existence.

This apparent agency available to rich young women in India today through the power of choice, contrasts to the situation in rural Hindu India, where women from high-class families have traditionally veiled, to indicate that the wealth of the family does not require its women to help in agricultural labour. These women remain confined in, and defined through, their relationships within a strict patriarchal authority. (A novel such as Rama Mehta's *Inside the Haveli* (1977), analysed in this chapter as a pivotal text, portrays the educated heroine's journey from a modern urban upbringing back into the traditional world behind the veil, where the severe restrictions of etiquette and subservience dominate life.)

A review of the historical situation in India now elaborates how this polarised position came about.

HISTORICAL VEILS: THE RAJ AND NATIONALISM

In the nineteenth century, the figure of Indian woman was configured either as 'nothing other than the sentimental erotic' or as the feminised colonial land, over both of which the coloniser had power. Moreover, the veiling of women was 'an inviting but still uncrossable difference', which, by extension made the *zenana* (harem) 'the essential space of Indian femininity' (Suleri, 1992a: 92). As indicated in the previous chapter with reference to the French in Africa, to the conquering colonialist, it is 'only after such a sanctum has been penetrated that the Anglo-Indian can claim to "know" the Indian' (Suleri, 1992a: 93). Hence, the trope of India as a female body to be raped (as discussed by Said and earlier by Fanon in the context of Algeria) can be seen as an extension of the figure of the veiled woman in the forbidden *zenana*, who arouses rage, desire, fear and, above all, frustration in the colonial male.

Within British colonial discourse, the trope of India itself encompassed shifting, multiple meanings. Geographically, the discovery of India was mostly accomplished in the seventeenth century. The early adventurers of the East India Company who 'discovered' the new land often imaginatively fabricated an India based on polarities of identity and difference, civilisation and barbarity, modernity and tradition. Once again the invaded land was taken to be a 'blank' landscape, a meaningless palimpsest waiting to be written over by the 'enlightened' invaders. By the mid nineteenth century, 'Britain has fixed and normalised its "discovery/discoveries" of India by defining the land as "an unchanging text" of a primitive and static

Hinduism – one which continually reaffirmed the British Raj as a necessary moral and civilising order' (Singh, 1996: 3).

Indian women at the turn of the last century found themselves positioned between two discourses of 'otherness': they had to 'consolidate two selves, the self constructed by British imperialism and the self engendered by Indian patriarchy' (Hubel, 1996: 146).[4] The trend to essentialise the female body continued at the end of the British Raj in the nationalist discourse of Jawaharlal Nehru and Mahatma Gandhi. Conflating discourses of nationalism, politics and religion, Nehru and Gandhi upheld the configuration of India as a female body.

Woman had already been a trope of nationalism in the earlier Swadeshi movement in Bengal. Tagore's 1915 novel, *The Home and the World*, dramatically illustrates the position of woman in this discourse, and in the world of purdah.

Within the economy of Hindu idealism, Rabindranath Tagore's *The Home and the World* (1915, 1985), set in Bengal at a time of the upsurge of the nationalist movement, employs many of the conceits of Mata Bharata (mother India) later utilised by Mahatma Gandhi and Jawaharlal Nehru in their invocation of an Indian (Hindu) motherland. In her introduction to the novel, Anita Desai points out how *The Home and the World* is a dramatisation of the clash between the old and the new, realism and idealism, tradition and the rapidly changing world. In traditional households, the secluded *zenana* (harem) and all the customs associated with it, were designated by the term 'purdah'. In this novel, a young wife is given her liberty from behind the veil of purdah, urged to 'come into the heart of the outer world and meet reality' (Tagore, 1915, 1985: 23) – by her benign and loving (if ineffectual) husband, a situation analogous to the need to modernise and liberate Bengal. Bimala, a devoted Hindu wife, is deified by both her husband and his revolutionary friend Sandip as the embodiment of 'the Shakti of the motherland ... the goddess herself' (33). While the possibility exists for Bimala to represent the middle-class educated 'new woman', she is, however, corrupted by her experience of politics and sexual awakening in the 'outside world'. Homi Bhabha regards this episode as analogous to the *Unheimlich*, the uncanny: from a masculinist perspective again 'outside the home' equates with 'out of control' (Bhabha, 1994: 10).

Bimala's unveiling, while being undertaken seemingly without shame (84), in fact exposes the shame of the nation itself.[5] One must question what Bimala's 'liberation' from purdah – and indeed that of other women at the time permitted into the world from woman's 'separate sphere' solely for the nationalist cause – achieves either for the nationalist movement or for her/their own independence. Here, as elsewhere, 'Women are typically constructed as the symbolic bearers of the nation but are denied any direct relation to national agency ... the "motherland" of male nationalism may not signify "home" and "source" to women' (McClintock et al., 1997: 90).

Although the nation changed from imperial subjection to nation state, the imbrication of women's body and the 'motherland' continued.[6] When India reached its independence from Britain, the female body and how it was or was not dressed, and the geographical space it occupied, still retained metaphoric symbolism both for women themselves as well as for men.

Yet, the rise of nationalism and Mahatma Gandhi's call for women to participate in it meant resurgence in the representation of women in public life. Gandhi enabled women to become both politically and professionally empowered: they participated in giving political speeches, in the satyagraha demonstrations, as well as being jailed. Gandhi was also active in attacking patriarchal cruelty against women (Dastur and Mehta, 1993: 23–4). Amongst other 'social evils', including child marriage, the dowry system, and prostitution, Gandhi spoke out against the 'barbarous custom' of purdah, which 'has now become useless and doing incalculable harm to the country'. Describing women as being 'caged and confined in their houses and little courtyards', in an interview in the journal *Young India*, Gandhi openly argued:

> All the education that we have been receiving for the past 100 years seems to have produced little impression on us, for I note that the *Purdah* is being retained even in educated households, not because the educated men believe in it themselves but because they will not manfully resist the brutal custom at a stroke. (Dastur and Mehta, 1993: 75)

Here, interestingly, Gandhi subverts and reverses the tradition of the male suppression of women being *a part* of manliness.[7] He also refused to accept as sacrosanct the Vedic texts, such as the laws of Manu, which stated that there could be no freedom for women. (These laws reject woman as a temptress, claiming that she is unworthy to be trusted with her own life and must be under the care of her father, then husband, then son.) In contrast, Gandhi deified women as the embodiment of the virtues of selflessness, passive endurance and non-violence – qualities he had observed and admired among the Suffragettes in London – which became the basic tenets of his satyagraha political philosophy. Yet these ideals of the upper-caste Hindu woman arguably formed another patriarchal discourse 'about' but not by women. Whether or not Hindu women are indeed the embodiments of such 'feminine' virtues has been contested both during and since Gandhi's time.[8]

The tradition that Gandhi addressed was rationalised by generations of myths and stories that justified why women had to cover their entire face and crouch down to make themselves invisible when men entered the room. The 'Vedic' concept of a woman as *shakti*, meaning mystical female energy (as personified by the goddess Shakti, Siva's consort), has also been used and abused for centuries.[9] Although at one level this mythology depicts woman as the source of all energy and well-being, and the spiritual nucleus of the family, it also, in the words of one critic, 'appears to be the justification for the subordination of woman to man devised by crafty old brahmins' (Nanda, 1990: 73). Amongst other 'spiritually-sanctioned' restrictions, Brahmin rituals created role boundaries for women, denying them access to sacred rituals and texts.

Whereas the *eroticised* female body had been the site of colonial desire, the 'new' discourse put forward by Nehru and Gandhi therefore in many ways resorted to a Hindu idealisation or deification of women – a stereotyping of women that may have equally stultified any emancipation of women in real terms. While the role of women in Indian society may seem to have remained unaltered for over a thousand years, some writers perceive that women's status has even 'regressed in significant ways' since independence (Bumiller, 1990: 20).

VEILED WOMAN IN INDIAN LITERATURE

While emphasising the issue of the interconnectedness of subjectivity, identity and power, 'Indian' literature aims to give expression to a 'national experience'. Yet both resident and diasporic writers stress the frequent 'non-place' of women within this rapidly changing national identity. Within this wider scheme of gender relations, women's fiction (both pre- and post-independence) highlights issues of sexual positioning within both narrative and power, as women negotiate personal spaces of agency. Expressions in short stories by Indian women writers,[10] such as 'The Library Girl' by Vishwapriya

L. Iyengar, written in terms of distinct binaries of light/dark, hope/despair, life/death are indicative of the fear passed down through generations of women, who are placed under the veil by the requirements of religious patriarchy. The widely-revered Urdu author Ismat Chughtai indicates the traditional symbolic importance of the veil in marriage, as well as the possibility for its subversive use. Other contemporary writers, such as Ginu Kamani, suggest the option of rebellion against traditional values through the expression of women's sexuality. Ruth Prawer Jhabvala's fictions contribute to the discussion of the various possible tropes of the veil as disguise and self-discovery. My reading of the story 'Draupadi' by Mahasveta Devi, however, questions how far Indian women writers are able to extricate themselves from traditional stereotypes of the Indian woman, and to what extent the mythical past still determines an essentialisation of the female body even within contemporary – and controversial – modes of expression.

Also included here is an examination of Salman Rushdie's work, which is rich in allusions to veiling and the trope of women beneath the veil. A discussion of his novels *Shame*, *Midnight's Children* and *The Satanic Verses* reveals how the veil is used as a self-conscious literary device and means of social and religious comment. The 'slippage' of text to disrupt and problematise both 'women' and their involvement in history is highlighted by the frequent reference to characters 'slipping' behind and beneath veils, sheets, carpets, curtains, and *burqas*.

The most extreme example of women's subordination is arguably that described in the elaborate rituals of veiling and avoidance detailed by Leigh Minturn in her anthropological account of Rajput women, customs that allowed Minturn to imagine herself in medieval rather than present-day India (1993).

Upper-class Hindu women observe purdah customs that act as deferential rituals denoting the status of family members. Women veil before men and older superior women by drawing down their saris to cover the face with the *gungat* (sari veil). This is a sign of respect for the man's status and a symbol of her own inferior status. Contact between husband and wife is restricted in order to maintain his bond with his mother and lessen his attachment to his wife. Minturn describes how a wife will squat, her face completely veiled, when conversing with her husband (1993: 75). Daughters-in-law, irrespective of age, remain subservient to their mothers-in-law and never unveil, or speak, in their presence. Rama Mehta (1990) describes how some women had never seen the faces of their daughters-in-law even though they had lived in the same house for 25 or 30 years. The practices of veiling and purdah are upheld by a complex system of religious rituals, social codes and strict discipline, any violation of which could mean the threat of loss of social respectability – the ever-present spectre of shame. In fictional terms this veiled lifestyle is described by Rama Mehta in her novel relating to Rajasthani customs, *Inside the Haveli*. An analysis of this novel will elaborate how far some of these theoretical and social concerns may be a 'lived' reality.

A taste of purdah: *Inside the Haveli*

Rama Mehta's *Inside the Haveli* (first published in 1977) has been hailed as a classic that maintains strict authenticity to the life it portrays. The author herself was both a novelist and leading sociologist, whose insight into the lives of women was based upon her own experiences of life in Udaipur (Rajasthan). (Rama Mehta was the first woman to be appointed to India's Foreign Service, a position she had to resign upon marriage.) Her novel is built on her non-fiction text 'From Purdah to Modernity', a fascinating study which reflects Mehta's concern with women and her country's coexisting and conflicting trends of time. Anees Jung describes the situation of women in India as being 'in-between' times, living in a 'vacuum' between the past and the present, between tradition and modernity. A woman brought from life in town to life in a village (as a wife in purdah) remarks that 'time [has lost] its validity ... There are curtains on the doorways ... There is nowhere to go, no one to talk to' (Jung, 1987: 52).

In *Inside the Haveli*, the protagonist, Geeta, experiences a similar shift between two eras, leaving behind the modernity of her parents' home for the traditional household of her aristocratic in-laws. While apparently typifying 'silenced woman', Geeta finds satisfaction in observing without being observed. She finally not only accepts the power of the patriarchs but ultimately perpetuates their values into the next generation. Brought up and educated to speak her mind and to associate freely with both men and women, she is shocked by the strict enforcement in her new home of ancient rules and behaviours, most particularly that of purdah.[11]

A description of when Geeta first arrives in Udaipur as a new bride, introduces both Geeta and the reader to the reality of her new life. On stepping down from the train: 'She was immediately encircled by women singing but their faces were covered. One of them moved forward and exclaimed in horror, "Where do you come from that you show your face to the world?"' (Mehta, 1977: 17). This comment is the start for her of a re-education in the traditional behaviour of 'respectable' women. As the car taking her to her new home enters the narrow streets of the city:

> Geeta had lifted her face and pulled back her sari to see. 'No, no, you cannot do that,' Pari [a maid] had snapped, pulling back the sari over her face. 'In Udaipur we keep purdah. Strange eyes must not see your beautiful face'. (17)

The main theme of the novel concerns Geeta's alienation from the life of the *haveli* and her gradual acceptance of its mores and rules. She is forced to live by the rigidly enforced codes of behaviour, which centre on the ritual avoidance of both men and older women through veiling. She learns that in order to retain her respectability, she must keep her head covered, even when no men are in sight (18). Purdah has been characterised as an extreme form of sex role differentiation, as well as providing 'separate worlds and symbolic shelter', typical of the rules of seclusion of women generally found in India 'even where they have not been formalised by an extra piece of clothing' (Minturn, 1993: 133). Covering the face is the outer sign of respect; not to do so would invoke the most heinous indictment of shame and dishonour.

Veiling the face is also the overt symbolism of an inner masking of emotion. This concealment of emotion could be compared to the traditional Indian theory of aesthetics, where the power of a work of art (be it text or performance) lies in the 'suggested possibility', or flavour of emotion, *rasa*. This theory of *rasa-dhvani* focuses on the dynamic interplay between concealment–suggestion–revelation–meaning. The 'suggested content' of *rasa*, which is necessary to incite subtle modes of approaching art and performative experience, could be thus linked to the multiple and shifting meanings of the veil.

As Geeta gradually learns the rules of the *zenana*, she discovers that just as an unveiled face would elicit shame, so too would an unveiling of raw emotion. The spontaneous and lively Geeta painfully learns to keep her feelings concealed, for 'in the haveli no one really expressed their feelings. They covered their emotions in an elaborate exchange of formal gestures and words ... Everyone moved cautiously, every word was weighed before it was spoken' (32). The importance of *rasa* (or aesthetic emotion) lies in its power to transcend 'superficial' mental states to ensure that the outward experience or object of perception gains inner meaning; it is appreciated inwardly, not merely on the sensory level. Thus *rasa* produces a 'totality of effect' that could synthesise intellect and emotion, senses and mind, and offer a point of reconciliation.[12]

Even after Geeta has been in the *haveli* for seven years, she has no friends – a result, perhaps, of the strict class divisions within the *haveli*. She finds that although the other women thrive on gossip, they

> never expressed an opinion and never revealed their feelings. They seemed like little canaries in a cage who sang and twittered but seemed to know no passion. Their large eyes full of yearning and longing looked dreamily on the world beyond from behind their veils. Though young, some unknown fear seemed to have eaten away their natural exuberance … It seemed to Geeta that they were waiting for the day when they would be freed from their confinement. (87)

Geeta too gradually changes. Although she envies the freedom of women she sees outside the walls, she accepts the discipline of the *haveli* without protest (91). At times of extreme crisis, when she rages behind her veil with anger or frustration, she remains silent. As Parikh and Garg point out in their discussion of the lives of Indian women, the misery of the upper-class woman is 'more poignant as she cannot express her anger in public or make a scene' (1989: 91). Similarly, the silence of women and the necessity for Geeta not to voice her concerns or anxieties to anyone (other than her maid, who is lower down the social hierarchy), for silence before her mother-in-law and any older relatives, for the taboo on speech at all in front of a male relative, all emphasise that Indian women in purdah were effectively silenced from within the social system. The silencing of subaltern woman was therefore not a phenomenon that depended upon an external colonial regime. At no point in *Inside the Haveli* are the British, or their influence in India, mentioned.[13] The traditions of the Udaipur *havelis* remained untainted by modern or liberal influences of other parts of India, since 'modern western influences were kept away from them, not by threats but by keeping alive the Indian model of behaviour' (Mehta, 1990: 125). Education for women was not considered important. The power of the feudal social structure and the belief that the traditional restrictions placed on women were intrinsically right were so entrenched that women were incapable of breaking the traditional mould (Mehta, 1990: 114) – a situation that would explain Geeta's eventual capitulation.

Yet while the silencing and invisibility of woman in these circumstances may seem to be overwhelmingly oppressive, Rama Mehta's novel does not play upon such judgements. Silence, like veiling, is ambivalent. Silence, like the veil, has many facets. It can be subversive when it frees itself from 'the male defined context of absence, lack, and fear as feminine territories … silence as a will not to say or a will to unsay and as a language of its own has barely been explored' (Minh-ha, 1988: 73). For women, the basic human right 'to remain silent' has far-reaching connotations: in the Indian context, silence is a possible way to reappropriate space and re-articulate self.

Geeta, for example, soon discovers positive aspects of veiling and silence. In the large family gatherings, she finds it difficult to determine who all the relatives are, especially since all the women remain veiled behind their saris. She is grateful to her maid's warning that she must never speak; in company all questions are answered by her mother-in-law. Most significantly, Geeta

> came to love the veil that hid her face, this allowed her to think while others talked. To her delight she had discovered that through her thin muslin sari, she could see everyone and yet not be seen by them. (22)

Anees Jung – referring to the secluded *havelis*, such as the one in which her mother still lives, as 'energy-filled spaces of silence', and 'the microcosms sustaining quality of life within the macrocosm of a vast land' – suggests that 'silence could be a language through which women in this land realised themselves' (1987: 20). Jung's fascinating account of encounters with women across India highlights ambiguities and utilises a more positive scenario, where often instead of disempowerment, the veil, harem (*zenana*) and purdah are regarded as features of 'psychic empowerment' and possibility rather than social oppression.

Other 'myths' of the harem/*haveli* are similarly dispelled in Rama Mehta's work. As opposed to western colonial representation, the *haveli* is not an erotic space – just the opposite. Contact between the sexes is controlled and strictly limited; tradition especially regulates and restricts intimacy (or indeed any private time) between a husband and wife. Husbands may only visit the *zenana* and their wives' room (or in some cases where women share a room or courtyard, their bed) for a limited number of hours at night.[14] Early in the novel, when she desperately needs advice and comfort, Geeta is filled with anger and depression at her isolated situation. Geeta hopes to be consoled through advice from her husband, 'but she only saw him in the night ... Though men could come to the women's apartment when they wished, it was not considered dignified to do so' (21). This picture of life in the *haveli* belies the orientalist representation of the 'erotic' and sensuous nature of harem life.[15]

A subplot of the novel illustrates the importance of the rigid codes of conduct in the *haveli*. Modesty and self-effacement are highly valued attributes, as are discipline, respect and loyalty. The character of the maid, Lakshmi, is structured as a foil to Geeta. Young, outspoken and rebellious (as Geeta is when she first arrives as a new bride), despite her good intentions and hard work, Lakshmi violates the purdah of the *haveli* – she unwillingly accepts a gift from one of the male servants, aware that such gifts are forbidden. Tormented by the shame of her predicament, she is too terrified to admit what has happened to the other women. Her husband discovers her 'crime' and publicly humiliates her. Eventually she runs away from the *haveli* (leaving her baby) into a life of self-imposed exile, while the man who has 'taken away her honour' (66) continues to work for the family. When the other female servants go to find her, they are shocked to see she has uncovered her face – a symbolic rejection of the hypocrisy of the *haveli* and the shame it has cast upon her (80–1). For the *haveli*, shame (as for many women in Islamic culture) lies in *un*veiling. Lakshmi reverses such logic, unveiling to retaliate against and expose the shame of the patriarchal system.

While Lakshmi is marginalised into poverty when she does not play by the patriarchal rules, Geeta learns to live by the rules and is gradually assimilated into them. (One could question how far class difference between the two women accounts for their respective fates.) By the end of the novel, Geeta no longer questions the validity of the *haveli* mores. Yet whether or not this process of assimilation corresponds to her losing her own identity is not clear. When her father-in-law dies (and her mother-in-law descends to the low status of widow) she becomes the head of the *haveli*. The reader is left with little doubt that from this position Geeta will perpetuate and endorse the traditions of the *haveli* – which she has come to love and respect – into the next generation.

This novel centres around the concept of women having their existence on the border-zone of being/becoming. They belong on the edge of the male world, behind the curtain, on the far extremity of the courtyards, behind the lattice wall, concealed beneath the veil. Bhabha speaks in terms of 'in-between spaces [that] provide the terrain for elaborating new strategies of selfhood – singular and communal – that initiate new signs of identity and innovative sites of collaboration, and contestation' (1994: 2). Here, a pertinent question is whether the in-between spaces occupied by the *haveli* woman can be a space for elaborating any sense of selfhood, or if all sense of identity is prescribed and predetermined.

When Geeta discovers 'to her delight' that she can see while not being seen, she places herself on that border threshold of not belonging in either world. Furthermore, as we have seen, she is at home neither in the world of the women, nor the world of men, which is forbidden to her. Woman's position is both at the border of male space and a border of time, situated in a non-time between past tradition and present modernity. Furthermore, in the world of *Inside the Haveli*, veiled woman has been displaced by the traditions of patriarchy into a borderline (migrant) location: migrant since she must forever be traversing the realms of male and female spaces (physically represented by interconnecting courtyards) her only real location being ever watchful on the threshold between the two.

From a sociological approach, contemporary Indian society still defines and restricts the identities that women are able to adopt. Their roles and their 'life-space' are circumscribed from birth by their gender. From an early age a female child is made to feel her inferiority to male children, 'She experiences no space for herself and learns to be *invisible*, obedient, conforming ... She learns to accept herself as unwanted, or as a *transient* to be cared for, but never to belong' (Parikh and Garg, 1989: 101, my italics). Woman in India must 'cultivate for herself a mask' (regardless of whether or not she is physically veiled), and yet 'carving out a space and a meaning for herself without threatening her well-defined prescriptive roles is not a risk she can easily take'. A woman is 'always in somebody else's space. There is no space which [she] can call her own' (Parikh and Garg, 1989: 102). The restriction upon space is one way of ensuring a woman's conformity and obedience. Denied physical, personal and spiritual space, a woman must learn to live within the system without any legitimate space for the self. (This description of the female sense of transience and non-belonging again relates to Bhabha's terminology of liminality, or existence on a threshold. Since Bhabha takes the image of the mask to indicate an unrepresentability identity, within this position of having no space, the identity of veiled woman is doubly non-locatable.)

Women's short stories

While *Inside the Haveli* negates a colonial stereotype of the 'erotic' eastern *haveli*, the next examples from fiction reveal a context in which gendered space is eroticised. The three stories here all deal with how young Indian wives deal with this search for a space of agency within the prescribed patriarchy. The young wife in Ginu Kamani's 'Younger Wife' could be said to idealise her role as wife and lover. Yet, unlike most other women in Indian literature, she expresses a great inner happiness (which to the reader may appear more as an alarming naivety).

Ismat Chughtai (1915–1992) was amongst the boldest and most outspoken Indian female writers in Urdu, at a time when it was revolutionary for a woman to write and publish at all. She was one of the very few women allowed to enter a Muslim university to study, on the condition they sit in purdah behind a curtain at the back of the class. She was greatly admired by her contemporaries, such as Saadat Hasan Manto, although her story *Lihaaf* ('The Quilt') written in 1942, was charged with obscenity by the British government. Her trial in Lahore lasted two years (during which time Manto was one of her few supporters). Her stories explore the oppressions of middle-class family life as well as the inhibitions of sexuality. Before looking at the controversial lesbian story 'The Quilt', I will analyse another short story, *Ghunghat*, 'The Veil'. Like the Egyptian writer Nawal El Saadawi, Chughtai tackles women's struggles within their designated culture, and her female protagonists may be broken by poverty but not defeated by patriarchal oppression. Both stories I analyse here suggest strategies whereby women may confront, or ridicule, the arrogance of male chauvinism. In 'The Veil', a bride challenges convention through her stoical silence. 'The Quilt' then offers one possible alternative strategy for survival within the bounds of marriage.

'The Veil' opens with the description of Goribi, a white-haired, 80-year-old virgin, who 'had never known the touch of a man's hand' although she is married (Chughtai, 1991: 1). At the age of 14 she had been married to her mother's (young) uncle, an egotistical man who was overwhelmed with feelings of resentment and aggression towards her. Failing to lift his bride's veil after the completion of the

8   *Portrait of a Noble Lady*, Moghal School (eighteenth century). This example of exquisite Moghul portraiture of an affluent Hindu woman shows how the veil evokes femininity, denotes prestige and hints at modesty. It also suggests how the end of the sari, the *ghungat*, could be drawn down to cover the face. (Victoria and Albert Museum, London, UK/Bridgeman Art Library)

ceremonies, he ordered her to 'lift the veil yourself' (3). When she failed to move – for this would be a violation of tradition – he accused her of arrogance and left. Knowing the bride had not been touched, the relatives interrogated him:

'She is defiant', he proclaimed.
'How do you know that?'
'I told her to lift her veil and she ignored my request.'
'You fool! Don't you know that a bride does not lift her own veil? Why didn't you do it yourself?'
'Never! I have sworn. If she will not lift her veil herself; she can go to hell!' (4)

He left the town for seven years; time he spent 'indulging in all the vices that were available to him; he consorted with prostitutes and homosexuals and ... all this while Goribi quietly smouldered away behind her veil' (4). Presumably she had no other choice, since she was, as Chughtai puts it 'suspended between her parents' home and that of her in-laws' (4) – in social terms, in fact, a migrant.

The husband eventually returned when his mother fell ill, and the relatives urged the couple to try again. Once again she was decked out in her bridal finery, now 'a flowering beauty' of 21. The story is repeated: he ordered her to raise her veil and she did not stir (the reason, whether from terror, shyness, or defiance is never explained). Leaving again that night, he never returned. Thirty years passed, and when he was brought home 'burdened with disease', he requested to see her so he may die in peace. Goribi took her wedding finery from her trunk and with her long veil arrived at his bedside:

'Lift your veil', Kale Mian whispered convulsively.
Goribi's trembling hands reached up towards her veil, and fell.
Kale Mian had taken his last breath.
That very moment Goribi calmly sat down on the floor beside his bed, smashed her glass bangles against the bedpost, and instead of the bridal veil, pulled the white veil of widowhood over her head. (6)

Here is not only a woman trapped within the traditional confines of identity, but also one whose loyalty to the traditions of marriage consumes her whole life. Both fictional and sociological writings reveal that, as propagated through the ongoing stereotypes of the

Hindu epics, being a wife and mother are the only possible roles available for many Indian women. Again the deeply-embedded assumptions about women's role also define their space, as one woman explains, 'Women as persons do not belong to any system except in a role. Essentially they are outsiders' (quoted in Parikh and Garg, 1989: 170). As a daughter-in-law, Goribi would have been received as a guest; at home, she no longer belonged. She would have been unable to find any legitimate space, until her ritual transformation to widow at last gave her a clearly defined role.

The use of the veil here is both as the traditional wedding veil and also the white veil of the Indian widow. Thus in these contexts the veil stands as the threshold between two different states of life, both wife and widowhood. Again, the veil is the borderline from one state of being to another. Here, because Goribi's veil is never lifted (and as we are told, she is still a virgin), she is immobilised on the border – unable to resume life as a bride, unable to return to life as an unmarried girl. She is in limbo, until the veil comes to symbolise death, rather than life. (Indian widows traditionally have no status in society and are forbidden to participate in any of society's festivals or rituals where they have a polluting and unlucky influence. This taboo status of widowhood is symbolised by the new widow smashing her bangles, removing her jewellery and dressing in white – the colour of mourning.)

The central use of the veil in this story also suggests that the husband's behaviour can be explained as a response to his frustrated gaze. He never sees his bride: he is 'melted' by the desire of the thought of a night with her; his body 'yearns for her like a tiger anticipating its prey' (5); but he is unable to lift her veil to claim what is his by right (5). The veil here, and Goribi's refusal to lift it, denies him his power as the rightful owner of the gaze, in Freudian–Lacanian terms. She, however, sees him; in fact he pleads, 'If you don't do what I say I am never going to show you my face again!' (5). He never sees *her* face at all. In this story, Goribi is depicted as leading a miserable and meaningless life. Since her refusal to lift her veil is never explained (another form of silencing, perhaps) one may interpret the story more positively as showing one woman's way of exerting her agency in the only way possible to her. Although one can only speculate as to the reasons the author did not explicate more extensively Goribi's motivation, Chughtai may be suggesting that a life with such an obnoxious (and violent) man could hardly have been better than the one without him.

This story also suggests the symbolism of the veil as hymen. Derrida formulates the hymen as both token of virginity and symbol of marriage, situating it as a boundary between inside and outside, through which Manichaean opposites are produced and reproduced (Derrida, 1981). Thus, while on the one hand promoting assimilation (in the context of marriage) it also articulates difference (through its function of separation). The hymen as dividing line is at the basis of economies governing inside/outside, sameness/difference, and public/private. Thus, for example in 'The Veil', the symbol of union – the lifting of the veil (symbolic rupture of the hymen) – becomes also the symbol of separation.[16]

Ismat Chughtai's controversial story 'The Quilt' again concerns the traditional values of society and their subversion, achieving, like the veil itself, 'a superb balance of reticence and suggestiveness' (Tharu and Lalita, 1993: 128). While not concerned specifically with physical veiling, it nevertheless uses the imagery of the quilt to symbolise the possibility of subversion beneath a traditional covering. The story involves a frustrated housewife whose husband 'totally forgot her presence' (Chughtai, 1991: 130). In fact he fills the house with young male students – a hint of his own sexual preference (8). Broken-hearted, his wife finds sexual and emotional solace in the companionship of her female servant, Rabbo. Their lesbian relationship is seen from the point of view of a small girl, so that it remains vague and understated. The girl does not understand what she sees or hears, although she is more than curious to discover the meaning of the noises that are coming from beneath the cover of the quilt (18–19)!

The story 'Younger Wife' by Ginu Kamani, written half a century after 'The Quilt', is far more explicit in its treatment of female sexuality. The volume of short stories *Junglee Girl* (1995) deals with many aspects of female sexuality, and was significantly described in a review as containing 'pithy tales of lust, longing and not belonging'. Negotiating intersections of sexuality, gender, and culture, the stories present different facets of the quest for sexual identity and fulfilment. They expose areas of life usually associated with shame: areas psychically and experientially difficult to access. Kamani recently spoke of the importance of telling stories about sex: exposing areas of shame as a part of her social activism (Kamani, 2002). The story 'Younger Wife' expresses one of the most evocative – and poetic – narratives of the experience of living beneath the veil. Written in the first person, the story opens with a surprisingly sensuous description of a man's feet:

The father of Harinath has the most beautiful feet in the world. His big toes are juicy knobs of ginger and his small toes cured cloves of garlic. His soles are as red as chillies, from the mud of the fields where he works. At dinnertime, I jump up when I hear the loud voices of the men returning home. I grab a small pot of water and sit by the door. I wait. (Kamani, 1995: 95)

This opening paragraph is pure magic: for the reader soon realises that the (unnamed) narrator never actually sees her husband's face, so she has fallen in love with the only part she sees from the viewpoint of her bent head under a veil, his feet. As the men enter the house, the narrator explains, 'being the youngest wife I cannot look at any of them, but I know by their feet who they are' (95). She washes her husband's feet and drinks the 'blessed water', as according to tradition. Then she describes massaging his toes, an erotic experience for her (96).

The narrative details her memories of the first years of her marriage, particularly the birth of her daughter, an event that caused her mother-in-law to demand she be sent back to her father's house and the baby buried. Fortunately, she was soon blessed with the birth of two sons, and despite her hard-hearted mother-in-law, who calls her 'a dangerous outsider' (97), her status was supported by her husband. (This story confirms the gender roles that are instilled from birth by parents, and that girls are generally unwelcome.)[17]

Her husband, she informs us, now 'wants to make more sons'. After he 'does the work' to her in the dark, she turns quickly so that she can caress his feet: 'They are my own special toys, for licking and sucking, like nipples for a baby' (98). She then describes how, before she left her father's house to be married, she would play the part of 'younger wife' to her father and take her mother's place when she was alone with him. (It is in this context that the title of the story makes sense, for she is the only wife of her husband.) Similarly, the husband reverses his expected role and sucks the milk vigorously from his wife's breasts – an act that makes his mother 'cover her face for shame' and run from the room (100). The highly-charged story ends with the narrator describing how her daughter (whom she has disowned on the basis of her gender and calls an 'orphan girl') will soon take on the role of 'younger wife' for her husband.

One of the few stories to describe the erotic life of a veiled woman – and one in which she is unquestioningly happy with her situation – 'Younger Wife' also depicts many of the traditional facets of patriarchal and patrilocal life. The contentment of the wife here contrasts with Bumiller's summary of rural women as either 'prisoners' if in purdah, or 'slaves' if working on the fields (1990: 79). The story contributes significantly to the varied 'lived experience' of women beneath the veil. Similarly it enhances the analysis of the world of *Inside the Haveli*, which described the large household of both upper-class women and their servants (both classes rigidly veiled). Here, the story involves a small rural middle-class family, whose traditional rules of decorum (which in turn dictate the roles of women) are based upon the same patriarchal and religious hegemonies.

In 'Younger Wife', the wife could be argued to gain agency and a strength of self-identity through the close sexual relationship she has with her husband; their bond certainly gives her the confidence to stand up to her mother-in-law. She knows her own traditional worth as a fertile mother of sons. The husband in this story is also able to defy his mother's overarching authority to defend his wife: 'Don't talk to me that way in front of your wife-slave', the mother screams at her son. 'My man laughed ... and in the broad daylight, in the front room of the house for receiving visitors, he did the man's work in me' (100). (The husband thus asserts his power over *both* women.) This short, and yet rich, story challenges ethical codes – especially in its theme of incest – and counteracts the discourses of essential-ising binaries that see women as victims rather than as complex agents. It also suggests that freedom is not located in external physical space so much as internal cognitive space.

However, a very different depiction of veiling is found in the bleak short story by Vishwapriya L. Iyengar 'The Library Girl', published in 1985 (in Holmstrom, 1990). This story, specifically about the Muslim community in India, describes a girl's first experience of wearing the *burqa*, using imagery that presents clear-cut contrasts of light/dark, joy/despair, freedom and agency/entrapment and invisibility. In this story, the young girl, Talat, is known by the local community as 'the library girl' due to her passion for reading and her daily visits to the library. Talat thinks of the library building as 'the eye' of the neighbourhood, a significant image considering the equivalence between the 'eye'/I of identity, since it is the library that formulates her identity, her nickname and her self-concept as a reader/scholar.

At 16 or 17 years old, Talat represents 'a bolt of sunshine' for the people of the *basti*, 'neighbourhood' (146). Whenever she visits the library, she smiles and politely greets the shopkeepers and residents along her path. They have come to know her and expect her daily visit. Although she is bright and intelligent, her father without explanation has recently stopped her schooling. She overhears her mother quarrelling with her father over her education, which he regards as worthless for a girl.[18] Her mother is afraid for the future of her daughter, and in her we see the mirror image of what Talat is likely to become: a fearful, uneducated, and trapped woman. As her mother sews a new *shalwar-kameez* for her, embroidered with star-shaped sequins, mother and child significantly gaze at each other in the mirror: Talat sees her mother's eyes 'like crows trapped in the cage of her face' (147).

Talat, unlike her mother, is able to escape the house to her sanctuary of the library, although she keeps the books she borrows well hidden from her disapproving father. One night the father returns home with a large package for her: a black silk *burqa* from 'Persia', as he prefers to call Iran (148). As Talat admires the fine black mesh of the face-mask, her mother continues to cook, she 'rubbed salt into the goat's breast and did not know if glass crystals were not being rubbed into her own' (149). Her grandmother says nothing, but lowers her eyes onto her crochet work. Only her father's eyes 'shone with pride and pleasure' as Talat tries on the *burqa* for the first time. Laughing, Talat turns to look at her reflection in the mirror, but

> She saw her own veiled face in the mirror and felt afraid. She had also seen her mother's face. In the cage the crows had died. Her father said, 'I have some business to attend to,' and left. The old woman [the grandmother] let out a scream of exasperation. The skull-cap had disintegrated into a confusion of knots. (149)

The cleverly integrated imagery here of death and horror indicates the silent, unspoken misery of the older women as they watch the young girl's identity being countered by the father's power, symbolised by the *burqa*. The mother in particular, 'saw her beautiful sun and star child become night in the mirror' (149).

Still wearing the *burqa*, Talat finds the book she had hidden and hurries out to reach the library before it closes. However, her entire experience of the world changes. Although she greets her friends along the way, no one responds to her. One man, the baker, burns his fingers in his confusion: 'The library girl had not come today and he watched instead a burqa-ed woman turn the corner.' Above the bakery, other friends continually glance out of the window, but soon 'it was turning dark and the library girl had not come' (150).

Gradually, from the points of view of the members of the *basti*, the reader realises how much they had come to depend upon Talat's cheerful presence. Now she has become invisible, a presence of 'no presence'. One man waits for Talat to give her a small gift, wondering, 'Why hadn't the child gone to the library? Had the bud already begun to wither?' But 'When Talat smiled at him through the black net he had turned his back. Neither the mad dog nor the enchanted child had stalked the streets today' (150).

For Talat herself, the *burqa* has gradually changed her; it has in fact robbed her of her identity as well as her voice:

> Within the veil, a darkness seized Talat. It bandaged her mouth, her eyes, and sealed her voice. Today her smiles had lit nothing. Blank faces had become ash in her gaze. She wanted to lift the veil and say, 'Look ... it's me. Only me in a Persian robe. It's a joke.' But the robe had hands that clasped her mouth. (150–1)

Finally, she approaches the library, but the doors are locked before she can reach the entrance. The librarian looking out for Talat sees only 'a woman in a *burqa* waving her hands, falling down and weeping' (151). Talat is left with the impotence and horror of the life of a woman behind the veil: 'Talat cried and Talat screamed inside her black veil. But they did not hear and did not see. Long after the name of Allah had turned evening into night she walked home slowly, very slowly' (151). This last sentence of the story can be interpreted in two ways. Literally, the 'name of Allah' would be called from the mosques at sunset to indicate a time of prayer at the onset of the night. Metaphorically, the passage suggests the name of Allah (and by implication the religion of Islam, meaning of course, 'surrender') has turned the light to darkness for the society. For women such as Talat, this is literally experienced by putting on the *burqa*. The *burqa* in this story generates fear and doubt, loneliness and loss of identity. The veil symbolically covers day to become night, transforms light to dark. Thus, this story returns to the argument of the veil being mainly a means of restricting and denying women's agency, rather than bestowing any positive attributes to life.

In contrast, however, the use of the veil in rendering women invisible and unrecognisable often does have 'positive' connotations, as demonstrated in the following stories, which involve European women. Here, veils are used to facilitate secrecy and anonymity. The female protagonists in Ruth Prawer Jhabvala's *Heat and Dust* (1975) and her short story 'Desecration' (in Jhabvala, 1976) both use the disguise of the *burqa* in order to facilitate actions that would otherwise be impossible for them. Olivia, the English wife in *Heat and Dust*, disguises herself beneath a *burqa* in order to visit the local village women and obtain an abortion (166). Sofia, a seemingly devoted wife (a hybrid of Indian and Russian descent) in 'Desecration', similarly disguises herself under a veil in order to undertake an affair with the local Indian police chief. Yet the appropriation of the veil leads to events that have disastrous consequences for both female characters. Olivia's abortion – resulting from fear of the possible consequences of her affair with the Nawab – goes disastrously wrong and leads to a scandalous divorce and expulsion from the English community. Sofia's agonising affair is one in which she is mentally and physically abused and ultimately ends in her suicide.

Mahasveta Devi's short story 'Draupadi' (translated by C.G. Spivak, in Holmstrom, 1990), depicts another use of veiling in literature – the metaphorical use of the veil as covering for the 'sacrosanct' female body and all it symbolises. This story is relevant to a consideration of the female body as both a symbol of nationalism and female agency – as well as being an example of the continued use of classical female icons. The story takes place during the violence between east and west Pakistan in the early 1970s. Draupadi's body is the site for political revenge; her rape and torture symbolise the defiling of the principles of freedom and nationalism. The story also intersects with the erotic aspect of (un)veiling.

In the Hindu epic the *Mahabharata*, Draupadi is the loyal and faithful wife of the five Pandava brothers. She is the embodiment of the essential qualities of female goodness, purity, honour and *dharma*. Putting aside vanity, and controlling desire and anger, she serves the five brothers equally, and they in turn are devoted to her. However, as Sara S. Mitter points out, she is 'probably the most complex and controversial female in ancient Hindu literature' (1991: 93). This is perhaps because of her unique status of having a polyandrous marriage, with its erotic as well as devotional aspect – harking back to the matriarchal culture of northern India before the Aryan invasions. However, Draupadi is best remembered for one incident in the *Mahabharata*. Her husbands lose their entire wealth in a game of dice played with their cousins, the Kaurava family (against whom they are later to fight the yuga-altering battle of Kurukshetra). Finally

Yudhisthira, the eldest brother, stakes their last possession on the throw of the dice: Draupadi. She is dragged into the room by her hair and, accused of being a whore and a slave, ordered to disrobe in an attempt to defile and shame both her and her family. As they endeavour to remove her clothes by force, none of her family comes to her aid, so Draupadi calls upon Krishna (the incarnation of Vishnu) to save her. Miraculously, as they try to disrobe her, her sari becomes endless and Draupadi remains fully clothed. She utters a terrible oath of vengeance for the dishonour done, the Kauravas repent and Draupadi is praised for her courage and virtue.[19]

In Mahasveta Devi's eponymous short story, the character Draupadi (shortened to Dopdi) is a tribal woman involved in peasant uprisings in West Bengal. She is eventually captured by the police, and consequently tortured and raped by her captors (102). After being stripped, however, she refuses to reclothe herself: 'You can strip me', she says defiantly to the police chief, 'but how can you clothe me again?' (104). In her defiant nakedness, exposing the extensive wounds she has had inflicted on her, she becomes more powerful. As in the *Mahabharata*, Draupadi's dignity shames the men. (Spivak emphasises here that the modern Draupadi is not a refutation of the ancient.) Here, however, she easily loses her clothing and she refuses to reclothe, remaining publicly naked. Hence the scene is more powerful since Draupadi is not shamed by her nakedness but subverts and uses it for her own purpose: 'Draupadi pushes Senanayak [the police chief] with her two mangled breasts, and for the first time Senanayak is afraid to stand before an unarmed target, terribly afraid' (104). Here the subaltern body becomes the signifier of a covert essence that is threatening to patriarchy, because no longer under its control. Spivak comments that 'this is the place where male leadership stops' (in Abel, 1982: 262).

Judith Butler writes that women are 'other' in so far as they are defined from a masculine perspective, on the condition that women occupy their bodies as their 'essential and enslaving identities' (1993: 141). Here, Devi's Draupadi (Dopdi) identifies with a self-concept that is beyond merely the physical body. She is not shamed by her nakedness because she knows that in her essential self – just like her namesake – she can never be defiled or disrobed. Dopdi sees her body representing a political cause (not just an individual who can be so easily beaten up by men). Her 'reality' as woman is both 'revealed' and hidden – Dopdi is unveiled and yet no physical essence is reached – hence the possibility of a more 'essential' concept of woman is inevitable. Here, the possibility of 'essential woman' would explain the 'essence' that would not (and perhaps cannot) be violated, not even by all man's brutality. If women are *more* than their bodies, then women's essential selves take on a quality that cannot be repressed, denied, or dismantled – literally 'dis-robed'. (To dis-robe, according to Chambers Dictionary, is 'to strip so as to render useless'.) For both Draupadis this metaphorical dis-robing was impossible. In Gayatri Spivak's words, Draupadi (in the *Mahabharata*) remains 'infinitely clothed' (in Devi, 1995: 268). In terms of semiotics, the infinite unravelling of her sari can be compared to an endless chain of signifiers; the exposure of her body – like the transcendental signified – is infinitely deferred.

Citing Mary Anne Doane's essay 'Veiling Over Desire: Close-ups of the Woman' (1989), Bhattacharya expands upon the concept of an essence of woman, proposing that the subaltern female body 'is in itself a veil, a "second screen"' (1998: 157). From the viewpoint of psychoanalysis, she also finds that the subaltern female body's 'very opaque embodiedness is a signifier of a covert essence' – an essence which she suggests is equally threatening to both western bourgeois patriarchy and feminism. Thus, 'the veil embodies in itself the problematics of the essential locus of desire, by infinitely problematising the very notion of essence' (Bhattacharya, 1998: 158).

Woman's self that is 'more than the body' offers an explanation of why Roland Barthes found the act of striptease an un-erotic event. 'Woman', he wrote, 'is desexualised the moment she is stripped naked.' As Barthes would have it, 'the end of the striptease is ... to signify, through the shedding of clothing, nakedness as a natural vesture of women' (1973: 85). Barthes returns us to the realm of fantasies of the male gaze, as well as to the concept of male fear/loathing of woman and the power of her sexuality, whether or not it is used erotically. In the passage quoted above, when Dopdi pushes her torn bloody breasts into Senanayak's clean white shirt, he is confronted with the other he has failed to destroy, and he is terribly afraid. In fact here Dopdi resembles Kali, the goddess who, dripping blood and laughing, dances on men's graves. 'The dance which accompanies the striptease from beginning to end is in no way an erotic element', writes Barthes (1973: 84–5). Perhaps in his mind's eye he sees the spectres of Kali (and Salomé) dancing.

Drawing upon Taussig's notions of the mask and Derrida's formulations of the hymen, theoretical notions confirm cultural definitions of the veil as trope of both cover and segregation. As outlined in Derrida's *Dissemination* (1981), the 'hymen' functions as mimesis (representation/imitation) occupying a space between inner and outer worlds, a place of 'conceptual opposition' demarcating public and private space. This 'in-between' character of the hymen acts as a sign of '(con)fusion between identity and difference', between play and appearance, an inter-medium coming between binary terms of opposition. Conversely also simulating sameness, the hymen 'abolishes the difference between the gaping void of absence and the fullness of presence'; it is – like Draupadi's endless sari – 'a play of signs over the abyss' (Gebauer and Wulf, 1995: 161).

For Taussig, in the revelation of unmasking, truth *is* the endless procession of masks, each one revealing the next. A similar infinite deferral is argued by Derrida for whom 'the veil can never be ripped away to reveal a fully illuminated truth' (Jay, 1994: 523). The hymen ultimately stands for the undecidability of meaning – arguably reflecting the ambiguity of the veil in cultural interpretations. The erotic could also be argued to play upon 'titillation' as undecidability: through the play and display of concealed/revealed, demonstrated by the erotic connotations of Scheherazade's infinitely deferred ending of narrative (the delayed fulfilment of desire). To arouse-through-concealment is also discussed by Freud as implicated in the uncanny (a concept I have already linked to patriarchy's need for veiling women) highlighting the power of oscillating (in)visibility.

Like Salomé's dance of the seven veils, an eroticised unveiling is simultaneously enticing and threatening, sexual and macabre, suggesting an eternal – and unnatural, or uncanny – dimension of woman's sexuality usurping male power. Such imagery, alarmingly perhaps, continues to be prevalent in contemporary writing, including that of Salman Rushdie. Of central concern here is how he utilises such imagery, whether to endorse or subvert masculinist symbolism of woman as 'veiled threat'.

Salman Rushdie and the veil

The literary examples above demonstrate how in discourse Indian women (and the female body) have been a trope used by both colonist and nationalist for the land or nation, and also how the trope of veiled woman in particular has been eroticised. Salman Rushdie's early novels (from the 1980s) also confront the conflation of the female body with nation and with historical process. The body of history, like the body of evidence, of narrative and of text, is juxtaposed with the body of the Indian female. Whether considered beautiful, diseased, sexualised, fragmented or endowed with supernatural power, the female body embodies the structuring of India's turbulent history.

A dominant theme pervading Rushdie's novels is that of migrancy and exile and their inherent opportunity for freedom. Even within his paradigm of subverting established political, social and religious structures, the ironic and challenging tone of his novels presents the concept of women's space, the border-zone on the periphery of male-dominated society, as a threatening space of potential female agency. The concept of going beyond thresholds, limits and frontiers also presents a threat.[20] In Rushdie's depictions of female space, the borderline is frequently defined by doors, locks, screens and veils. The world of the female is 'beyond the pale' (as it was for Kipling) – an area of fear for the male characters, similar to the 'void' beyond the frontier. In Baudrillard's postmodernist view (1990), woman is located at the borderline, beyond which lies the void. Colliding postmodern and Islamic world-views, one could argue that Rushdie parodies the attitudes and prejudices of both.

In Rushdie's three novels discussed here, the borderline typified by the veil, purdah and the *zenana* (harem) is the threshold beyond which woman is placed by patriarchy within the dichotomy of innocent/whore and/or mother/vampire. The veil for Rushdie signifies modesty (Bilquis's 'dupatta of modesty' and 'womanly honour' in *Shame* (1989: 65)), erotic enticement (the 'perforated sheet' in *Midnight's Children* (1995: 9–23)), and male sexual fantasy (the 'Hijab' brothel in *Satanic Verses*) – juxtaposing images of 'pure and impure, chaste and coarse' (Rushdie, 1991: 401). Rushdie's uses of the veil/*hijab* are varied, as well as subtle and nuanced. At the core of his representations, however, is a tendency to eroticise the veil, possibly reinforcing masculinist hegemonies: the overriding fascination of woman's unveiling before the male gaze – and within this unveiling lies the inherent threat of female sexuality.

Some feminist critics have disputed to what extent Rushdie fulfils his stated intent of writing women into the narrative of history, arguing that Rushdie does little more than repeat the dynamics of women's oppression.[21] Does, however, Rushdie's ambivalent attitude towards women offer them any alternate mode of being? A masculinist viewpoint in which he demonises women as 'those who must be feared' (Grewal in Fletcher, 1994: 124) or as 'monsters', would do little to subvert tradition but much to reinforce woman in her subjugated Muslim positioning. Hopefully, Rushdie provides a more subversive depiction of women's identity, with an aim to expose rather than replicate misogynist attitudes.

The 'Perforated Sheet' in Midnight's Children

Midnight's Children (first published in 1981) was the first of Rushdie's novels to be critically acclaimed. Its narrative structure has been compared to that of *The Arabian Nights*, which also plays with acts of concealment (Batty in Fletcher: 1994). The concept of 'the perforated sheet' is a perfect symbol of Rushdie's attitude to history itself, and indeed the author describes his novel as being about memory, which is both fragmented and partial (1991: xii–xiv).

The notion that history is a collage or body of 'badly fitting parts' sutured together by the thread of narrative is an image pervading the novel. Naseem, hidden by the perforated sheet, is a corporeal example of the breakdown of metanarrative into a series of local narratives. The seductive image is one that offers hope that the fragments, both geographic and historic, will form a perfect unity. While Rushdie's narrator, Saleem, strives like his grandfather Aziz for a complete corpus of knowledge, the opposing characteristics of history reveal that such a completion is impossible. The oppositional process of revelation/concealment governs both historical record as well as the characters' interpersonal involvement with history. Historiography, Rushdie's novel suggests, is a process of continual veiling and unveiling of the past. Whether reality is literally 'swept under the carpet' (as Rushdie would have us believe of the Muslim movement to reject partition) or disguised by the perforated sheet, history becomes a fiction in which 'complete history' is veiled, an 'eternal opposition of inside and outside' (Rushdie, 1991: 237), a continual process of disclosure and disguise. At the core of the novel, then, is the need to veil both woman and memory, both desire and historical 'fact'. Relying on the veiled narrative of the unreliable narrator, who plays tanta-lisingly with concealment/revelation in both form and content, the reader must piece together the fragments of 'body' and 'history'.

Within the narrative of *Midnight's Children*, the veil itself is an image both of erotic allure and conversely of woman's unassailable purity. The episodes involving the perforated sheet implicate the veil as the *hijab* originally brought down to separate male and female space. Rushdie, having depicted it in its literal sense, proceeds to use the trope as an ongoing metaphor of fragmentation and division. The veil holds the promise that the truth (whether a body of woman or the body of history) might be eventually unveiled. Rushdie's fragmented writing style (in which he never completely removes the curtain between himself and the reader) also tantalisingly withholds the whole story, giving us glimpses of a unified perspective only to immediately withdraw and renounce the authenticity of the narrator's memory or of his narrative.[22]

The function of the sheet in dividing space also suggests the Partition of India in 1947, an event with which the protagonist's family is fully implicated. In the beginning of the (hi)story Dr Aziz falls in love with Naseem as he glimpses her various parts through the 'crude circle about seven inches in diameter' cut into the centre of the sheet. Later in the novel, literalised once more, a white sheet is installed between Jamila Singer (Aziz's granddaughter) and her audience. As Jamila presses her mouth to a small aperture to sing, the whole of Pakistan 'fell in love with a fifteen-year-old girl whom it only ever glimpsed through a gold-and-white perforated sheet' (313). In both instances, male sexual fantasy conjures up an eroticised picture of 'woman' as object of desire. While Dr Aziz eventually proposes marriage to 'this phantasm of partitioned woman' (28), Jamila 'begins to receive a thousand and one firm proposals of marriage a week' (313).

Compounding Rushdie's ongoing questioning of what constitutes reality/unreality, history/make-believe, the perforated sheet is an obvious symbol of both cover and revelation. In the early episode, Dr Aziz is summoned to visit a female patient. He finds a darkened bedchamber, where two women, built like professional wrestlers, stood 'each holding one corner of an enormous white bedsheet, their arms raised high above their heads so that the sheet hung between them like a curtain' (24). Of course, Rushdie's perforated sheet is a comical exaggeration of the real purdah that is part of Muslim culture.[23] In terms of a spatial analysis, the act of perforation is one of 'boring or piercing [which] implies the existence of an interior space communicating with an exterior space by means of the perforation itself'. It also signifies the 'accidental or pathological formation of a hole through a part of the body or the natural orifice of an organ', for example, the hymen (a concept which relates the perforated sheet to Derrida's veil/hymen discussed earlier in this chapter) (Levy, 1991: 28).

The girl's father explains that the doctor must examine Naseem standing behind the sheet 'like a good girl' while she positions 'the required segment' of her body against the hole in the sheet for inspection (25). During his frequent visits, gradually he falls under 'the sorcerer's spell' of the sheet (26) and begins to

> have a picture of Naseem in his mind, a badly-fitting collage of her severally-inspected parts. This phantasm of a partitioned woman began to haunt him, and not only in his dreams. Glued together by his imagination, she accompanied him on all his rounds ... he could smell her scent of lavender and chambeli; he could hear her voice and her helpless laughter of a little girl; but she was headless, because he had never seen her face. (28)

Haunted as he is by the erotic and sensuous memories of Naseem's body parts, his erotic 'fantasy' reaches a Joycean epiphany when he sees her 'celestial rump' through the hole in the sheet (29). Gradually over three years, he sees all the parts of her body except her face. When Aziz finally proposes marriage to her, the sheet is dropped between the lovers. '"At last," said Aadam Aziz, "I see you whole at last. But I must go now ..."' (33). The anticlimax portrayed through this moment is all too clear. Although the 'mutilated bed-sheet' (31) sentimentally forms part of Naseem's dowry given to Dr Aziz – and is symbolically on the bed as the marriage is consummated – their relationship has lost its erotic associations. Naseem, who Aziz had 'made the mistake of loving in fragments ... was now unified and transmuted into the formidable figure she could always remain' (40).

Dr Aziz attempts to persuade his wife out of purdah, although she refuses on the basis of the shame that revealing her face, tantamount to walking 'naked in front of strange men' (39), would incur: (a cultural response similar to those seen in Djebar's novels). Eventually, Aziz incinerates all her veils. Taking her revenge for 'the obligation of facial nudity', Naseem installs herself behind a regime of barricades, domestic rules that 'were a self-defence so impregnable that Aziz, after many fruitless attempts, had more or less given up trying to storm her many revelins and bastions' (48). He leaves her 'like a large smug spider' to her rule in her own chosen domain. 'It was enough for her to live in unveiled, barefaced shamelessness' comments the narrator/Saleem, adding provocatively that her barricades were possibly not 'a system of self-defence at all, but a means of defence against her self' (48). While Naseem is a comic figure for Rushdie, in many ways a 'typical Indian woman', she also represents Bharat Mata (Mother India), an India that can only be seen and understood in fragments. When Aziz tries to change Naseem's character it is impossible, suggesting the 'difficulty if not impossibility of changing traditional India' (Goonetilleke, 1998: 22).

Later in the novel, Saleem's sister Jamila (also called 'the Brass Monkey') takes on a similarly essentialised role as 'Pakistan's angel' and 'Bulbul of the Faith' (306). Unlike Naseem, however, Jamila maintains her illusion and therefore her success as object of male religious, national and sexual fantasies. By remaining behind the cover of an elaborately embroidered white sheet (possibly a metaphor for the palimpsest of history itself), Jamila keeps within the prescribed limits of female space as defined by Muslim patriarchy. Thus, men can – in safety – make of her what they will: superimposing their own desires onto the *tabula rasa*. Just as subaltern woman is spoken *for* by patriarchal discourse, stories and rumours abound as to the reason Jamila is veiled. Her audience assume that what lies beneath the surface is 'a superhuman being ... an angel who sang to her people' (314) – a situation that alludes to the nationalist positioning of woman as deity. When she sings at the Presidential Residence, her voice is described as 'a sword for purity', the symbol of patriotism. Meanwhile, Rushdie cleverly highlights the fact that while Jamila can sing patriotic songs of 'truth beauty happiness pain', she herself is 'imprisoned' behind a 'gilded tent' (ibid). Here, the irony of Rushdie's narrator undermines the role she has been persuaded to adopt. Her own desires are edited out of the story in such a way as to expose patriarchy's exploitation of her life and talent.

Likewise, this episode illustrates the human desire to (un)veil the truth: Jamila is not disfigured, as her uncle asserts, in order to maintain the falsehood of her status as veiled woman. Her untouchability is enforced in order to make her more seductive. The veiling of both her beauty and talent are unnecessary; the veil itself is a lie, superimposed to fragment wholeness. The veiling of Jamila's body ('the sacred temple, if you will') illustrates simultaneously the impossibility of the narrator's dream 'to preserve this wholeness' (237), and patriarchy's method of forcefully imposing an artificial wholeness upon fragmentation, conformity upon individuality. The former bestows meaning while the latter obliterates it: a coexistence of opposites.

The treatment of the perforated sheet, associated with both Naseem and Jamila, confirms that men can often only conceptualise woman as a whole autonomous being but cannot handle her in reality. As long as Naseem remains fragmented and Jamila invisible, men are able to adore the entity they represent, according to their own delineation. This superimposition of a 'reality' or 'identity' onto the

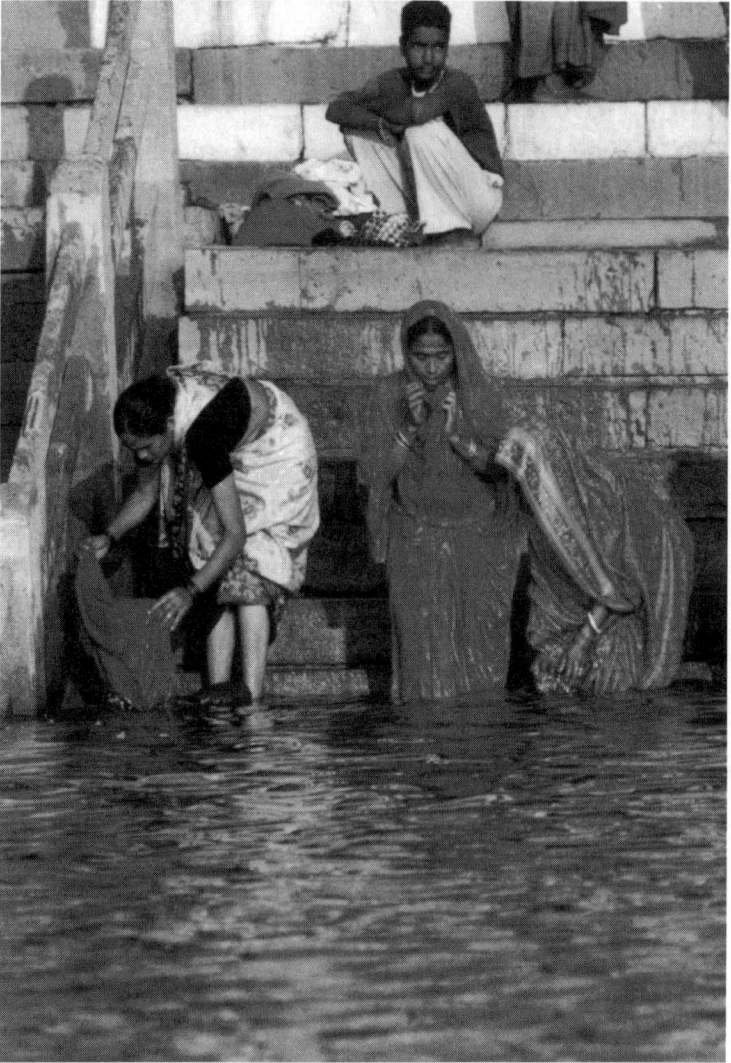

9   Hindu women bathing on the Ganges, Varanasi, India, 2002. Two women take a ritual dip in the holy river. One of the women – perhaps a maid – supports the other who maintains her dignity and privacy from the intrusive male gaze behind her gold-bordered sari. (Photo: Craig Pruess)

identity-less veiled woman is also brought into play in *The Satanic Verses* (Rushdie's most comical, and controversial, novel).

'The Hijab' in The Satanic Verses

In *The Satanic Verses*, Rushdie extends his parody of the origins of Muslim society and the traditions upon which the Islamic faith is based.[24] My discussion here focuses first on Rushdie's interpretation of the overthrow of the female goddesses worshipped in Mecca before its conversion to Islam; then on the episode of the Hijab, where Rushdie parodies the occasion of Mohammed calling for the partition of a curtain to safeguard his new wife from other men – the historical event about which, 'One can only be astonished at the dispropor-tion between the incident and the response' (Mernissi, 1991: 100).

The incident of Mohammed's withdrawal of a verse he had recited is well known, although it appeared neither in the Qur'an nor Hadith, but only in the work of the tenth-century historian Abu Jafar at-Tabari. The story goes that Mohammed was distressed by a rift that had sprung up between him and most of his tribe after he had forbidden the cult of the goddesses. In the 'Satanic Verses', he spoke allowing Al-Lat and the goddesses to be venerated as intercessors. Later, the angel Gabriel told Mohammed that these verses were inspired by Satan and should be replaced by lines declaring that the goddesses were mere fragments of the imagination. From this point, 'Mohammad became a jealous monotheist, and *shirk* (idolatry; literally, associating other beings with al-Lah) became the greatest sin of Islam' (Armstrong, 1993: 173). Henceforth, although Mohammed respected women and vastly improved the position of women in his society, the iconography of women was structured through a refutation of any female association with the divine – a belief that was to later be expressed through women's exclusion from mosques and sacred space. Woman was more typically to be associated, in fact, with the devil.[25]

Rushdie's depiction of the episode is subversive in that in his – highly ironic – version, not only does the goddess Al-Lat 'exist' even after her statues have been destroyed, but also, in his private moments, Mahound (Rushdie's controversial 'Mohammed' figure) both fears and venerates her. Mahound's sickness and death, for example, are depicted as Al-Lat's triumphant revenge upon him (394). Again Rushdie's actual position here is problematic, since the 'subversive' elements of the text are shot through with satire. While Rushdie is acknowledging the power of the pre-Islamic goddesses, an assertion of a feminist past and espousal of the cause of women, this episode can also been read as antithetical to women, another instance suggesting their inherently dangerous nature.

As Rushdie continues his satire on the history of Islam, 'The Curtain' becomes the name of the most popular brothel in Jahilia (Mecca), a labyrinthine collection of rooms guarded by large Circassian eunuchs. Rushdie here perpetuates the orientalist fantasy of the eastern harem: the madam of the brothel sits 'shrouded by black veils'. Baal, the satirical poet and enemy of Mahound, hides 'behind the Curtain' to escape detection and arrest (377).[26] Disguised as a eunuch, he infiltrates the female space of the brothel – again replicating the colonial male's desire to penetrate the forbidden regions of the harem. It is his idea for the 'girls' of the brothel to name themselves after the wives of the Prophet and to imitate their personalities, in order to improve business. According to Rushdie's narrative, rather than the 'hijab' providing a curtain of sacred privacy to women, this new idea is a tremendous erotic turn-on both for the customers and the girls alike, all of whom were 'secretly disgruntled with the new Islamic code'. Gradually, the prostitutes' 'previous selves began to fade away' (382). They take on the identities of Mohammed's wives after whom they are named, so much so that when they are finally arrested they have forgotten their own names and identities. They have to register by numbers as 'Curtain No 1, Curtain No 2, and so on', an ultimate degradation of their humanity (390).

While it seems initially that the Hijab brothel acts as a feminist 'border-zone' that allows space for transformation, we find that the women's identities change merely to become the passive, obedient and docile sex objects of men. In fact, 'even in their heart of hearts they wished to turn themselves into the oldest male fantasy of them all' (384). The imaginative crossings that should be available at the border become instead the sexual fantasies of a male elite. Significantly, the 'clandestine excitement' of The Curtain is augmented by the clients wearing masks. As one of the courtesans says of the *hijab*, 'No wonder Mahound secluded them [his wives] ... People fantasise more about what they can't see' (380). Thus, the 'in-between' space that should 'provide the terrain for elaborating new strategies of selfhood' (Bhabha, 1994: 1) turns instead into the orientalist male fantasy harem *par excellence*.

As Rushdie explains in his justification 'In Good Faith', the conflation of the harem and brothel is intentionally invoked as a crystallisation of the 'opposition between sacred and profane worlds' (a distinction parallel to Mernissi's definition of *hijab* concealing both the sacred and the obscene). He also explains that the brothel is named 'Hijab' after the name for modest dress as an ironic means of further highlighting 'the inverted echo between the two worlds' (Rushdie, 1991: 402). Yet harem and brothel are both female spaces that exist primarily for the convenience of men and the gratification of male desire, and the same equation has been made by generations of minds espousing orientalist attitudes and excuses.

Rushdie, however, maintains his intention is to avoid insulting or abusing either Islam or women (particularly the Prophet's wives) but merely to demonstrate issues of morality and the power dynamics inherent within strategies of Islamic doctrine *and* sexual domination. Rushdie in fact aims to 'liberate' notions of Islamic women, through his insightful parody (and indictment) of Islam, and fundamentalism, as a whole.

His novel *Shame*, set in 1980s Pakistan, further elaborates problematic power relations between the sexes, and contemplates the controversial role of the harem as secluded female space – most especially how it functions as a way of segregating women from the male headquarters of power: society.

Shame: *exposing veiled woman*

Set in a 'fictionalised' Pakistan, the novel *Shame* (1989) deals with issues of migrancy, and questions the political 'truths' of history. Within these major themes, woman, as in traditional Islamic society, is situated on the border, a domestic female space on the periphery of the male political world. One of the central motifs is that of space and the possibility of transgressing borders, an option which is apparently unavailable for women in Muslim society.

Rushdie's depiction of the border as an area of exile and marginality is comparable to Bhabha's concept of liminal space but with some salient distinctions. For Rushdie in *Shame*, borderlines of territory are also the borders of sexuality and sanity, of fantasy and reality, waking and sleeping. Rushdie's concept of the borderline is one of the possibility of going-across, of 'translation', but beyond the frontier also lies the void. The frontier can also be a trap – just as the sinister dumb waiter in the Shakil sisters' house acts as a border between the inner and outer worlds of 'male-defined' and therefore safe society. These borders (as in Bhabha's formulation) are places full of contrary logic and ambivalence.

The dangerous nature of thresholds is also implicated in the division of private and public, and the purdah of segregated gendered space.

The female characters Sufiya, Bilquis, and Rani (and others such as Farah Zoroaster) are all exiled to remote geographical and social borders. Two of the wives are banished initially by their husbands (fictionalised versions of two of Pakistan's most ruthless leaders) for bearing daughters rather than sons. Both sexually and politically, the women are exploited and rendered powerless 'at the edge of the world'. Rushdie's fictions exploring postcolonial displacement concur with Bhabha's theoretical discussion of the dynamic possibility of agency inherent within migrancy (Salgado, 2000: 36). Yet in *Shame*, the women are displaced (and in this sense migrant) but their position offers no possibility of renegotiating self or of gaining agency. They are denied agency since ultimately they remain under the control of men (whether husbands or fathers). The wives of the two major political figures both end living in an isolation similar to purdah, where their voices are silenced. Such expressions as are attempted – for example Rani's silent protest against her husband's career of atrocities in the shawls she embroiders while 'stranded in the backyard of the universe' (94) – are rendered ineffective as a counter-discourse.

While apparently sympathetic to this plight of silenced women, Rushdie can also be accused of himself silencing and ridiculing women's role within history.[27] (Even the controversial political career of Benazir Bhutto is reduced to farce through his characterisation of Virgin Ironpants.) He also portrays women who are violent, demented, and dangerous both to men as individuals and to male-ordered society as a whole – women who are also better locked up and locked away. The most horrifying episode in the novel is when Sufiya, the character who symbolically embodies both the shame of the nation and the vengeful wrath of women, escapes from the room in which she has been confined and drugged. She too becomes the *Unheimlich*, the woman who has escaped from the home. (Ultimately, even the female space of the home is depicted as threatening to men, as two of the main characters meet a terrible end within the Shakil sisters' domestic sphere – poisoned by tea and cake.)

An analysis of the main female characters in *Shame* illustrates how the tropes of the veil and purdah form a central key to the novel. The plot begins (and ends) with the three indistinguishable Shakil sisters, the joint mothers of Omar Khayyam. The 'imprisonment' of the sisters, first in an extreme purdah by their father, and then in a self-willed isolation (which is more threatening to those remaining outside), suggests Rushdie's ongoing fascination with the theme of exile. The sisters' unusual sense of identity is compounded by the closed world in which they live, a house sealed off from the outside world except through access via the large dumb waiter, lined with hidden 18-inch stiletto blades (10). An obvious symbol of this bizarre gothic version of purdah is the house as womb/tomb complete with *vagina dentata*. Like the impenetrable barriers that Naseem builds around herself in *Midnight's Children*, the sisters build an inner world of female space that men attempt to penetrate at their peril. Catherine Cundy claims that these destructive female images 'become a direct image of the threat posed by female sexuality which seems to lie behind so many of Rushdie's characterisations of women' (1996: 54). This 'threat' is, of course, analogous to the Islamic notion of *fitna*, so that rather than promoting a patriarchal voice, Rushdie is engaged in depicting facets of women's traditional positioning in society and exposing how women have long been viewed. In *Shame*, women are situated within the female domestic space of the home, men in the dynamic public space of politics.

The other main female characters in *Shame* are the two wives of the central political leaders, Bilquis Hyder and Rani Harappa, and their daughters Sufiya and Naveed 'Good News', and Arjumand 'Virgin Ironpants'. As throughout Rushdie's oeuvre, the traditional and the modern are woven together in a *bricolage* of ideas, metaphors and concepts. The use of the veil as metaphor takes many shapes: the 'dupatta of modesty' which saves the young Bilquis from the shame of nudity; the shawls embroidered by Rani Harappa depicting the shameless and 'unspeakable' events of her husband's career; the endless lengths of black cloth ('shrouds for the living') sewn by Bilquis which eventually become the *burqas* enabling the men to escape disguised as women.

The character of Sufiya, the personification of shame, is in one chapter directly depicted as a veiled woman.[28] The second child of Bilquis and Raza Hyder (the first being a stillborn son), Sufiya contracts a brain fever which leaves her an idiot (also a parody on her name meaning 'wisdom') thus placing her on the fringe of 'normal' society and culture.[29] Yet, filled with shame 'for all of Pakistan's political corruption' (35), she also comes to represent the guilt of the nation. Gradually she is transformed into a vengeful and terrifying 'beast', whose only expression of agency lies in wreaking mayhem and committing murder.

The narrator exonerates Sufiya from these crimes, possibly because even when an adult, her mental age remains that of a child, and also because she is the embodiment not only of shame, but also of the feline, dangerous side of woman – a grotesque parody of a stereotype that is so pervasive in patriarchy that such actions need no further justification.[30] Sufiya is a tool for the narrator/Rushdie to portray the binary nature of woman – patriarchal myths of the innocent/demon, virgin/whore dichotomy.

Dangerous to man and society, Sophia functions, as mentioned above, to demonstrate the Muslim tenet of *fitna*, woman's destructive influence on society through her innate sexual nature. Significantly, when Sufiya commits her murders, she appears as a *veiled* woman – in an image that invokes both fear and loathing. (Rushdie introduces the episode in the simple title, 'The woman in the veil: a horror story'.) The police chief sees a woman

veiled as usual in a head-to-toe black burqa, moving down a darkened corridor. As she passed him without glancing in his direction he was appalled to see that her burqa was sodden and dripping with something too thick to be water. The blood, black in the unlit corridor, left a trail down the passage behind her. (239)[31]

Her father, Raza Hyder, finds the bloody *burqa* and destroys it, in order to cover up her crime and the family shame it betokens. Without Sufiya's thoughtful use of the veil as disguise, their lives would be, as Raza puts it, 'funtoosh, kaput, good night' (240). Shortly after the murders, and the suicide of the other daughter, Naveed, Raza's wife, Bilquis, retreats behind 'the secrecy of the veil' (251) while blaming her husband for the shame that has brought all this about. Thus Rushdie uses images of veils of secrecy, and the need to cover up one's sins and crimes, in addition to the veil as denoting woman's secret nature, erratic, uncontrollable, and violent.[32]

At the end of *Shame*, Sufiya is the hybrid of woman/beast, human/animal, a feral child whose function is to 'terrorise authority' through mockery and mimicry – acting, in fact, in the capacity of Bhabha's hybrid. According to Bhabha, the function of the hybrid is to disturb the systematic construction of knowledge, so that the normal mediums of cultural authority become 'virtually unrecognisable' (1994: 115). As Sufiya indeed terrorises both community and the figures of authority – Raza Hyder, Talvar Ulhaq, and Omar – she fulfils Bhabha's description of the 'paranoid threat of the hybrid [that] is finally uncontainable because it breaks down the authority of self/other, inside/outside' (1994: 118). While Bhabha suggests that the boundaries of authority are always besieged by hybrid phantoms, the productions of terror and fear, Rushdie ultimately describes the shadowy figure of Sufiya as 'a chimaera, the collective fantasy of a stifled people' (291) – hinting at his broader political concerns.

Finally, Sufiya can be seen as a personification not only of shame gone out of control, but also of rampant fundamentalism. She is 'the woman in the veil' (the title of Chapter 10) who covers up in order to stalk the streets and kill, and also the newly-veiled woman who symbolises political Islamism. The narrator interjects his own comments on the Islamic revival, suggesting that eventually a nation will 'get sick' of any authority based on 'myth' imposed from above (278).

In a final episode involving veils, near the end of the novel General Hyder (now President) and Omar Khayyam Shakil realise that their past deeds have caught up with them and they must flee. Since their faces are well known, this initially seems impossible, until Bilquis gives them the lengths of black cloth she has been sewing. 'Burqas, Omar Khayyam realises, as hope bursts upon him; head-to-toe cloaks of invisibility, veils. *The living wear shrouds as well as the dead*' (290, original italics). The black-veiled fugitives escape from the presidential palace, since 'nobody questions women wearing veils' (291). In a humorous episode, providing light relief after Sufiya's murders, three veiled figures – the two men and Bilquis – board a bus, heading towards the land-border beyond the town. In a moment of near-crisis, the bus driver (guessing that two of the veiled figures are men) jokes that 'even the transvestites are going into purdah now'. Bilquis prevents the veils being torn off by humiliating the men on the bus, evoking the same word that has haunted all the characters in its different facets throughout the novel: shame (297).

Continuing the paradigm of borders as possible sites for the re-negotiating of identity, the text here reveals a gendered discrepancy. The border, the peripheries of national and social space, disallow agency or identity for women. For the men, however, the border functions as a site comparable to Baudrillard's void, which, according to Sadie Plant, is a 'forbidden zone outside all human domain ... the zone most feared but also which is most desired' (1993: 88). Here, transformations of self are possible, but – the void being associated with female seduction – terrifying. For Omar Khayyam, returning to the open frontier of wasteland – 'the edge of his world, the rim of things' – enlivens the worst of all his nightmares, 'the gaping mouth of the void' (296). The men's identities have already undergone a transformation, from ruling male elite, to outcast leaders mistaken for *hijras* (297). Significantly, the characters approach the borderland dressed as veiled women: shame symbolically hidden behind the dark cover of the *burqa*. Here, once again, the border becomes associated with the female space behind the veil, a 'no-*man's* land'.

The beyond, as for Bhabha, signifies 'spatial distance, marks progress, promises the future' (1994: 4). Yet the act of *going beyond*, is unknowable and unrepresentable, and constitutes a break in the sequential flow of time. Hence for Omar Khayyam, the border is both a spatial and temporal threat: a place where his past, present and future will collide. It is here, in the uncanny location out of normal space–time, that Sufiya, as the embodiment of shame, at last wreaks her revenge on Omar, the embodiment of shamelessness.

To conclude: Rushdie's use of images and stereotypes that endorse the fear of women's sexuality and violence in this novel put women into positions of passivity and powerlessness (Rani, Bilquis) or alternately violence and madness (both Sufiya and Arjumand) – replicating 'traditional' roles available to women in patriarchal discourses and societies. Most importantly, the trope of the veil is associated with violence, terror and the 'gaping mouth of the void' beyond the frontiers of safety. Women are both consigned to the margins and implicated in the terror inherent within them. Symbolically, the veil also marginalises women to the border zone. Here, the veiled woman, neglected and despised, suffers on the border of sanity and becomes a destructive force threatening both man and society.[33]

Yet these representations demonising woman as destruction stand in distinct contrast to Rushdie's non-fictional espousal of the feminist cause. They can be read as *part of* his indictment of corruption and extremism in Pakistani and Islamist politics. Rushdie's concerns towards religious fundamentalism, human rights, and the position of women in Islamic society are repeatedly exposed through his ironic narratorial voice(s), and through his agile ability to 'stand canonicity on its head' (Suleri, 1992a: 191).

CONCLUSION

The Hindu or Muslim veiled woman may appear to be a relic of traditional class and religious values, despite the impact of modernisation/globalisation. She may also stand as an icon of the eroticised female body of colonial or male desire. Yet in her various representations she still appears as a powerful – and ambiguous – indicator of meaning in Indian literature.

Taken from the vast subcontinent of India and Pakistan, the literary examples above highlight a few instances and experiences of veiling, but are not intended to be representative of the continent as a whole (with its plethora of languages, traditions and writers – most of whom remain untranslated), nor privilege certain languages or states above others. Similarly this chapter cannot take into account the tradition of oral narrative in India, the medium through which both sacred and secular texts have been preserved and handed down for millennia. Yet the literature in this chapter, as well as documenting the past century of social attitudes, is indicative of current concerns in drawing political and social parallels. The stories also serve as a means for women to address directly their experiences and their own perspectives on their cultures and their lives within the political/religious frameworks of Hinduism (or, more accurately, *Sanatanadharma*) and Islam (not to forget the large Christian minority in India). The literature examined here also exposes the ongoing problems of women in these countries, in which many avenues for self-empowerment are illegal (traditional dance, public singing, and so on have been banned since the 1970s in Pakistan); or where a woman may face social disgrace, divorce, and even exile from her country if she insists on pursuing her own career and creative interests. In some cases, opting to veil bestows a vestige of respectability to activities not otherwise permissible (as seen with the veiled Jamila Singer's opportunity/exploitation in *Midnight's Children*).

This chapter places women both as 'other' and as outsider, traditionally on the borders of discourse and society. Throughout the twentieth century, the veil, regardless of the literature we study, seems to offer little access to a 'third space' of agency, new ideas, or the possibility for fulfilling self-definition. As Sara Suleri argues, throughout the nineteenth and twentieth centuries, cultural and ethnic realities remained patriarchal, so that 'it is surely the task of radical feminism to provide an alternate perspective' (1992a: 756). Today, however, feminists active in countries dominated by the political powers of religious extremists, whether Hindu or Islamic, are aided by their awareness of the work and achievements of feminists elsewhere and of the possibility of appealing to universal principles of human rights and international law.[34]

The works of Rushdie discussed here, while elaborating and satirising a cultural scenario, foreshadow many events since their publication, for example the rise in political Islam in Pakistan in 2003 since (and as a direct result of) the American war on Afghanistan. Veiled woman is again becoming an important political and religious signifier in today's Pakistan. Recent reports[35] suggest an increasingly Islamicised government may well formally introduce Sharia law – one of the first acts of which would be to make purdah (and veiling) compulsory.

Thus, within the area considered in this chapter, the veil continues to be a site of contested meaning, although Indian women writers refer to it less as a source of feminist protest, than as a location – even opportunity – through which women must forge a significant and meaningful role for themselves in society. (Here, as in other countries, writing remains one of the avenues through which women are able to (re)define positions of agency and convey their complex social positioning.)

A more politicised positioning of the veil is found in the novels of Salman Rushdie – a fact that complies with the previous tendency of men to bestow both sexual and political meaning onto the body of woman – although here we could argue that Rushdie's intention is to invoke and yet simultaneously challenge stereotypes that feed male notions and fantasies of women.

Through this elaborate analysis of the iconic status of the veil, we can finally see that while covering woman's face or body, the veil serves to expose, if not woman herself, then at least the liminal space she occupies and the problematic status of women in Hindu and Muslim society today.

7
Conclusion:
Liberating the Veil

The legacy of the fiction analysed here is to indicate the need for a broader awareness of women's indefatigable and innovative resourcefulness in negotiating new avenues of agency. It also raises issues of women's silencing – problematised within postcolonial studies – suggesting the importance of incorporating the many ways that women fight for justice, and, how they, despite being silenced by 'mainstream' patriarchal discourse, are able to transcend and defy conventional hegemonies.

This analysis of veiling, chiefly written from within the framework of postcolonial and postmodern discourse, also exposes the limitations of its inherent *Weltanschauung*. The 'postcolonial' assumptions through which academics now view reality in the wake of Said's blueprint of orientalism and Spivak's formulation of disadvantaged 'subaltern woman' form another system of *hijab*, a curtain behind which 'real women' are compartmentalised and commodified, appropriated for the sake of intellectual satisfaction, highjacked by and veiled behind western academic discourse. Such postcolonial debates stand in danger of again homogenising the diversity of women's experience and resourcefulness. While 'subaltern woman' as an academic construct may be silenced, women across the 'third world' may also be outspoken, defiant and resilient to the challenging demands of both tradition and modernity (Shirin in *A Good Place to Die* is a good example) – forging new channels of speech and expression. Like the protagonist, Ruhiya, in *The Honey*, woman's powers of communication need not be limited to the physical, nor her social role constrained within prescriptions of religion or social conformity. Neither must the human experiences of imagination and resourcefulness be limited nor contained within academic/intellectual discourses. The danger of doing so is to obscure rather than clarify, to place a veil between cultures, peoples, and experiences of life on the planet that we all share. Furthermore, in this context, I would argue that postcolonial studies, which delineates and defines in terms of power dynamics (and violence), is itself in need of redefinition.

The future of postcolonialism is surely to transcend fixation on power – which is essentially a masculinist and culturally-limited notion of what constitutes 'reality'.[1]

SOCIO-CULTURAL CONTEXTS

Questioning and problematising previous readings of the veil in terms of 'negative' or 'positive' interpretations, the analysis of literature here has highlighted some of the salient problems facing women in the world today. Whether or not a woman wears a veil, a number of the issues that women must deal with in terms of agency, silencing, and accessing the means to and opportunities for fulfilment (in whatever way each woman seeks it) are common throughout the patriarchal world. Few societies allow women the liberty to 'be themselves', to speak freely, or to determine and maintain rights over their own bodies. Mobility has been located as one of the prime determinants of freedom and agency. Importantly, in the cross-cultural context of my discussion, the physical dimension is only one aspect of mobility, another being the intellectual space of creativity: freedom of mind (Braidotti, 1994: 256).

Having analysed the veil in terms of its many socio-cultural contexts, it is questionable how far the gendered aspects of debate are indeed expressed and polarised as binary representations. Even within feminist debate, or within the texts of female writers, representations of the veil are diverse. A return to veiling has been described as 'turning back the clock' (Sharpley-Whiting, 1998: 60) in Islamic societies, but many Arab thinkers (male and female) regard it is a step *forwards*, a step *towards* agency and identity (in direct opposition to a traditional Euro-American 'orientalist' viewpoint). The veil, although seeming to define invisible borders and impose rules of space and sexual difference (a 'prison' according to some writers such as Fatima Mernissi), nevertheless allows some women *increased* physical mobility within their social and spatial world. Addressing Braidotti's extended notion of mobility (cited above), it is also arguable that the veil also allows access to mobility in a broader sense. In some circumstances, the veil 'liberates' women since it enables them to be viewed by their society as intelligent human beings rather than sexual objects. (Moreover, while observing and existing within certain limitations of dress code, they are freed from cultural expectations and the aggressive marketing of 'fashion' imposed by the western media.)

Yet while the veil apparently promotes agency within some specific cultural milieus (as well as providing a protection against harsh climatic conditions) it is 'instructive to see how an item of clothing with so many positive, practical uses has, over many years, been hijacked as a means of controlling the female sex' (Buonaventura, 1998: 97). The veil may provide both symbolic and practical protection, and a degree of camouflage through anonymity (allowing the wearer to 'see without being seen') yet such limited agency does not appear to compensate for other patriarchal institutions suppressing women's freedom of movement and speech.

Ultimately, women's oppression is culture specific and often defies western 'orientalist' or feminist notions. Patriarchal domination is also by no means universal. Yet my findings reveal that while veiling may not seem cross-culturally to implicate masculinist laws of control (whether in the name of religion, national or colonial rule), it is exactly the male need for mastery (both literal and symbolic) that is at the basis of the veiling of women.

The power of the male gaze, both eastern and western, and the power of surveillance inherent within both power systems are a continuing cause for concern. Foucault feared that the external gaze can become an internalised and self-regulating mechanism, perpetuated through the extension of old religious preoccupations, such as the smallest details being 'in the sight of God' (Jay, 1994: 382).[2] This type of 'interiorising' of surveillance, I would argue, is inherent within religious power structures, seeking to control the lives of their followers, whether Judeo-Christian or Islamic. So long as such fear, together with the fear of the 'dark continent' of the feminine (dominating western thought since the Victorians and Freud), is promulgated in society, and so long as the Islamic world similarly fears and restricts the disturbing 'sexual nature' (fitna) of woman, then the veiling of women will persist. The oppression of women will continue in both Judeo-Christian and Islamic countries as long as women are the scapegoat and focus for man's fear – whether in the name of religion, nationalism or politics.

We have seen how Nawal El Saadawi links the practices of veiling to international politics, connecting the revival of fundamentalism in certain parts of the world and the increasing demands that women be excluded from public life, secluded and kept at home. Arguing that neo-colonialism/religious fundamentalism are two sides of the same coin, she describes capitalist neo-colonialism as a system that corrupts both men and women into being oppressors. Feminism, she claims, is not aimed at fighting men, but at what makes men oppress women (El Saadawi, 1999: 67).

Analysing gender oppression as multilayered, these critics highlight the problematic axis of sexism, racism, and classism in which women and women's bodies have been assigned the status of 'culture bearer' for past and future generations (Peterson and Runyan, 1999: 172–4). Veiling is frequently conflated with the enforcement of dress codes to denote women's role as preserver of 'authentic' national, cultural and religious 'identity'. The control of women's sexuality and their domestic lives is perceived by androcentric society as central in maintaining cultural control by the male elite.

Paradoxically, emerging side by side with material modernisation, other aspects of 'westernisation' such as the heightened liberalisation of women and the expansion of their access to power and space in society are denounced as threatening. Meanwhile, the encounter between patriarchy and modernity has resulted in the development of 'neopatriarchy': far from being eradicated or modernised, patriarchal structures have been reorganised and reinforced by giving them 'modern' forms and appearances (Sharebi, 1988: 4).

A QUESTION OF CHOICE

While some models of feminism are involved with problems of essentialism, many feminists are centrally concerned with both colonisation/globalisation and the need for transnational feminist resistance. While awareness of the failure of the western democratic model of society increases, many issues of human rights are now being hailed as justifying a transcultural approach. Endorsing the recognition of individual difference still allows black and Asian feminists such as bell hooks and Haidah Moghissi to deplore the apathy towards many violations of women's rights witnessed in the world today. Even when bearing witness to atrocities performed in the name of 'freedom', 'patriotism', 'religion' or 'liberation' (wherever they may be) the liberal/humanitarian world seems powerless to offer a secure alternative. In the countries covered by the present discussion, the voice of political Islam and the desperation of those willing to die for their own vision of freedom seem at present the only manifestations of an alternative option.

The relationship between women and Islam and the position of women within Islamic states are both volatile and ambivalent. While western feminists once took up the veiling argument to illustrate the oppression of women in Islam, it is no longer viable to talk in such Manichaean terms while women all over the world are actively *choosing* to veil as an expression of their own sexual, religious, and national identity. Ania Loomba points out that in 'fundamentalist' discourses (that is to say, where Islam assumes a political agenda) women are subjects as well as objects, 'targets as well as speakers of its most virulent rhetoric' (1998: 227).[3]

Lila Abu-Lughod rightly locates veiling/unveiling as a term through which the east has long been devalued and the west has constructed itself as superior (2001: 108). Yet she argues that Arab feminists see both 'tradition' and recent developments in Islamism as threatening to women. Moreover, both these expressions of patriarchal Islam advocate the veil. Even without conflating western feminist attitudes, the ongoing debate between different factions of Arab feminists in the Middle East – caught in the identification of feminism with 'westoxification' and 'colonial hegemony' – demonstrates why the veil continues to be a paradoxical and highly emotive trope of debate.

One indication of whether or not veiling eradicates agency and identity involves the important question of women's ability to make choices. For some women, to choose to wear the veil is an act of free will, agency and often insurgency (as seen in revolutionary Algeria, for example). However, since it is based on a notion of individuated identity, which is culturally specific, the notion of choice raises problematic issues of essentialism – and may suggest the superimposition of a 'western' Enlightenment concept onto a different cultural milieu. The concept of choice, related as it is to the notion of being an 'isolated individual', indicates liberal western models of citizenship and social behaviour, which may be irrelevant in societies based on the extended family group.[4] Yet in situations devoid of choice, a woman may be coerced by male (or older female) relatives, or indoctrinated by phallocentric arguments related to either 'religion' or 'traditional culture' – such attitudes being imbibed unwittingly by women. Again, women can be confined within the family through economic and political dependence on men – which is often upheld through religiously sanctioned patriarchy.

Yet the location of 'oppression' permutates according to cultural perception. As Trinh Minh-ha argues, 'If the act of unveiling has a liberating potential, so does the act of veiling. It all depends on the context in which such an act is carried out, or more precisely, on how and where women see dominance' (1988: 73). Yael Tamir also confirms that, in some European countries, young girls' freely-chosen act of veiling is a complex one that both remains within and challenges tradition, and 'to see it merely as a symbol of their subordination ... is to miss the subtle dialectic of cultural contestation' (in Okin, 1999: 71).

SHIFTING STRUCTURES OF RELIGION AND NATION

In the framework of religion, we have seen that in both Islamic and Hindu contexts women are consigned to segregated spaces during religious practices and in the home. They may be required to wear clothing that conceals not only their physical form but also their individual identity. (Men are also required to wear modest clothing, but not to the extent of their individuality being covered or regarded as a threat.) In the Hindu household, the wearing of the veil also connotes social deference to men and inferiority to older women. In such a patriarchal restricted physical and intellectual space, veiled woman, like the subaltern woman, 'is a signifier, whose distinction is that she is shifted from one position to another without being allowed any content' (Young, 1990: 164).

Gayatri Spivak, meanwhile, locates the meaning of the veil within the violence of imperialism, since veiled woman becomes the 'essence' of the nationalist struggle. The veil is simultaneously a site of colonial fantasy, nationalist ideology and gender identity. In the struggle between colonialism and nationalism, what is arguably lost in this 'battle of the veil' is woman's freedom. Conversely, the attempts of western feminists to lift the veil and 'liberate' oriental woman can be seen as part of the orientalist obsession with 'othering' the east. This misleading emphasis on a single cultural signifier to articulate identity, is opposed to women themselves who reclaim the veil as a positive, self-affirming force – either political or personal. More subtle nuances of veiling also reveal the limitations of a viewpoint that labels women as either veiled or unveiled. This restricted definition of being/nonbeing, even within feminism, risks the connotation of denying a woman's identity as something other than her clothing – an assumption for which feminists have indicted both colonialists and patriarchal religions.

An example from Algeria illustrates the distinction between cultural and religious practice, and between genuine choice and external enforcement. In her article 'Veils of my Youth', Ghania Hammadou expresses her concern that the traditional women's cover of the white (often raw silk) *haik* has rapidly been replaced by the black *chador*:

'the uniform of fundamentalist Islam [which has] swept away ancestral tradition' (1999: 69). This change most importantly symbolises a curtailment of freedoms for women, which has included the outlawing of women's traditional outings to the 'female space' of religious shrines (see also Mernissi, 1977). The nostalgia and affection with which Hammadou remembers her mother's *haik* can also be read as a nuance that destabilises the binary of the veil as oppressive/liberating.

THEORETICAL POSITIONS: THE VEIL AS MASK AND MIRROR

Within a psychoanalytic paradigm, the veil's dialectic of vision and obscurity is related to the male desire to hide woman. While the owner of the gaze, according to Freud, may desire to see, his overwhelming urge is to conceal, to contain and to obscure woman as lack and as threat. Fearful that the female may eventually threaten to return the gaze, men place the veil over the female face to keep it from contaminating the male subject. Freudian theory has thus proved useful as an example of a theory that condemns women to the role of 'other' and the reverse of rational man. As we have seen in the chapters on the Arab world, Freud's concepts are in concord with many notions about women found in Islamic thought. Male discourse can centre around women's supposedly dangerous sexual nature (as in the Islamic context) or the idea that woman represents a deeper fear of death or castration (fears endorsed by Freudian theory). In a phallocentric world, veiling reinforces women as 'nothing to be seen', and this association of veiling with lack – and man's consequent mastery of her both in discourse and life – can act as a means to empower men.

Within the scopic regime of the colonial gaze, Yegenoglu argues that the veil delineates an inside/outside dichotomy (1998: 108–9). The panoptic gaze discussed by Foucault, through to the phallic gaze of Freud and Lacan highlight the male 'I/eye' as implicated in the ownership of both knowledge and power. Hence the uneasiness of the (colonial) male when the object of his vision is thwarted, and hence his desire both to veil and unveil the oriental woman who has become 'the object of a look that turns her into a particular object of fascination and fixation' (Yegenoglu, 1998: 111). In the context of this theory, one may postulate that the veil in fact provides an 'escape' from the patriarchal 'eye' (both colonial and colonised) and is in fact a means of subverting the male ownership of the gaze. Yet paradoxically, by covering herself from the male gaze, the veiled woman becomes the *'belle inconnue'* and as such arouses man's sexual curiosity and desire. The veil thus assumes a role of both concealing and revealing: concealing the truth, or according to Richards, 'what we most need to know, the substantial presence of the wearer' (1994: 295), while simultaneously revealing a non-identity upon which man can superimpose his own meanings, sexual or political.

The veil not only acts as a mask but also as a mirror. Denying woman a face of her own, the veil is the blank surface, the screen of male representation, which reflects back man's own narcissistic image, his mastery as the subject of the phallocentric universe. Similarly, the veil reflects back the colonial gaze, in a reverse voyeurism.

Theoretical works postulate whether an 'escape' from the omnipresence of patriarchal control is possible, and shed light on the possibility of female space not only being empowering but also strategic in the renegotiating of women's identity in terms of a feminine spirituality.[5] Irigaray proposes a place of female escape, *'la mystérique'*, an underground world located *behind* the phallocentric mirror. Combining mystery, hysteria, and mysticism, it is a world hidden from the surveyor's gaze where women might 'whirl and dance out of the glare of the [patriarchal] sun' (Irigaray, 1985: 192). Here, women are able to 'slip away' from the male gaze, a process that involves breaking the walls of the prison and transgressing distinctions of inside/outside. It is in this metaphorical space that the veil may have the effect of turning the woman inward towards a 'core self' that is not defined by appearance – such as an inner sense of consciousness itself.

Similarly, Elaine Showalter advocates a 'wild zone': the female space outside the male domain of time/space, where a woman is free from restrictions on expressing her creativity and unique identity.[6] She proposes that women 'constitute a muted group, the boundaries of whose culture and reality overlap, but are not wholly contained by, the dominant male group', suggesting problems of both language and power. The wild zone of women's experience comprises aspects of creativity and imagination, a place for revolutionary women's language that is elsewhere repressed, an area of interpersonal experience and awareness inaccessible to men, an area of female consciousness (1985: 262). Whether or not such female spaces remain theoretical and ultimately utopian, depends on how women are individually able to access the potential 'opportunity' to explore within themselves, as distinct to relying upon opportunities in the restricted 'outside' world. In a recent chapter analysing the position of women in Islamic cities today, Tariq Ali claims that Muslim women have 'devised elaborate methods to transcend their spatial and social confinement' (2002: 65). The fact he does not cite a specific example perhaps shows that these 'secret lives, usually undiscovered by husbands or male relatives' (Ali, 2002: 65) do indeed take place in a 'wild zone' outside male spheres of experience.

GENDERED LITERARY REPRESENTATIONS

To conclude, this study must evaluate how far literary representations have successfully expressed and exposed the cultural problems and attitudes, and illustrated the theoretical concerns, surrounding the veil. Also, it must be considered whether these representations are gendered. How far do male authors express masculinist attitudes, and how far does such literature collude with theoretical expressions of fear, misogyny, and woman as 'other'?

In contrast to the female writers, many of the male writers considered here focus on images of woman's sexualised body as site of both desire and repulsion,[7] locating the sexual/reproductive nature of women as their foremost identity as individuals and as representatives of the nation/traditional culture. The veil becomes a necessary manifestation born of man's fears (either of loss of family honour, sexual energy, or social stability). The discussion of the previous chapters has revealed that male representations of veiling have predominantly been 'positive' towards the practice, whether for reasons of erotic allure, from the desire to isolate woman on the periphery of society/commerce/power, or out of fear of what 'uncovered' woman may represent for man. The veil is both normalised and necessary. The century separating Oscar Wilde's Salomé and Salman Rushdie's Sufiya does not seem to have forged a radically different position for women (or at least their fictional representations) within traditional masculine 'public' space. Male writers emphasise the veil's function to reveal (provocatively as with Rushdie's perforated sheet) or to conceal (Jamila Singer, also in *Midnight's Children*). This paradox of the veil as masquerade in a dialectic of vision and obscurity sheds further light on the reason for the veil's problematic ambiguity.

For women writers, the depiction of veiling has been seen to be more multifaceted. While some writers, such as Mernissi, refer to the veil as a prison, others, Jeffery and Jung for example, refer the reader back to an original concept of the veil, like the harem, being a place of female spiritual sanctuary. Texts such as the novel *Inside the Haveli* suggest that veiled woman can and must adapt to the physical and social restrictions placed upon them. Few other writers are so optimistic. Yet the opposition between perspectives may be confused or obfuscatory. In Assia Djebar's fiction, for example, an ambivalent stance is evident, perhaps with the intention of highlighting the paradoxical nature of the veil in society due to its multifaceted symbolisms. Aware of writing in the wake of Fanon's positioning of the veil as a symbol of national 'purity' and of anti-colonial insurgence, Djebar is perhaps unable categorically to condemn the practice of veiling. Instead, she uses it in more nuanced terms: as confining and 'backward' in practice, and as a symbol of a desirable return to traditional values in *Sister to Scheherazade*, and as a metaphorical symbol of the stifling of women's voices in *Fantasia*.

The multiple viewpoints within the texts of female writers, or indeed the fact that few authors take the veil as an issue in itself, suggest the ambivalence of the writers themselves. Sensitive to the veil's magnified importance in hegemonic colonial and anti-colonial discourse, as well as the shifting symbolisms in its religious and nationalistic connotations, women writers prioritise concerns of the woman behind the veil, rather than privileging the veil itself. Such fictional works attempt perhaps to illuminate 'women's strategic uses of the veil and what goes on under the veil' which, Marnia Lazreg argued in theory, 'remain a mystery' (1994: 14).

The plight of the veiled woman still largely remains determined within masculinist discourse, confirming that female history is always 'disfigured', confined to the shadows of colonial and phallocentric representation. It now appears that veiled subaltern woman is once again in danger of being 'rewritten' by the newly emergent US world-imperial discourse, being represented without recourse to opportunity for self-expression or transaction between speaker and listener. (Women in Afghanistan, for instance, are caught within discourses constructed by both western media/political propaganda, and traditional tribal laws – whether of the Taliban or the opposing mujaheddin. In both, they are silenced and voiceless.)[8]

The veil for both male and female writers appears both emblematic and symbolic, and as such, a final definitive articulation is problematic. Although many Arab feminists and sociologists have vehemently emphasised the negative aspects of veiling for women, even a forceful voice such as Nawal El Saadawi, who has condemned the veil as 'un-Islamic dress' in her essays, does not use the veil in her novels as a central trope around which to condemn oppressive patriarchy. (She has also condemned the 'post-modern veil' of make-up as being 'as pernicious to the humanity and authentic identity of the woman who wears it as the so-called religious veil'.)[9] Many writers, such as El Saadawi, have claimed that the veil has become too central in Euro-American feminism to be a topic of strategic argument or meaningful opposition for Arab feminists.[10] In short, the veil itself is in danger of having been overexposed.

Women fighting for social and individual liberties, for education, work, or the ability to access 'forbidden' space, speak of other more fundamental needs. One Saudi woman describes her lack of agency thus: 'I resent not being able to drive an automobile more than I resent having to wear a veil' – highlighting other facets of life that may be central to many women's redefinition of identity (Davies, 1994: 2). Likewise, in literature, other concerns, such as lack of mobility, lack of choice in marriage, punitive divorce laws, and even harsher laws against adultery (in some countries punishable by stoning to death), are more crucial than the question of veiling. Many of these issues are not restricted to female discourse and complaint: some, such as the need for social contact with the opposite sex before marriage, are also topics of concern to male writers.

In Saudi Arabia, for example, the veil represents variously a terrifying symbol of women's oppression and a stifling enclosure. These images are not far removed from those of the social and sexual frustrations caused by the veil that lead to the equally tragic events in the male author Bandula Chandraratana's novel *Mirage*. On the basis of this novel, we could argue that it is men as well as women who suffer from the ramifications of veiling; in fact the author suggests that the whole of society suffers from the enforcement of such archaic practices.

Returning to the context of the unresolved (forgotten?) crisis in Afghanistan, the central focus on veiled women by western media overemphasised gender inequalities, which hide class inequalities and class warfare. Western writers' stress on the veil (*burqa*) reinforces enormously oppressive gender stereotypes, and simultaneously ignores that veiling is a method of controlling men *through* their women and thus society as a whole. The veil as trope and reality is exploited in order to serve various national and imperial interests as well as to shape public opinion – by the press, by international aid agencies, as well as by groups such as the Taliban. While the enforced veiling of women was clearly part of the Taliban's abuse of women's rights, it has been argued that the western media's blinkered focus ignored more important social issues (Lindisfarne, 2001).

10   Ladies of Caubul in their In and Out-of-Door Costume, engraved by Walker, 1848 (litho) by James Rattray. Combining fantasy and portraiture, the details of décor and dress suggest both refinement and austerity. As today in many cultures, the elegant indoor dress contrasts with that of outdoors. The outdoor *burqa* (illustrated here in the mid nineteenth century) has more recently been endowed with both religious and political significance – and is a familiar contemporary image in the media. (Stapleton Collection, UK/Bridgeman Art Library)

Interestingly, the media did not emphasise the Taliban's rigorous enforcement of beards (another facial cover) as an infringement of men's rights as they did the veil, although violations of both invoked punishment.[11] The discrepancy in logic here is highlighted by the 'surprising' fact that (more than a year later) since the fall of the Taliban women have mostly not discarded the burqa, although men have shaved off their beards.

METAPHORICAL MASKINGS

If, however, ethnographically situated readings of the veil are ultimately limited by their susceptibility to cultural misconceptions, the metaphorical significations of veiling remain of some lasting interest in literary studies. In connection with the Egyptian veil of Isis, which encapsulates the coexistence of illumination and deception, revelation and concealment, traditionally the veil is associated with 'darkness, a pre-dawn, an unenlightened state either cosmic or spiritual, as well as with esoteric knowledge' (Warwick and Cavallaro, 1998: 132). We have seen how, in a Sufi context, the veil is defined as that which separates human perception from divine awareness. Associated with spiritual sight, unveiling or mystical illumination (*Kashf*) is the process whereby the doors of perception – and the human heart – are gradually opened.

In Indian philosophy, *maya* is the veil of illusion that takes the appearance of concrete 'reality' and thereby conceals the true nature of existence. Iris Murdoch discusses the 'veil of maya' in the context of Schopenhauer's differentiation between appearances and reality, concluding also that both Plato and Kant 'envisage some deeper reality which lies beyond normal superficial appearances' (Murdoch, 1992: 298). In Vedic philosophy, reality, the state of pure knowledge, is divided into the three levels of *rishi* (the knower), *chhandas* (the known) and *devata* (the process of knowing – which links the knower and the known). The word *chhandas* literally means 'that which covers'. Its purpose is similar to that of *maya*; it hides the real (*rishi*, the 'knower') through a process of covering – identification with the material, physical world. The inner silence and intelligence on which the world is based are ever-present but always hidden from view. Thus, in the usual human condition where perception is unenlightened, what is taken for 'the real' is merely the cover of *chhandas*. The unified, balanced state of these three constituents is *samhita* (togetherness), an integrated state where the unity of diversified values is revealed.

In this context, concealment takes on a different perspective. Irigaray speaks of 'the question of perceivable concealments that only mystical formulas can capture' (1985: 157). 'What if', she asks, 'matter had always, already, had a part but was yet invisible, beyond the senses, moving in ways alien to any fixed reflection' (Irigaray, 1992: 197). From this perspective, Mernissi's definition of the multiple levels of veiling, and the veil as an 'abstract reality in the realm of ideas' (1991: 93) takes on a central and definitive role. In a sense, every woman who is not awakened to her full spiritual (and thus social) potential is veiled.[12]

Repressive rules, customs and superstitious beliefs have been used for millennia to exploit, subjugate and degrade women in every culture. Women have been 'veiled' by their own minds, by the fear and distrust they have been forced to experience. They have lived under the shadow of assuming the masks placed upon them are natural, that the illusions of limitation are real. To give an example: in Anaïs Nin's short story 'Hedja' (1976) a veiled Muslim woman throws off the veils of custom, education and sexual stereotyping. She rediscovers her power as a woman, that she 'possesses her own source of vitality and direct relation to creation without the need to rely indefinitely on man' (Spencer, 1981: 99). It is as if, having broken the walls of her prison, and found a way out of the labyrinth to the heart of her own 'secret' feminine self, she has been lead via 'different configurations and chains' back to *la mystérique*, back to her 'unity'. Once Hedja redefines her own rules and identity, her veils, both mental and physical, disappear.

Veils and masks are thus codes of disguise (and not only in 'other' cultures) based upon and perpetuating narratives that in turn structure representations of power or otherness. Michael Taussig has emphasised not the importance of wearing the mask, but the significance of its removal. Demasking for Taussig again both reveals and conceals: revealing the reality of the spirit world as a chain of masks – like the endless chain of signifiers 'masking' the transcendental signified. He posits that in many rituals of initiation, it is the reality of demasking, not the illusions of masking, that is crucial (1993: 230). (This hypothesis may explain the potent impact of the symbolic forced unveiling of Algerian women by the French colonists in 1953, as discussed in Chapter 5.) Yet, like Derrida's 'theatrical mask', which covers what it represents, the paradoxical role of the veil is both to conceal and reveal (1981: 193). Viewed positively, veiled woman both conceals and exposes the 'truth' by being able to give 'familiar realities an unknown turn'.

The veil, as we have seen, acts as hymen and as mask.[13] It acts to articulate and yet to cover difference. Haddour argues that 'the universalisation (better still the mythologisation) of the structure of the hymen makes all differences the same ... it makes oppression the same, which is a form of oppression, a form of utopianism which overlooks actual differences' (2000: 162). Cultural hegemonies that encourage (or enforce) veiling are indeed 'utopian' economies seeking to eliminate difference/dissension. Thus the veil acts as an attempt by men to 'essentialise' women by making them super-ficially (a word literally meaning 'over the face') identical, abolishing difference yet establishing a fraudulent 'unity'.

The covering of the veil represents a symbol of indeterminacy: it is self-deconstructing since it hides both difference and unity.[14] When it hides one, it does not reveal the other. When the veil hides unity, for example, it does not reveal difference, because it superimposes a superficial homogeneity that is neither 'essence' nor 'difference'. The veil leads to indeterminacy in the sense that when a woman covers up, she hides her natural features, her appearance, and therefore her difference from other women in a literal sense. The woman's distinct identity in terms of difference cannot be determined on the level of appearance. She becomes part of an amorphous mass. Viewed in this way, the veil is both anti-essentialist and anti-differential. In both cases the veil frustrates the search for identity. Here, the veiled nature of identity can be compared to Foucault's *phantasm*, in which 'neither the elements of totalisation nor difference can be definitely achieved or dispatched' (cited in Young, 1990: 83–4).[15]

This act of imposing on all women in diverse cultures the rubric of a transcultural (religious, patriarchal or class) ideology – simulating sameness – can be viewed as an act of violence. Meanwhile the west observes the east and seeing veiled women supposes that their oppression is also 'all the same'. Overlooking actual differences, veiled women are the 'face of Islam', or, the face of 'backward woman' in India, Pakistan, or Afghanistan. These notions are refuted in the writing of women themselves.

Significantly, while much is written about the moment of unveiling women, representing either oppression or liberation – with all its erotic connotations for men, and 'liberating' potential for western feminists – little is said about the moment of veiling itself, an act of initiation into womanhood for Muslims. However, one of the most dramatic and memorable depictions of the psychological impact of wearing the veil is in the short story 'Library Girl', where the young Muslim girl experiences a transformation of identity – in terms of social and emotional loss and a smothering of identity – when she first wears the *chador* (see Chapter 6). This story remains one of the few to speak categorically against the practice, revealing the otherwise unexplored experience of first becoming an 'invisible' woman. Other stories analysed here depict women's lives continuing *despite* the veil, or the veil being manipulated by the woman in the pursuit of her own purposes, as she struggles to negotiate other problems.

Unveiling has long been a metaphor for self-knowledge, of the symbolic liberation of the mind from the boundaries of civilisation, education, political, or cultural expectations (as used by El Saadawi and as a trait of the Indian 'new woman'). Mernissi answers her own question 'what is it that is being veiled?' in terms of patriarchy's desire to hide both 'the obscene' and 'the sacred' (1993: 184). Here, veiled woman has been depicted as *both* in the context of religion, nationalist politics and sexuality, while women struggle to liberate themselves from such stereotyped binaries, to emerge free from the ideology of female inferiority and 'unveiled' from centuries of palimpsestic existence.

Finally, Elaine Showalter asks, what happens when women *choose* to unveil themselves in defiance or seduction?

> From the feminist point of view, the woman behind the veil might not only be splendid but perhaps *normal*. As Hélène Cixous declares, 'You only have to look at the Medusa straight on to see her. And she's not deadly. She's beautiful and she's laughing'. (1992: 156)

The veil acts to cover and protect, to hide and disguise, to limit agency, to obscure women's participation in society, yet make visible and tangible women's status with regard to freedom and human rights. Through its translucency (as muslin) it simultaneously conceals and reveals. This paradox is at the root of its problematic ambiguous and ambivalent status in women's lives and in literary representation. The veil is, and will continue to be, a central figure of debate around which issues of women's struggle for meaningful existence and renegotiation of identity revolve.

Notes

1   BACKGROUND TO THE VEIL: HISTORY, THEORY AND CULTURE

1. In discussing veiling within terms of patriarchy and phallocentric cultures, patriarchal systems are defined as male dominated hierarchies in which control is maintained from the top. The patriarchal system is associated with class and gender oppression; since it cannot survive without war, it must constantly create new enemies. The apex of the pyramid can be filled by either a man or a woman (as for example Margaret Thatcher, Indira Gandhi) without the basic patriarchal structure being changed.

2. A discussion on the veiling of women within the Islamic world could also consider the practice in Turkey, Malaysia, Indonesia and South-east Asia (and 'new' veiling in Britain and South Africa) but for reasons of space these are not included here.

   Also I have limited myself here to quoting works as they appear in their English translations. I am aware that language itself creates 'veils' in terms of layers of meaning and interpretation, indicated by the motif of veiling in the art of translation, which is literally a 'bearing across' (see Rushdie, 1991: 17). Yet, like Rushdie I would like to think that if in translation something is lost, something can also be gained.

3. In the media, coverage of 'the veiled woman' has also frequently been ethnocentric, ill-informed and hostile. Popular representations of Islam use the veil as a marker of cultural and *ethical* difference. Where the Islamic world is concerned, the western press often reveals a long-standing Eurocentric fear and prejudice, unaware perhaps of the many layers of social and cultural meaning denoted by the veil, and of its occurrence in western as well as eastern cultures. Edward Said highlights this problem, attacking the western press for its covering/covering up of historical and current events in the Arab world, arguing that 'the result has been the triumph not just of a particular *knowledge* of Islam but rather a particular *interpretation*' (1981: 160).

4. *Guardian*, 12 February 2002, p. 17.

5. A recent autobiographical account of the 'war' on the Taliban/Al'Qaida (following the bombing of the World Trade Centre) and the years leading up to it, *Zoya's Story* (Zoya et al., 2002), highlights that the Afghan civilian population had been terrorised by the brutal regimes of both the mujaheddin and the Taliban. The installation of the Northern Alliance warlords following the bombing merely replaced one set of 'brutal subhumans' (Zoya et al., 2002: 225) with another.

6. *Arena*, BBC, March 2000.

7. Geertz concludes, however, that the veiling of women is essentially a social constraint to maintain their sexuality within tightly limited bounds.

8. Nawal El Saadawi, Leila Ahmed and Fadwa El Guindi have traced the historical appearance of veils to pre-Babylonian times in Sumeria, Persia and in Hellenic and Byzantine cultures. Leila Ahmed describes how in Athens prior to Christianity (550–323 BCE) 'women were expected to confine themselves to their quarters and to manage their household ... Their clothing concealed them from the eyes of strange men' (1992: 28).

9. It is important to note that the word *hijab* is used differently by Muslim Sufis. This will become evident in the discussion of Zehna B. Ghandour's novel, *The Honey*, in Chapter 4.

10. Many such misconceptions of Islam are also discussed by Karen Armstrong, who argues that Mohammed emphasised the absolute moral and spiritual equality of the sexes. She clarifies:

> Unfortunately, as in Christianity, the religion was later hijacked by the men, who interpreted the texts in a way that was negative for Muslim women ... The Koran does not prescribe the veil for all women but only for Muhammad's wives, as a mark of their status ... Muslims adopted the customs of veiling women and secluding them in harems from Persia and Christian Byzantium, where women had long been marginalised in this way. (Armstrong, 1993: 184)

11. Ali concludes that the origins of this attitude lay in pagan Arab society, where women played a central role in commerce, politics, and sex. He could have also cited the importance of the female goddesses in pre-Islamic Arab tribal religion: a topic I discuss further in Chapters 3 and 6. Such female power and the inherently harmonious societies it generated could not endure in the face of (violent) masculinist religion.

12. W. Buonaventura, writing from a (non-academic) Eurocentric perspective on the veil, argues that:

> Throughout history, men have invented rules and taboos to deal with that which they fear. By a cruel twist of fate, a device which was originally used by women for their own protection against men who sought to subjugate them has become a means whereby women continue to collude with their own oppression. (1998: 98)

She concludes that in strict Islamic countries a woman may live out her whole existence behind the veil (in Saudi Arabia from the age of four onwards) as 'an anonymous figure so devoid of identity that even when she dies her veil may remain in place, as much a part of her body as her skin itself' (Buonaventura, 1998: 98).

13. Similarly, the word 'Arab' is taken to denote anyone Muslim, despite the fact that a huge minority of Arabs across the Middle East are Christian (in a variety of sects and churches). The propaganda for the bombing and invasion of Iraq (April 2003) failed to mention that a sizeable number of Iraqi Christians would also be killed in the assault. A significant shift in propaganda during the Iraq war occurred when a blurred photo of a veiled woman was identified as Saddam's chief expert in chemical warfare: 'veiled woman' was hence not to be pitied or rescued, but an integral

part of the enemy to be feared and destroyed. Any bombing that involved mass killing of the female population (collateral damage) was thus not only excusable, but justified.

14. The shifting symbolism of the veil is clearly seen in the example of Iran's recent history. Following the collapse of the Shah's regime, women became the focal point of the anti-west phobia (the fear of what has sometimes been referred to as 'westoxication') which resulted in the call for universal veiling. The Islamic state issues slogans such as: 'Lack of coverture is the extreme of westernisation, and westernisation is the extreme of prostitution!' (Shahidian, 1998: 27). In Iran veiling is a central site of both sexual and revolutionary politics.

    (In this book I do not deal with Iran in detail, since veiling in Iran, with its changing and complex history and meaning, is a topic too vast for the space available here. Also, due to its differences in language (Farsi), history and culture from the Arab Middle East (Iran is a Shii as opposed to Sunni Muslim country) it would justify a book in itself.)

15. It is now possible to include Afghanistan under the Taliban to Mernissi's list.

16. Mouna Ayoub, the ex-wife of Saudi multimillionaire Nasser Al-Rashid, for example, has her veils designed by Christian Dior. See *The Sunday Times: Style*, 18 June 2000.

17. See *Radical Fashion*, Victoria and Albert Museum Publications, October 2001.

18. It is difficult to know which terminology to adopt, since all currently-used terms seem inadequate or non-representational. The terms 'east' and 'west' are fraught with Orientalist import; 'north' and 'south' are often inaccurate, although recently the terms 'Global South' and 'Global North' have been adopted. Most importantly, 'feminism' is not a 'western' phenomenon: the struggle for liberation against oppression is embedded within every culture.

19. A new trend in feminism is seeing a return to the need for a universal approach to identity. Some feminists, such as Avtar Brah, discuss difference as *experiential* diversity. Brah posits that while it is now widely accepted that 'woman' is not a unitary category, the question remains whether it can be a unifying category. She believes 'it is possible to develop a feminist politics that is global' (1996: 31). In similar vein, Jodi Dean proposes a 'reflective solidarity' that upholds the possibility of 'a universal communicative "we"' as a bridge between universality and difference (1996: 8). This terminology offers the hope for a 'transnational mobility' that demands a rethinking of theory and criticism, and a qualitative leap of the feminist political imagination.

20. See Alexander and Mohanty, 1997, reviewed by S. Ahmed (1999) in *Interventions*, 3, pp. 476–80.

21. Many female critics attack Said's *Orientalism* for its exclusion of reference to women or gender difference in the colonial world. Others have sought to explicate the role of women and the question of sexual difference within orientalism. Yegenoglu in particular emphasises the veiled woman as a site of fantasy of colonialism, and as a highly-charged symbol articulating cultural and sexual east/west difference.

22. The twentieth century began with the fascination with the 'orient' (usually meaning the Arab world) with such figures as Nijinski (who danced in 'oriental' costume in *Schéhérazade* and *Les Orientales*), Rudolf Valentino's persona as an Arabian lover, Mata Hari (an erotic/exotic dancer accused of being a spy), and T.E. Lawrence – all of whom 'fictionalised'/romanticised the oriental character through elaborate masquerades.

23. A questioning of identity that is not shared by all postcolonial critics.

24. An experience described by Rama Mehta in *Inside the Haveli* (discussed in Chapter 6).

25. The terminology here is reminiscent of Keats's poem 'Lamia', a nineteenth-century example of male misogyny and fear of woman – whose human appearance hides a deadly serpentine nature.

26. Their use of the word 'gaze' here, however, is a general rather than Freudian one.

2   IMAGINING VEILED WOMAN

1. Said gives the representations of women in Verdi's *Aida* (priestesses, dancing girls, slaves) as an example of the display of feminine eroticism 'articulat[ing] power relations and reveal[ing] a desire to enhance supremacy through representation' (1994: 146).

2. In the Ottoman harems of Turkey, no man – even the pasha or sultan himself – was allowed to enter the 'sacred space' of the women's quarters without permission. A system of civility protected the harem women from intrusion or violation by men. Similarly, even the most powerful man in the Ottoman Empire could not deny a woman's rights to wealth, property or her inheritance (see Melman, 1986: 95).

3. L.S. Hanimefendi's autobiography *The Imperial Harem of the Sultans* was first published in French as *Le Harem Imperial* in 1925, having been edited by her nephew and published after her death in 1922. Leyla Hanimefendi (an honorific name, meaning 'great lady') was maid of honour and then lady of the palace under no less than seven sultans, from Sultan Abdul Aziz (1839–1861) to Mehmet IV and V and then the Caliphate in the 1920s. (The sultanate was finally abolished in 1922 with the deposition of Mehmed VI.) I use her honorific name since westernised 'surnames' were not introduced into Turkish culture until Attatürk's Republic in the late 1920s.

4. In Wilde's novel *The Picture of Dorian Gray* the orient is used as a glamorised and exoticised locale offering alternative modes of expression and behaviour (including homosexuality and opium smoking) in contrast to the conventional confines of English mentality (associated with hetero-sexuality). See Sedgwick, 1992: 241.

5. Wilde's mother was a devoted Irish nationalist who wrote poetry under the pen-name 'Speranza'. She had caused a major sensation in calling the people of Ireland to rise up in arms against their colonial masters and drive them from Dublin Castle. See Woodcock, 1989: 251.

6. Ed Cohen expands on this concept of 'maleness' being firmly entrenched within 'Englishness' in late Victorian discourse – which designated Wilde's

behaviour as the antithesis of 'normal' middle-class male behaviour. Wilde was inscribed as 'the visible enemy', the embodiment of a threatening 'difference', and was made into a scapegoat in the same manner as the 'foreign other' (1993: 172). He became 'the other', not in terms of a 'white nigger' as the Irish were termed at the time, but as the scapegoat of hypocritical Victorian sexuality.

7. See G.P. Landow, in 'The Victorian Web' on the internet at <landow.stg.brown.edu/victorian/gender>. The viewer's eye is then caught by the bookcase in the foreground and the books that lie on a shelf beneath the bottles, powders and perfumes. On closer perusal, the titles of the volumes are all-important: Zola's *Nana*, the Marquis de Sade, *Manon Lescaut*, and lastly, *The Golden Ass*. The theme that unites all these works is man's fear of woman's power – a fear that in every case leads to the destruction of the woman. These works are all concerned with women who threaten the security of male-ordained society and are made to pay the consequences: Zola's Nana is, like Madame Bovary, a woman who must die for her sexual pleasures, in this case a horrific death by smallpox. Manon Lescaut (in the original story by Abbé Prévost and also the operas by Puccini [1893] and Massenet [1884]) is forced into becoming a courtesan/ prostitute and dies in desolation and despair. The Marquis de Sade's Justine is infamously degraded and destroyed by her male oppressors. And lastly, *The Golden Ass*, the story of a man punished for his curiosity and desire for women, a work that includes the story of Psyche, a woman who ultimately betrays her lover, Cupid. I would suggest that the title *The Golden Ass* is a commentary on the men who pursue and waste both their time and energies with women. As the translation of Apuleius' *Metamorphosis*, *The Golden Ass* may also suggest a fear of women's capability of metamorphosing to her 'real nature' – that of the deadly lamia, the 'venomous' woman. Bram Dijkstra (1996: 10) discusses Victorian man's fear of being made a fool by woman's sexual domination. He cites the 1915 film *A Fool There Was* (the title of which is the first line from Kipling's poem 'The Vampire') in which an ordinary man falls victim to a woman's vampire-like predatory enticements.

8. All devices used as central elements in Beardsley's illustrations to *Salomé*, and indeed, in the play itself. A century later, in 'The Precession of Simulacra', Jean Baudrillard discusses how, in the postmodern 'hyperreal' world of simulations, we are seduced by images. He writes, 'It is the reflection of basic reality – it masks and perverts a basic reality – it masks the absence of a basic reality – it bears no relation to any reality whatsoever: it is its own pure simulacrum' (cited in Jay, 1994: 544).

9. 'The ancients believed that a peek behind the veil often meant a view of one's own death, which is why the Goddess's hidden face was dreaded and thought deadly, like the face of Athene-Gorgo, or Medusa' (Walker, 1988: 161).

10. Richard Dellamora also regards the Beardsley drawings as 'especially helpful in emphasising a host of perverse sexual acts connoted in the script'. He cites, amongst others, the drawing called *The Climax* which draws attention to the 'forbidden subject of female sexual climax'. See

'Traversing the Feminine in Oscar Wilde's Salomé' in Freedman (ed.), 1996: 105–6.

11. The original biblical story was the focus of several representations in the nineteenth (and twentieth) century, including novels by Flaubert and Mallarmé and paintings by many artists, such as Gustav Klimt, as well as a German opera by Richard Strauss (1905).

12. Elaine Showalter interestingly describes *Salomé* as 'a milder *fin-de-siècle* version of *The Satanic Verses*' (1992: 150). Some critics (see Dellamora, 1996: 100) have since argued that Wilde's play was found offensive and banned because Salomé asserts her desire as a woman.

13. For a fascinating account of the staging of *Salomé* see Tydeman and Price, 1996.

14. I use the English translation of the text, the authorship of which itself is not without ambiguity. Wilde at first credited his friend Lord Alfred Douglas with the English translation, but this was in fact so inadequate that Wilde is known to have translated it again himself, with the aid of various friends, including possibly André Gide. (See Showalter, 1992: 149.) All references to the text are from *Salomé: A Tragedy in One Act*, trans. Lord Alfred Douglas, with illustrations by Aubrey Beardsley (New York: Dover Publications, 1967).

15. Despite the early ominous references to unnatural and strange events, Salomé is repeatedly depicted as innocent and virginal. Bram Dijkstra argues that the figure of Salomé epitomises woman's ability to destroy men's souls while they remain nominally chaste in body. He argues that the Victorian image of woman as depraved and perverted views a virgin as almost the worst type of dangerous woman: 'Virgin or whore, or virgin-whore, all women are the same and will attempt to unman you either way … virginity is the worst form of feminine whoredom, because in her virginity woman maintains her self-sufficiency and hence her power to "decapitate" the male' (1986: 385).

16. J.-K. Huysmans, *A Rebours* (Against Nature) (first published 1884) was used by Wilde as the 'yellow book' which corrupts Dorian Gray ('the strangest book he had ever read' [105]) in *The Picture of Dorian Gray*.

17. Unlike the biblical story in which Salomé's mother, Herodias, demands that she request the head of John the Baptist, Wilde's version has Salomé demanding the head as her own reward for dancing – and she does not reveal what her reward is to be until after she has finished her dance and her unveiling.

18. Sybil Vane (like Salomé) is a figure representing female sexuality. In loving Dorian, she discovers the falseness of the 'masks' she wears as an actress. When she removes the masks to become 'herself', she loses her ability to act. Without the masks, Dorian cannot love her. After cruelly rejecting her in favour of worshipping his own image, Dorian Gray goes back to admiring, and hiding behind the mask of, his painting (demonstrating both fear of the real and 'exposed' female and fear of his own sexual desires). See T. Dawson, 'Fear of the Feminine in The Picture of Dorian Gray' <landow.stg.brown.edu/victorian/gender>.

19. Several notable dancers were famous at Wilde's time, and were praised for their artistry by him. The innovative Loïe Fuller (1862–1928) in

particular, who made use of veils and mirrors in her dance, was an idol of the Symbolist and Art Nouveau movements. She was to dance the role of Salomé in Paris in 1907. See Tydeman and Price, 1996: 138.

20. As Art, Salomé's dance, then, serves the function of art:

> Art may outrage the world by flouting its laws or by picturing indulgently their violation. Or art may seduce the world by making it follow an example which seems bad but is discovered to be better than its seems. In these various ways the artist forces the world toward self-recognition with at least a tinge of self-redemption. (Ellman, 1969: 34)

Perhaps it was this concept of art allowing the artist a glimpse of self-recognition that decided Wilde to dress as Salomé. The extraordinary photograph (published in Ellman's biography of Wilde) would confirm that it was Salomé as artist, and not Jokanaan as homosexual martyr, with whom Wilde identified.

21. I discuss the veil/hymen symbolism in Chapter 6.

22. At the end of the nineteenth century (as throughout) women suffered daily discomfort, restraint and pain although they 'accepted their inconveniences as inevitable'. Dresses were always made too tight, as waists were corseted to be 13 to 18 inches. Corsets were known as 'instruments of torture'; they prevented breathing, digestion, and gave permanent back and other pain. When corsets were first put on young girls at the age of about 13, they would scream with pain and rage. Women also had to endure bustles, crinolines (called 'the cage'), and garters so tight that their legs swelled up as the blood flow was restricted. From Waugh, 1970: 146.

23. The New Woman of the 1890s grew out of the construction of a new female sexual discourse, emphasising alternately female sexlessness and purity or sexual expression. She wanted to reinterpret relationships, without having to rely on men for political or emotional support. Salomé was seen as a sexually rebellious and possibly lesbian example of the New Woman. For a detailed discussion of the New Woman, see Showalter, 1992: 38–58.

24. Nina Auerbach delineates the Victorian myth of the 'explosively mobile, magic woman, who breaks the boundaries of family within which her society restricts her'. She sees that woman as a 'disruptive spiritual energy, which lived in defiance of the three cherished Victorian institutions: the family, the patriarchal state and God the Father' (1995: 1). Salomé, although only briefly mentioned by Auerbach, is the epitome of this 'female demon' who displaces masculine authority.

25. The historical Salomé was not killed however. She was later married to her father's half-brother, Herod Philip the Tetrarch, ruler of an area in what is now Syria. It would appear that Victorian mores and intolerance of the female made her brutal murder at the end of Wilde's play necessary.

26. Also a theme of Kipling's *The Man who Would be King*, and the conclusion reached by Kim: 'How can a man follow the Way [spirituality] or the Great Game [spying] when he is so-always pestered by women?' (Kipling, 1901, 1994: 314).

27. While many Arab women writers depict the 'traumas to which the female body is subjected in her society' (Al-Ali, 1994: 14), in *Ghazzah Street* the trauma might appear to be entirely within the mind of the English protagonist. It is interesting to note, however, how recent events in Saudi Arabia (the insurgence of terrorist bombings and the killing of British ex-patriot workers in Saudi in early 2003) bear comparison with Mantel's insightful plot.

28. Such discussions on women's 'invisibility' in the patriarchal order hark back to the dominant philosophical tradition that has, ever since Plato, devalued women because they were outside the truth.

29. A tradition from 'The Yellow Wallpaper' by Charlotte Perkins Gilman and *Wide Sargasso Sea* by Jean Rhys, through to Margaret Atwood's *Surfacing* and *Alias Grace*.

30. Published in the US as *The Persian Bride* (New York: Houghton Mifflin, 2000) – a title that creates an interesting conceptual juxtaposition to the English title *A Good Place to Die*.

3   REVEALING AND RE-VEILING: EGYPT

1. However, just as Gayatri Spivak argues that India cannot be taken to typify the rest of the orient (1988), so the 'Middle East' cannot be said to be representative of the whole Islamic or Arab world – which comprises a vast heterogeneity of cultures, languages and ethnic groups. North Africa and the Middle East also have ethnic minorities of Christians and Jews, such as the Copts in Egypt.

2. The inter-ethnic conflicts in today's Iraq and the ongoing Kurdish problem bear witness to the legacy of these artificial boundaries across cultural and linguistic groupings.

3. The concept of nationalism in the Middle East, or *watan* in Arabic, can be explained in two ways. The first is linked to the western idea of the nation-state, which the educated elite imbibed from contacts with Europe. The second is more indigenous in origin, related to the Arab *umma*, or community, the sense of belonging to a tribe or clan with religious or ethnic affiliation. See Milton-Edwards, 2000: 43–66 for a full discussion of the growth of nationalism in the Middle East.

4. Cynthia Enloe argues that all nationalisms 'have sprung from masculinized memory, masculinized humiliation and masculinized hope' (1990: 44), while Anne McClintock goes further in her view that all nations are but 'sanctioned institutionalisations of gender difference', a construction upon which male power is based (McClintock et al., 1997: 89).

5. If a sense of alterity aids in defining a nation, then it seems the relegation of woman to the figure of other must also uphold the maintenance of the masculine ethic of nationhood. Critics have pointed out that even though the reform of women's position in society seems to be a major concern within nationalist discourses (Egypt being a good example), women themselves seem to 'disappear' from the discussions about them. Women may be outside and 'hidden' in the various theorisations of nationalism and not full members of the imagined communities.

6. In a valuable work that analyses contemporary Islamic women's issues, Miriam Cooke defines the different agendas of Arab feminists and 'Islamic feminists': those who situate themselves within an overtly religious discourse and who specifically object to the exclusion of women from the physical and discursive spaces of Islam. Haideh Moghissi regards the term 'Islamic feminism' as an oxymoron, although Cooke argues that Moghissi inaccurately conflates Islam with Islamic fundamentalism. Cooke suggests that while Islamic feminists have a 'double commitment' both to faith and to women's rights, this juxtaposition 'describes the emergence of a new, complex self-positioning that celebrates multiple belongings'. She continues, 'To describe oneself as an Islamic feminist is not to describe a fixed identity but to create a new, contingent, subject position ... This linking of apparently mutually exclusive identities can become a radical act of subversion.' See Cooke, 2001: 59–60.

7. The organisation she founded, Solidarity of Arab Women, and her magazine, *Nun*, have both been banned, one before and one after the Gulf War: both are still illegal in Egypt.

8. See El Guindi, 1999: 140.

9. Interview with Ahdaf Soueif 'Lifting the Veil', *Guardian*, 2 August 1999.

10. Nawal El Saadawi, amongst other feminists, condemns these changes as being 'neo-colonialist': they include the southern hemisphere's dependence on the World Bank and the World Trade Organisation.

11. In personal conversation with Ahdaf Soueif, Conference on Inscriptions of Arab Women's Identity, Kent University, 20 November 1999.

12. Nawal El Saadawi's novels have been translated into English by her husband Sherif Hetata, a novelist in his own right. In conversation with him (November 1999) I asked if he felt 'something was lost in translation' from Nawal's original Arabic text. He replied with humour that, on the contrary, he felt he improved them.

13. Malti-Douglas discusses how,

> the male gaze is part and parcel of the complex Arabo-Islamic discourse on gender and sexuality. Legists [sic] taking their cue from the Qur'an have tirelessly warned against the potentially socially destructive power of this gaze ... warning men against looking at women. (1995: 205)

14. It is useful here to note the ocular activity of the male characters in Naguib Mahfouz's novels. For example, Yasin in *Palace Walk* spends his time staring at and whenever possible following (and inevitably assaulting) women: 'Visions of naked women began to swarm through his mind ... when he was looking at a woman ... They were created by a rash emotion that stripped bodies of their coverings and revealed them naked in the way God created them' (75). His desire for women is aroused by the sight of any female body: 'Just one beautiful feature was enough for him ... even ugliness, as long as there was a woman attached to it, was excused by his blind lust' (Mahfouz, 1957, 1991: 75).

15. The motto of the Arab Women's organisation founded by El Saadawi is 'To raise the veil from the mind'. See introduction to Toubia, 1988.

16. In mythical terms, El Saadawi may here be referring back to the myth of Isis, in which the goddess reassembles her murdered brother/lover Osiris limb by limb by her gaze. The interaction between real and unreal in the process of veiling also harks back to this 'dismembering' of reality, and the need for its restoration. For an excellent telling of the Isis myth, see the prologue to Katherine Frank's *Lucie Duff Gordon: A Passage to Egypt* (1995: 6). El Saadawi has written extensively on the significance of this myth: see her autobiography *A Daughter of Isis* (1998b).

17. Similarly, according to the Qur'an 'Satan tempted them, so that he might reveal to them their private parts that had been hidden from each other' (Sura 7: 20). An ethnographic example of how women adopt the rules of the phallocentric system occurs among the Bedouin, of whom Abu-Lughod writes that: 'veiling indicates a woman's recognition of sexuality's place in the social system and her wish to distance herself from it, thus asserting her social sense to conform to the system's ideals' (1986: 162).

18. The power of the unnamed female employee can also be explained with reference to Luce Irigaray's concept of the Speculum, which reverses the direction of the gaze and redefines 'otherness'.

19. H. Moghissi cites other instances of the use of rape to dishonour the enemy within the Arab world – Arab women being the 'ubiquitous target of cruelty' – in Sudan, Algeria, Pakistan, and Afghanistan (1999: 2–3).

20. Personal conversation with Nawal El Saadawi, 19 November 1999.

21. F. Malti-Douglas, introduction to N. El Saadawi, *The Innocence of the Devil*, p. xvii.

22. This suggests a significant state of total knowledge comparable to Eve's after eating the forbidden fruit, which opened her eyes to her nakedness. See Warner, 1985: 294 where she cites the Old Testament refutation of woman's evil body, associating forbidden knowledge/the eye/genitals: unless Eve repents of her evil ways, Yahweh threatens 'I will also pull up your skirts as far as your face and let your shame be seen' (Jer.,13:26).

23. Personal conversation at the Inscriptions of Arab Identity Conference, Kent University, 20 December 1999. El Saadawi also cites her novel *Woman at Point Zero*, where Firdaws redefines the game patriarchy is playing, and her death is seen as just the beginning of the battle. 'The execution of Firdaws does not mean the annihilation of her body. Neither does it mean the victory of male/patriarchal values' (in Al-Ali, 1994: 32).

24. Although Salman Rushdie's controversial satire on the goddesses and their suppression is a theme of *The Satanic Verses* (discussed in Chapter 6).

25. Illustrated in El Saadawi's novel *Woman at Point Zero*.

4   PIETY AND PATRIARCHY: THE ARABIAN PENINSULA AND THE EASTERN MEDITERRANEAN

1. As a result of the atmosphere of anti-orientalist discourse within academics, women have been left 'to speak for themselves' to such an extent that there is no direct challenge to fundamentalism, and opposition is reduced to the level of abstraction. Interestingly, Haideh Moghissi concurs with western feminists in condemning all 'degrading' practices such as veiling,

seclusion (purdah), and gender segregation as violations of human rights. Like Nawal El Saadawi she cites a catalogue of horrors perpetrated against women by their 'Arab brothers' in the name of 'cultural authenticity', which include forced 'Islamic' codes of seclusion and the veil.

2. Citing debates on the role of the veil in 'empowering women', Moghissi argues that 'Under the rule of fundamentalism in the Middle East and North Africa, women who are persecuted, jailed and whipped for their non-compliance with *hejab* find the dress code anything but empowering. One can appreciate why the individuals who express such ideas do not live in the region' (1999: 5).

3. Highlighting autobiography as a common genre of self-representation, Faqir explains 'within theocratic, military, totalitarian and neopatriarchal societies writing ... becomes an act of defiance and assertion of individual identity' (1998: 9).

4. In 'Resisting a Diet of Sex, Drugs and Rock N'roll', *The Times* (Supplement on Saudi Arabia), 28 November 2000.

5. Frances is the 'liberated foreigner', the westernised intellect, who sees all but understands little. Yet Mantel's novel is within the context of a fictionalised situation of 'the innocent abroad'. Frances's experience is offered as a suspenseful drama of a woman caught between European (her husband's) and Arab (her female neighbours') discourses of ethics and identity.

6. See Faqir, 1998: 13 who describes the heavy penalties, including jail sentences, for 'offending public taste'. Male writers go largely unpunished for flouting sexual codes.

7. In many ways she is comparable to Hester Prynne in Nathaniel Hawthorne's *The Scarlet Letter* (1850, 1994) who faced a similar predicament in an equally fundamentalist and puritanical society, and yet remained silent to protect the identity of her lover.

8. Comparable in theme with El Saadawi's story 'In Camera', in *The Death of an Ex-Minister*.

9. Moghissi explains how a woman may be stoned to death for the crime of *zena* (extra-marital relations), which may encompass both adultery and rape. In the legislators' view women are to blame for the sexual crimes committed against them. See Moghissi, 1999: 29.

10. See F. Mernissi *Beyond the Veil* (1975) for a full explanation of *fitna* and its social implications.

11. In Oman, for example, a woman without her face mask is 'unthinkable', for 'to be maskless is to be not fully dressed, and thus to be socially and sexually compromised'. Any woman who refuses to veil her face in fact 'courts social death'. See Chatty in Lindisfarne-Tapper and Ingham, 1997: 127–47.

12. The story of Sayeed's quest for justice/revenge is continued in the sequel *An Eye for an Eye* (2001).

13. These strategies can be compared to strategies used by Scheherazade in her manipulation of discourse in order to subvert the tyranny of the king Shahrehar. (In Arab countries, she is widely regarded as a heroine of literary, sexual and interpersonal achievement.) As Malti-Douglas points out, Scheherazade subverts male power, since her oral power of narrative

forces the king to become the passive auditor. Scheherazade brings together three elements: the power of woman's speech, the power of trickery, and the power of woman's sexuality (see Malti-Douglas, 1991: 24–9). The female characters in *Women of Sand and Myrrh* can be argued to utilise these same strategies, which they use for surviving in the severe regime by manipulating the social system to their own ends.

14. Lesbianism as an escape from patriarchy is not unique to this novel. Although declared unlawful (*haram*) there is no reference to it in the Qur'an, as is pointed out in El Saadawi's novel *The Innocence of the Devil*. See also Malti-Douglas, 1995: 133.

15. Al-Shaykh's comment that 'Suha ... has something of me and of many emancipated Arab women in the Arabian Gulf' is also relevant. (The author herself lives in Berkeley Square, London, rather than her native Lebanon.) Interview in *Literary Review*, 40, 2, 1997, p. 298.

16. For example, in the story 'Fall Nights' by Samirah Khashuqji, the female protagonist refuses to become a second wife, since she refuses to gain her happiness at the cost of another woman's unhappiness. See Bagader et al., 1998: 107–11.

17. The American feminist Diane Elam warns against any theory of feminism that believes 'it knows what a woman is and what she can do [since it] both forecloses the limitless possibilities of women and misrepresents the various forms that social injustice can take' (Elam, 1994: 32). Similarly, the definition of 'oppression' and 'injustice' varies according to subjective experience and perception.

18. Recent reports suggest that Hamas is aware it cannot maintain support solely through violence and is now offering 'a potent mixture of welfare and religion' to Palestinian women, in the form of food and medical aid (C. McGreal, 'Hamas Wins Hearts by Saving Lives where Arafat Fails', *Guardian*, 24 June 2003, 15).

19. Unveiling (*kashf*) is one of the three Sufi paths to knowledge, the others being revelation (*shar'*) and ratiocination (*aql*). *Kashf* (unveiling or 'mystical illumination') is the process whereby the doors of perception – and the human heart – are gradually opened. Each principle of Sufism directs the individual 'towards the path of recognition of the essence within the essence hidden behind the veils of change and the curtains of uncertainty' (Chittick, 1998: 95).

20. The word *haram* (with the root h/r/m) meaning something taboo or forbidden is linked etymologically with the words *harem* and *mahram*, which indicates the family members with whom one may associate without restrictions – i.e. without veiling (see Esposito, 1995b: 101). See also Jane Khatib-Chahidi, 'Sexual Prohibitions, Shared Space and "Fictive" Marriages in Shi'ite Iran' for a fascinating delineation of the principle of *Mahram*. In Ardener, 1997.

21. Sufi poem by Sa'ib. Qt in Lewison and Morgan, 1999: 47.

22. This work is also the basis of Salman Rushdie's parody *Grimus*: an anagram of 'Simurg'.

23. The relevance of Attar's poem has also recently (November 2002) been revived by the Iranian artist and film-maker Shirin Neshat in the multimedia event 'Logic of the Birds', which explores through film,

music and performance 'the consciousness of illusion and reality and individual and collective'. Neshat takes the fundamental theme of Persian and Islamic mysticism in order to make sense of 'our confused identity, to go back to our roots and translate them into a universal language' (Neshat, 2002). The mystical leader of the birds, the Hoopoe, is represented as a powerful *female* figure, an enigmatic figure whose nature is both human and divine, compassionate and fearless. In the performance, as the Hoopoe and her followers undergo their pilgrimage through trials of earth, fire and water to reach the Simurgh, a silent group of veiled women look on, witnessing but not participating in the spiritual journey. Since, as Neshat makes clear, Persian culture predates the Islamic invasion by 3,500 years, the image may suggest the peripheralisation of veiled Islamic women, yet more probably veiled woman as ego-less silent (silenced?) witness to the spiritual progress of mankind. The use of music (the 'otherworldly' singing of Sussan Deyhim) combined with the silent black-robed chorus of men and women also suggest a more universal meaning that transcends specific time–place or cultural boundaries. The poem, and this contemporary adaptation, produce 'an epic affirmation that true enlightenment comes from within' (Neshat, 2002: 2).

24. Other identity markers ignored by western cultural theorists, such as women's ownership of gold jewellery, have more recently been explored. For example, Annalies Moors compares wearing the veil and wearing gold in Palestine. She concludes that whereas the veil in western eyes has long been 'the most visible sign of the backwardness of Muslim societies' and the material expression of 'the particular subordination Muslim women had to suffer at the hands of their own men', the discussion of power relations associated with gold has been absent. (The ownership and wearing of gold jewellery in fact is suggested as an important factor contributing to women's economic and social agency, and a means whereby Middle Eastern women negotiate differences of gendered and class subject positions. See A. Moors in Spyer (ed.), 1998: 208–23.

5   VIOLENCE, LIBERATION AND RESISTANCE: NORTH AFRICA

1. I am grateful here to Valerie Orlando's *Nomadic Voices of Exile: Feminine Identity in Francophone Literature of the Maghreb*, a book that has informed and inspired much of this chapter.
2. See introduction to Alloula, 1986. Foucault proposes the phantasm as a way of accounting for some of the paradoxes (such as local relativity/universality) encountered in the problematic concept of history.
3. See Abu-Haidar, 1996: 73.
4. Although critics discuss Frantz Fanon in terms of his being the main instigator of psychic and social rebellion in Algeria, Albert Camus' conception of rebellion is worth consideration. In *The Rebel*, Camus outlines his concept of the ethics of rebellion: the fight against 'falsehood, injustice and violence' that refuses to give in to despair. 'Rebellion is the very movement of life and it cannot be denied without renouncing life. Its purest outburst ... gives birth to existence. Thus it is love and fecundity

or it is nothing at all' (1953: 271). Rebellion affirms human dignity: as Camus put it, 'I rebel, therefore we exist' (1953: 22). In contrast to Camus who insists on humanity, Fanon principally advocates violent uprising as a necessary stage of revolution. (Although Camus was born in the Algerian town of Oran of French parents, he was caught in what would now be termed the state of 'hybridity', belonging to two worlds and two cultures.)

5. For Fanon, the various and fluctuating representations of the veil in Algeria are of 'primordial importance'. Women were the 'lighthouse and barometer' of the struggle (Fanon, 1965: 50). However, as Sharpley-Whiting significantly points out, the Berber women of Algeria had never veiled, and prior to the nationalist resurgence in 1957 women in the cities had abandoned the veil. Culturally, one may therefore question Fanon's centralisation of the importance of the veil.

6. The film *The Battle of Algiers* demonstrates the use of veiled women for concealing weapons and as liaison agents, by alternately veiling or unveiling. (Dir. G. Pontecorvo: Algeria/Italy, 1965.)

7. These features have been both attacked and defended (by Homi Bhabha amongst others). In her analysis of the role of gender in *Black Skin, White Masks*, Gwen Bergner locates women as defined exclusively in terms of their sexual relationships with men, both excluding female subjectivity and oppressing women. As Bergner comments, 'though for Fanon colonial identity forms out of the mirroring relationship between white men and black men, this process is played out through the bodies of women' (1995: 80). Marnia Lazreg claims that Fanon 'waxes lyrical about the unveiled woman's body' to such an extent that his attitude 'stems from the same attitude as those voiced by his French contemporaries' – the very attitude that he has so persuasively condemned (1994: 128). Other women writers have retaliated against feminist criticism to claim that in fact Fanon was committed to women's liberation, reading his works as exhibiting a '*pro*feminist consciousness' that is a testament to women's resistance to oppression (Sharpley-Whiting, 1998: 73).

8. Richard's wife, Isabel Burton, refuted that he had violated or infiltrated the haj, since she was convinced that he was (secretly) a Muslim. See Blanch, 1954.

9. It is used, for example, to juxtapose past and contemporary masculine orientalism in Leïla Sebbar's novel *Sherazade: Missing, Aged Seventeen, Dark Curly Hair, Green Eyes*. It also features as a central motif in Assia Djebar's novel *Women of Algiers*, which exposes women's experiences through the colonial period, as I discuss later in this chapter.

10. Feminist criticism of Alloula, however, sees *The Colonial Harem* itself as a work of 'inverted colonial nostalgia' (Lazreg, 1994: 191).

11. Yet language is also a medium of colonial power, and in a polyglot country such as Algeria, Djebar is aware of the controversial stance she takes in choosing to write in French. In Djebar's case, however, she seems to create a fluidity in her language – she utilises expressions from her mother's Berber heritage for example – which crosses cultural divides, and creates 'a continuum of intersections' breaching divides of time, space and gender. This process is one in which 'language is taken to "bear the burden" of

one's own cultural experience ... to convey in a language that is not one's own the spirit that is one's own' (Ashcroft et al., 1989: 38). Djebar in fact describes her appropriation of French as 'one of the spoils of war' (1980: postscript).

12. It is important to note, however, that there are *four* women in the painting. Djebar dismisses the black slave although she is an integral part of the scene. Is Djebar displaying a racism/classism derived from her French education here, or imagining the slave to be eavesdropping, excluded from the conversation?

13. Marnia Lazreg argues that Assia Djebar unwittingly perpetuates this 'western viewpoint' in her utilisation of the painting *Women of Algiers*, and that Djebar fails to 'decipher the ways in which the women reacted to their *de facto* unveiling before a conquering stranger' (1994: 14). However, it seems evident that Djebar uses the idea of the women in the painting as a springboard to re-imagine other lives, which have greater pertinence to an active involvement in Algerian history.

14. Writers such as Monia Hejaiej have discussed the importance of female oral narrative in this context – a mode of narration that is 'both indirect and veiled', since such expression is 'a part of a condition inherent in her life behind the veil, behind closed doors, where she loves and suffers in silence' (1996: 35).

15. An opinion also expressed by Fatima Mernissi in *The Harem Within* (1994).

16. Djebar's suggestion of an alternative 'female' space of communication is not only an example of Homi Bhabha's 'Third Space' but more appropriately the place of 'la mystèrique' described by Luce Irigaray, an underground world combining mystery, hysteria and mysticism, a place where 'the feminine finds its natural home' (Irigaray, 1985: 103) – a concept I elaborate later.

17. The Moroccan filmmaker Farida Ben Lyazid also creates an all-female space in her 1989 film *Bab Ilsma Maftouh* ('The Door to Heaven is Open'), with which to point to a women's history within Islam 'that includes female spirituality, prophecy, and intellectual creativity as well as revolt, material power, and social and political leadership' (Shohat and Stam, 1994: 165).

18. Djebar also associates using French with veils in her introduction to El Saadawi's *Woman at Point Zero*.

19. This type of friendship between women and across antagonistic lines of nationality is remarkable when one compares it with the male relationships in Albert Camus' novels. Camus' world is entirely that of the *pied noirs* (the French Algerians); no cross-national friendships are mentioned at all. Mersault's famous encounter with the Arabs on the beach is an antagonistic one, in which the Arabs appear a remote and stereotyped 'other'. Women's experience is quite different to this sense of isolation: in women's traditional Arab world there is always space and time for friendship and companionship. (Being an 'isolated individual' appears a very western idea, a part of the 'Protestant ethic'.)

20. The first section of the novel ends with the narrator setting off at dawn with her little girl's hand in hers, just as her father had done with her. The same scene is also the end of *Sister to Scheherazade*, suggesting an

equation of the narrator of this novel, Assia Djebar, with the character Isma in the second novel of the quartet.

21. Djebar explains the use of the four languages available to Algerian women: 'French for secret missives; Arabic for our stifled emotions towards God-the Father ... ; Lybico-Berber which takes us back to the pagan idols – mother gods of pre-Islamic Mecca. The fourth language for all females, young or old, cloistered or half-emancipated, remains that of the body' (1985: 180).

22. In evaluating this concept, she discusses the violence inherent within the colonial project, the rending apart of a landscape to create a 'recovered and interpreted' space of colonial power. Heidegger's original idea that the structure of a work of art lies in the conflict in the making of a text is applied by Spivak to the postcolonial context. Heidegger suggests that a strife (*der Streit*), a 'violent concept-metaphor of violation' emerges out of the violence of the rift. Spivak compares this violence to the project of imperialism. She describes 'worlding', as the 'reinscription of a cartography that must (re)present itself as impeccable' based on 'the necessary colonialist presuppositions of an uninscribed earth' (Spivak, 1999: 114, 212). Spivak speaks of the epistemological violence (in religion, education, language) inherent within colonialism, a concept that becomes a reality for writers such as Djebar, who is constantly aware of the cultural violence and betrayal inherent in the use of the coloniser's language.

23. Azzedine Haddour implicates women in the Algerian colonial conflict as both *victim* and – because of the absence of indigenous women in the 'public space' of society – as *cause* of the increasing violence between coloniser and colonised. He sees violence as ultimately 'the only mediating agency of social intercourse' (2000: 128).

24. An instance of co-wives living 'like loving sisters rather than bitter rivals' is given by Geraldine Brooks describing a family in Palestine. On closer acquaintance, however, she realises how much the older, displaced, wife has suffered. See Brooks, 1996: 70–5.

25. Djebar (and other Arab writers) also do not avail themselves of the opportunities to explore the possible use of the veil as a powerful weapon which 'conceals the desire for revenge and/or the power to exact revenge thereby causing fear and anxiety' (Merini, 1999: 121). The only such use of a 'mask' known to me is in Bharati Mukherjee's *Jasmine*, where the heroine enacts her revenge for rape while assuming the mask/identity of the vengeful goddess Kali.

26. Fatima Mernissi also discusses the traditional male veiling of the caliph in Islam – a veil that has its historical origins in the need to cut off the caliph from his violent subjects. She writes, 'The *hijab* of the caliph, his veil, is an institution just as fundamental to political Islam as is the veil of women, and if it is never directly invoked in the desperate cry for the return to the veil, it is because it hides the unmentionable: the will of the people, the will of the '*amma*, the mass, which is just as dangerous as that of women' (1993: 178).

27. Bowles lived most of his life in North Africa, settling in the 1940s with his novelist wife, Jane, in Tangier, where he died in 1999.

28. Could Bowles in fact have this in mind and be playing a literary game in naming his female character 'Kit' as a parallel to Conrad's 'Marlowe'?
29. Jane escaped western convention by living in Morocco, significantly referring to Tangier as an 'interzone' where she was able to establish an alternate all-female family. For a fascinating chapter on Jane Bowles, novelist and travel writer, see Curtia, 1998: 113–54.
30. Gita Mehta, for example, in her novel *A River Sutra*, considers the 'muslin mask' of Jain monks in India. The white mask covering the nose and mouth symbolises the avoidance of human vanity as well as ensuring non-violence to insects: the two most important principles of Jainism being *ahimsa* (non-violence) and *apiragrah* (non-possession). Their mask announces the principle of the sanctity of all life, and a lifestyle that does not allow injustice or atrocity of any kind to flourish in society. (Veiling in India is dealt with in more detail in Chapter 6.)
31. Trinh Minh-ha writes,

> Difference should neither be defined by the dominant sex nor by the dominant culture. So that when women decide to lift the veil one can say that they do so in defiance of their men's oppressive right to their bodies. But when they decide to keep or put on the veil they once took off they might do so to reappropriate their space or to claim a new difference in defiance of genderless, hegemonic, centred standardisation. (1988: 73)

6   SUBVERSION, SEDUCTION AND SHAME: INDIA

1. Significantly, the word *sati* also means 'a good woman'. See Dalrymple, 1999, and Bumiller, 1990, for a discussion of the continuing relevance and ongoing controversy on recent *satis*.
2. Vandana Shiva, for example, persuasively argues how the impact of glob-alisation is removing traditional areas of agency from women. Women are the custodians of local knowledge of bio-diversity and are the primary food producers of the global south. As economic globalisation spreads, agricultural women themselves are devalued, removed from their traditional role as expert food producers who work in harmony with nature's processes. 'This deliberate blindness to diversity, the blindness to nature's production, production by women ... allows destruction and appropriation to be projected as creation ... Global law has created new property rights to life forms just as colonialism used the myth of discovery to take over the land of others as colonies.' See Shiva, 2000. Thus, the role of food provider becomes disassociated from women and is dependent on global agribusiness and biotechnology companies. Here we witness the ultimate result of male fear and envy of women's power to reproduce: multinational companies attempting to usurp women's reproductive nature through the development of animal/human cloning, and genetically modified foods. While this may seem an obscure form of veiling the feminine, these tendencies all demonstrate an interrelated – and extremely dangerous – trend. These are all imperative issues which

must now be addressed by postcolonial studies and literature, either in terms of concerns with neo-colonial land ownership, or the removal of agency from subaltern women.

3. Official social attitudes and statistics deny many problems facing women in their choice of potential partners, including the high incidence of homosexuality among Indian men, as well as the increasingly high risk from AIDS.

4. Importantly, however, it must be recognised that Indian culture, both Hindu and Muslim (Moghal), had long held an allure for the British, as providing an alternate mode of sexuality and belief (and thus dressing). Dalrymple, for example, writes of English *memsahibs* who voluntarily joined harems (1999: 35), and men who likewise crossed over entirely to Indian lifestyles (2003). Chilla Bulbeck (1998) also discusses how for many European women, a reversed binarism situates the Indian lifestyle as one more attractive than their own, with a spiritual wholeness that they lack. At the turn of the last century as faith in rationality and white, masculinist Christianity eroded, many women were drawn to Hindu culture and religion. Annie Besant's theosophical society, for example, as well as providing an informed translation of Hindu texts (such as the *Bhaghavad-Gita*, a sacred text which itself became associated with secular nationalist struggles) was linked with female rights. (In England, Besant was a social reformer and early advocate of birth control; later in India she was an ardent believer in Indian Home Rule and became president of the Indian National Congress in 1917.)

5. A role comparable to Sufiya in Rushdie's novel *Shame* (discussed later in this chapter).

6. In Nehru's *The Discovery of India*, first published in 1945, the figure of Mother India, Bharat Mata, has both mythical and romantic associations, through which Nehru binds together the vast variety of India into a unifying symbol of beneficence and plenitude. While Nehru makes the new nation of India into an ideal of liberalism and cultural development, he frequently relies on orientalist metaphors, evoking an India with 'an inscrutable, feminised identity' (Singh, 1996: 154). In his anti-imperialist rhetoric, Nehru graphically incorporates the stereotype of the female body representing the nation (as Fanon was to do in relation to Algeria):

> They seized her body and possessed her, but it was a possession of violence. They did not know her or try to know her. They never looked into her eyes, for theirs were averted and hers cast down through shame and humiliation. (Nehru, 1967: 272)

7. Traditionally one reason in Hinduism for the seclusion of women in purdah was to limit access to women since sexual activity was thought to sap men's strength, in much the same way as a disease (Minturn 1993: 207).

8. The contemporary novelist Anita Desai (1990) criticises the Hindu deification of women, a stance confirmed by other feminist writers who contrast this idealisation of women with actual feminist resistance.

9. The symbolic deification of women contradicts both women's sexuality and agency as intelligent, creative, individuals. Sukrita Paul Kumar argues how:

    The-deep rooted myths about women, the 'female' and the 'feminine' have not allowed women to lead an authentically free life ... Woman is delineated as mother and protector, as an inspirer and cherisher, as *Shakti*, the primal force and as the chaste, suffering wife, or then, as a charmer. No matter as what, but women in literature as in life have been projected generally as instrument secondary to the realisation of man and his destiny.' (in Dinesh, 1994: 41–2)

10. The texts I cite here are written in a variety of Indian languages, including Urdu, Hindi, and Bengali, which I access through their translations.

11. She is to enter the lifestyle graphically described by Indira Parikh and Pulin Garg, in which women:

    come as brides and leave only for the funeral pyre. The husband's home is their prison, their castle, their palace. They believe, or are made to believe, or have no other choice but believe, that this is all for their good ... However, within the walls of their home, within the feudal system of a large joint family, run parallel themes of exploitation, intrigue and counter-intrigue, all revolving around the control of resources through legacy and heritage. This is the only life they know as wives. (1989: 90)

12. For an elaboration on *rasa*, see Dehejia, 1996: 10–12.

13. The only cultural references to outside the *haveli* compound are to Udaipur University and to the old palace of the Rana (king) of Udaipur, whose throne and kingdom had been dissolved at Independence 25 years before the narrative starts. (The novel spans twelve years of life in the *haveli*, commencing in 1972.)

14. Rushdie satirises this tradition in his novel *Shame*, where he refers to husbands visiting their wives at night in the *haveli* as resembling Ali Baba and the Forty Thieves. One of these wives, Rani Hamayun, comments that, 'this arrangement which is supposed to be made for decency etcetera is just the excuse for the biggest orgy on earth' (Rushdie, 1989: 75–6).

15. The following passage exemplifies the distinction between modern and traditional worlds, as well as the traditions associated with gendered space:

    In the first few months of the marriage she had found the separation of men and women romantic, full of mystery. In her parents' home men and women talked quite freely, her mother respected her father but didn't hide behind a screen when his friends were present. But in the haveli men were regarded with awe as if they were gods. They were the masters and their slightest wish was a command. (21)

16. Interestingly, as Azzedine Haddour claims, Derrida's metaphor of the hymen is not neutral but 'interpenetrated and tainted with patriarchal

and heterosexist ideologies' (2000: 161). He cites Derrida's failure to see that the hymen as veil is a 'political frontier', suggesting that attitudes and economies of colonial racism are comparable with patriarchal misogyny.

17. See Parikh and Garg, 1989: 101, and Mitter, 1991: 115.

18. In her essay 'Writing Away the Prison' Hamida Na'na cites a *fatwa* (religious edict) in her community which forbade the education of girls (in Faqir, 1998: 93).

19. The Vedic sage Vyasa was the original author of the *Mahabharata*, composed several hundred years BCE. Several English translations exist. Here, I also refer to the summary of the Draupadi episode in Mitter (1991). A newly published version as retold by Krishna Dharma (Torchlight, 1999) features a fanciful depiction of Draupadi's disrobing on the cover.

20. My reading of Rushdie's novels will focus specifically on his treatment of women and veiling, a central trope in several of his works. Intentionally omitting several important issues within the scope of Rushdie's novels (due to restricted space), my argument, especially with reference to *The Satanic Verses*, may overlap with the ongoing 'Rushdie debate', although I am not seeking here to address his use/abuse of religion specifically. This novel is useful to my argument since it draws heavily upon the Islamic notion of '*hijab*', the original veil/curtain in Islam, thus presenting a postmodern interpretation of the tradition.

21. See, for example, Spivak in Smale, 2001: 123.

22. Uma Parameswaran outlines other important associations of the perforated sheet, which she takes to be one of the basic recurring metaphors that pervade Rushdie's meaning and method (1988: 41–54).

23. The sheet is also related to the screen or sheet held up at Hindu and Muslim weddings, which is then drawn away for the couple to take their 'first look' at each other. See Parameswaran, 1988: 42.

24. The *fatwa* against Rushdie was also based upon several other issues relating to the depiction of Mohammed – 'a sabotage of religion'. See Ruthven, 1990.

25. An association that informs Nawal El Saadawi's *The Innocence of the Devil*, the Arabic title of which (pointedly) links woman (Gannat) with the devil (Iblis) – a relationship that originated in the Garden of Eden (see Chapter 3).

26. See S. Aravamudan 'Being God's Postman is no Fun, Yaar' in Fletcher, 1994, for a fascinating elaboration of the importance of satire in pre-Islamic Arab culture: the function of Rushdie's characters of Salman and Baal.

27. The fact that Rushdie claims to be promoting women's cause by including women's history in his narrative has been challenged by Inderpal Grewal, who argues that although women do exist in his novel, they are largely ineffectual. While claiming to 'include' women in the retelling of history, Rushdie in fact gives them little or no part in the historical process at all. See I. Grewal, in Fletcher, 1994: 124.

28. Although critics usually cite her name as being a play on the word 'Sufi', it should also be pointed out that this is a Muslim spelling of 'Sophia', meaning wisdom, knowledge. Hence, it could be argued that she represents

the shame that is implicit in knowing the truth – as in T.S. Eliot's 'After such knowledge, what forgiveness?' (Gerontian).

29. She is possibly based on President Zia's mentally disabled daughter who was hidden from public view.

30. In Sufiya, Rushdie harks back to the nineteenth- and early-twentieth-century imagery of 'evil sisters' in the woman-as-vampire myth – a discourse in which, as Margaret Hallissy elucidates, 'evil women stand as representatives for all women' (1987: 10). See also Dijkstra, 1996.

31. Although both Talvar and Raza realise what has happened – that Sufiya 'had intercourse with the four young goondas before tearing off their heads' (240) – they agree to do nothing about it. Rushdie describes how 'in the ocean the sea-Beast stirs ... And as the girl grows, as her under-standing increases, the Beast has more to eat' (241). Aijaz Ahmed sees Sufiya as part of 'the oldest of the misogynist myths: the virgin who is really a vampire, the irresistible temptress who seduces men in order to kill them, not an object of male manipulation but a devourer of hapless men' (1994: 148). Sufiya becomes aware of her sexuality and the failure of Omar to do 'the thing that husbands make' (241). It is thus as a sexually mature and frustrated woman that she goes out, the epitome of *fitna*, 'to wreak havoc on the world' (242).

32. When her husband locks up Sufiya as a madwoman in the attic, Rushdie falls into using another nineteenth-century stereotype. Since she is then drugged senseless, Sufiya is both 'Sleeping Beauty' *and* the Beast, the 'emasculating, insane woman fatal to men', a myth that 'enables the suppression of women ... and re-creates their Otherness' (Grewal in Fletcher, 1994: 141). Rushdie evokes a similar association of woman as sexual predator in his novel *Grimus*, where the veiled figure of Liv exploits her sexuality to enact her revenge, 'plotted in centuries of darkened, still-seated brooding' (Rushdie, 1975, 1996: 221). Here, Rushdie's text combines a misogynist scene with sexual stereotyping of women's role: Liv's naked body, 'a headless Venus', is displayed – and described in detail – in order to arouse the male voyeur, Flapping Eagle. (The passage where Liv finally lifts her black veil is closely reminiscent of Rider-Haggard's *She*, when the mysterious Ayesha unveils herself – a moment of revealed beauty disguising the treachery beneath.)

33. Aijaz Ahmed champions a feminist complaint against Rushdie's misogynist rendering of women's experience, limited as it is to 'the zones of the erotic, the irrational, the demented and the demonic' (1994: 151). Although this reading emerges in the context of these novels: elsewhere, especially in his later novels, his treatment of women is more sympathetic. (I also exclude from my discussion his characterisation of Padma in *Midnight's Children*.) While highlighting here the depiction of women as 'monsters' it is also important to acknowledge the existence of similar male characters, especially in *Shame*, as well as their important role in Rushdie's biting satire.

34. See April Carter's discussion of feminism and globalisation (2001: 216–20).

35. See I. Hilton, 'Pakistan is Losing the Fight Against Fundamentalism' in the *Guardian*, 20 May 2003, and R. McCarthy report 'Destiny and Devotion' in the *Guardian Weekend* magazine, 17 May 2003.

7   CONCLUSION: LIBERATING THE VEIL

1. Bill Ashcroft in fact suggested several new directions for the future of postcolonial studies, in his keynote address to the Rethinking Commonwealth/Postcolonial Literatures conference, Santa Clara University, US, April 2002.

2. While Fatima Mernissi and Nawal El Saadawi have dwelt at length on the fear inherent within the Islamic world, Foucault's work highlights the dangers inherent in the western use of space as a locus of domination and the spread of fear (for example, through the invisible eye of the panopticon, which bestows totalitarian mastery over the environment). He discusses 'the diabolical aspect' of the idea of a centralised machine of surveillance in which everyone is caught. 'Power', he claims, 'is no longer substantially identified with an individual who possesses it or exercises it by right of birth; it becomes a machinery that no one owns' (Foucault, 1977: 156).

3. The identification of 'fundamentalism' with a power motive rather than one of faith is corroborated by Tariq Ali, for example, who argues that, as in all fundamentalisms, the 'religious' context is simply a means of gaining public support for repressive agendas (2001).

4. Marjo Buitelaar highlights how in Morocco, 'the western notion of privacy as the right of the individual to time and space for him- or herself is relatively weak and socially depreciated. Moroccans seldom withdraw from company ... and such behaviour is met with suspicion' (see Ask and Tjomsland (eds) 1998: 105). Rama Mehta's novel *Inside the Haveli* also demonstrates how women in India can be submerged within the family and have their identity defined by kinship structures.

5. The depiction by Rama Mehta in her novel *Inside the Haveli* of the separate gendered worlds of upper-class Hindu India, suggests that secluded female space could be a place of agency, albeit within traditional parameters (and also depending on one's class and position within the family hierarchy).

6. A concept Elaine Showalter adapts from Edwin Ardener (Showalter, 1985). The original definition of the wild zone by Edwin Ardener emphasises that women are 'overlooked', 'muted', 'invisible', mere 'black holes in someone else's universe' (qt. Showalter, 1985: 25).

7. Elaine Showalter poses the interesting question, could men also be allegorically veiled figures? She concludes that the idea of unveiling men is 'comic, implausible, and unthreatening, presumably because their bodies are not the symbolic carriers in modern society either of creative or destructive forces' (1992: 148).

8. Even an 'authentic' autobiographical account such as *Zoya's Story* (2002) suggests a palimpsestic 'rewriting' in accordance with the desired configuration of events for the Euro–US alliance readership. (Her politicised and applauded public unveiling on the *Oprah Winfrey Show* – in front of a crowd of 18,000 people – is also reminiscent of the French unveiling of the Algerian women in 1953, discussed in Chapter 5.)

9. El Saadawi, Keynote address at the Inscriptions of Identity in the Discourse on Arab Women conference, Kent University, 19 November 1999; also

in *The Nawal El-Saadawi Reader*, p. 170, where she refers to the veil of facial make-up as a supposed 'sign of progress' imposed by global neo-colonial media.

10. El Saadawi, in personal conversation at the Inscriptions of Identity in the Discourse on Arab Women conference, Kent University, 19 November 1999.

11. Men faced punishment if their beards were not the stipulated 8 cm long. See Pankaj Mishra, 2001: p. 43.

12. It is the crippling cultural concepts derived from the past centuries of patriarchal domination in society that have deprived women of their spiritual heritage. Women have been denied access to the spiritual and religious domain, which has been defined as an exclusively male sanctum. Men have blocked the way of the female creative life-giving power, whether perceived in terms of women's priesthood, or of mother nature. Here is a significant connection between the way men destroy the natural environment and their attitude towards women. Vandana Shiva locates among the giant multinational biotech food corporations

> The imperative to stamp out the smallest insect, the smallest plant, the smallest peasant comes from a deep fear – the fear of everything that is alive and free. And this deep insecurity and fear is unleashing the violence against all people and against all species. (2000)

Significantly in this light, the French writer Anaïs Nin perceived that, 'The man who has made the most definitive conquest of nature, the American man, is the one most afraid of *woman as nature*, of the feminine in himself' (Spencer, 1981: 97).

13. Rafika Merini offers an alternate interpretation of veils as masks, linked in many African countries to spiritual and physical transformation. Masks worn as an integral part of ritual ceremonies involving music and dance suggest a release from the restrictions of formal identity, and the possibility of the 'wearer of the mask taking on the power represented by the mask' (Merini, 1999: 120).

14. My definition of 'unity' here owes much to contemporary scholarship in quantum physics and neuroscience. While scientists working in the area of quantum physics have concluded that reality is an undivided wholeness, the quantum wave function, some have extended this logic to ask 'is human consciousness a type of quantum knowledge?' See *inter alia* Herbert, 1985: 249. Such arguments place the notion of 'essentialism' in a different context: that of a unity of consciousness, not only on the level of human awareness but even on the level of the quantum universe.

15. These arguments are based on the Indian (Upanishadic) philosophy well known to Foucault. See Schaub, 1989: 306–15.

Bibliography

Abdi, A.A. (1999) 'Frantz Fanon and Postcolonial Realities: A Temporal Perspective' in *Wasafiri*, Autumn.

Abel, E. (ed.) (1982) *Writing and Sexual Difference*. Brighton: Harvester Press.

Abu-Haidar, F. (1996) 'Unmasking Women: The Female Persona in Algerian Fiction' in L. Ibnlfassi and N. Hitchcott (eds) *African Francophone Writing*. Oxford: Berg.

Abu-Lughod, L. (1986) *Veiled Sentiments: Honour and Poetry Among the Bedouin*. Berkeley: University of California Press.

—— (1998) *Remaking Women: Feminism and Modernity in the Middle East*. Princeton, New Jersey: Princeton University Press.

—— (2001) 'Orientalism and Middle East Feminist Studies' in *Feminist Studies*, 27, 1, Spring.

Accad, E. (1978) *Veil of Shame: The Role of Women in the Contemporary Fiction of North Africa and the Arab World*. Quebec: Éditions Naaman.

—— (1990) *Sexuality and War: Literary Masks of the Middle East*. New York: New York University Press.

Ahmed, A. (1994) *In Theory: Classes, Nations, Literatures*. London: Verso.

Ahmed, A.S. and H. Donnan (1994) *Islam, Globalization, and Postmodernity*. London: Routledge.

Ahmed, L. (1992) *Women and Gender in Islam: Historical Roots of a Modern Debate*. New Haven: Yale University Press.

—— (1999) *A Border Passage From Egypt to America: A Woman's Journey*. London: Penguin.

Al-Ali, N.S. (1994) *Gender Writing–Writing Gender: The Representation of Women in a Selection of Modern Egyptian Literature*. Cairo: American University in Cairo Press.

—— (1997) *Feminism and Contemporary Debates in Egypt*. Exeter: University of Exeter Press.

Alexander, M.J., and C.T. Mohanty (eds) (1997) *Feminist Genealogies, Legal Legacies and Democratic Futures*. London: Routledge.

Al-Hibri, A. (1982) *Women and Islam*. Oxford: Pergamon.

Ali, T. (2001) 'Devout Sceptics', an interview BBC Radio 4, 16 August.

—— (2002) *The Clash of Fundamentalisms*. London: Verso.

Alireza, M. (1987) 'Women of Saudi Arabia' in *National Geographic*, 172, 4.

Alloula, M. (1986) *The Colonial Harem*. Minneapolis: University of Minnesota Press.

Almunajjed, M. (1997) *Women in Saudi Arabia Today*. London: Macmillan.

Al-Shaykh, H. (1980) *The Story of Zahra*. London: Quartet Books.

—— (1988, 1993) *Women of Sand and Myrrh*. London: Quartet Books.

—— (1997) *Literary Review*, 40, 2.

Anderson, B. (1983) *Imagined Communities: Reflections on the Origin and Spread of Nationalism*. London: Verso.

Angha, N. (1991) *Principles of Sufism*. Fremont, California: Jain Publishing Corporation.

Ardener, S. (ed.) (1997) *Women and Space: Ground Rules and Social Maps*. Oxford: Berg.

Arebi, S. (1994) *Women and Words in Saudi Arabia: The Politics of Literary Discourse*. New York: Columbia University Press.

Argyle, M. and M. Cook (1976) *Gaze and Mutual Gaze*. Cambridge: Cambridge University Press.

Armstrong, K. (1993) *A History of God*. London: Heinemann

—— (2000) *The Battle for God: Fundamentalism in Judaism, Christianity and Islam*. London: Harper Collins.

Armstrong, N. and L. Tennenhouse (eds) (1989) *The Violence of Representation: Literature and the History of Violence*. London: Routledge.

Ashcroft, B., G. Grifffiths and H. Tiffin (1989) *The Empire Writes Back*. London: Routledge.

—— (1995) *The Postcolonial Studies Reader*. London: Routledge.

Ask, K. and M. Tjomsland (eds) (1998) *Women and Islamization: Contemporary Dimensions of Discourse on Gender Relations*. Oxford: Berg.

Attar, F.D. (trans. C.S. Nott) (1954, 1974) *The Conference of the Birds: The Persian Poem Mantiq Ut-tair*. London: Routledge and Kegan Paul.

Atwood, M. (1977, 1997) *Surfacing*. London: Virago.

—— (1997) *Alias Grace*. London: Virago.

Auerbach, N. (1995) *Our Vampires Ourselves*. Chicago: University of Chicago Press.

Augé, M. (1997) *Non-Places: Introduction to an Anthropology of Supermodernity*. London: Verso.

Bagader, A., A. Heinrichsdorff and D. Akers (eds) (1998) *Voices of Change: Short Stories by Saudi Arabian Women Writers*. London: Lynne Reiner.

Barber, B.R. (1996) *Jihad Versus McWorld*. New York: Ballantine.

Barker, F. (ed.) (1984) *Europe and Its Others: Proceedings of the Essex Conference on the Sociology of Literature*. Colchester: Essex University Press.

Barthes, R. (1973) *Mythologies*. London: Grafton.

Battersby, C. (1998) *The Phenomenal Woman: Feminist Metaphysics and the Patterns of Identity*. London: Routledge

Baudrillard, J. (trans. B. Singer) (1990) *On Seduction*. London: Macmillan.

Becker, U. (trans. L.W. Garmer) (1994) *The Continuum Encyclopaedia of Symbols*. New York: Continuum.

Benhabib, S. and D. Cornell (eds) (1987) *Feminism as Critique: Essays on the Politics of Gender in Late-Capitalist Societies*. Cambridge: Polity Press.

Ben Jalloun, T. (1987) *La Nuit Sacrée*. Paris: Seuil.

—— (trans. A. Sheridan) (1988) *The Sand Child*. London: Quartet Books.

Bergner, G. (1995) 'Who is that Masked Woman? Or the Role of Gender in Fanon's *Black Skin, White Masks*' in *PMLA* 110, 1, January.

Bhabha, H.K. (1983) 'The Other Question' in *Screen*, 24, 6.

—— (1987) 'Interrogating Identity' in ICA Documents, 6: *Identity*. London: Institute of Contemporary Arts.

—— (1994) *The Location of Culture*. London: Routledge.

—— (1999) 'The Manifesto in Reinventing Britain' in *Wasafiri*, 29, Spring.

Bhattacharya, N. (1998) *Reading the Splendid Body: Gender and Consumerism in British Writing on India*. London: Associated University Presses.

Blanch, L. (1954) *The Wilder Shores of Love*. London: Gollantz.

Blavatsky, H.P. (1877, 1976) *Isis Unveiled: A Master Key to the Mysteries of Ancient and Modern Science and Theology*. Pasadena: Theosophical Society Press.

Boone, J.A. (1995) 'Vacation Cruises; or, The Homoerotics of Orientalism' in *PLMA* 110, 1, January.

Bowles, P. (1949, 1993) *The Sheltering Sky*. London: Harper Collins.

Brah, A. (1996) *Cartographies of Diaspora: Contesting Identities*. London: Routledge.

Braidotti, R. (1991) *Patterns of Dissonance*. London: Routledge.

—— (1994) *Nomadic Subjects: Embodiment and Sexual Difference in Contemporary Feminist Theory*. New York: Columbia University Press.

Brennan, T. (1989) *Salman Rushdie and the Third World: Myths of the Nation*. London: Macmillan.

Brooks, G. (1996) *Nine Parts of Desire, the Hidden World of Islamic Women*. London: Penguin.

Buchan, J. (1999) *A Good Place to Die*. London: Harvill Press.

Buchanan, I. (ed.) (2000) *Deleuze and Feminist Theory*. Edinburgh: Edinburgh University Press.

Bulbeck, C. (1998) *Re-Orienting Western Feminisms: Women's Diversity in a Postcolonial World*. Cambridge, Cambridge University Press.

Bumiller, E. (1990) *May You Be the Mother of a Hundred Sons: A Journey Among the Women of India*. New York: Ballantine.

Buonaventura, W. (1998) *Beauty and the East*. London: Saqi Books.

Burton, R.F. (1885) *The Thousand Nights and a Night*. London: Burton Club.

Butler, J. (1990) *Gender Trouble: Feminism and the Subversion of Identity*. London: Routledge.

—— (1993) *Bodies that Matter*. London: Routledge.

Camus, A. (1953) *The Rebel*. London: Penguin.

—— (1966) *Exile and the Kingdom*. London: Penguin.

Carter, A. (2001) *The Political Theory of Global Citizenship*. London: Routledge.

Castells, M. (1997) *The Power of Identity*. Oxford: Blackwell.

Chandraratana, B. (1999) *Mirage*. London: Weidenfeld and Nicolson.

—— (2001) *An Eye for an Eye*. London: Weidenfeld and Nicolson.

Charrad, M.M. (1998) 'Cultural Diversity within Islam: Veils and Laws in Tunisia' in H.L. Bodman and N. Tohini (eds) *Women in Muslim Societies: Diversity within Unity*. London: Lynne Reiner.

Chatty, D. and A. Rabo (eds) (1997) *Organizing Women: Formal and Informal Women's Groups in the Middle East (Cross-Cultural Perspectives on Women V. 17)*. Oxford: Berg.

Chittick, W. (1998) 'Between the Yes and the No' in R. Forman (ed.) *The Innate Capacity: Mysticism, Psychology and Philosophy*. Oxford: Oxford University Press.

Chughtai, I. (1991) *The Quilt and other Stories*. London: Women's Press.

Cixous, H. (1976) 'The Laugh of the Medusa' in *Signs*, 1, 4.

—— (1986) *The Newly Born Woman*. Minneapolis: University of Minnesota Press.

—— (1990) *The Body and the Text*. London: Harvester Wheatsheaf.

—— (ed. S. Sellars) (1994), *The Hélène Cixous Reader*. London: Routledge.

Cohen, E. (1993) *Talk on the Wilde Side: Toward a Genealogy of a Discourse on Male Sexualities*. New York: Routledge.

Cohen, R. (1997) *Global Diasporas: An Introduction*. London: UCL Press.

Cole, E.B. and S. Coultrap-McQuin (eds) (1992) *Explorations in Feminist Ethics*. Bloomington: Indiana University Press.

Cooke, M. (2001) *Women Claim Islam: Creating Islamic Feminism through Literature*. London: Routledge.

Croutier, A.L. (1989) *Harem: The World Behind the Veil*. London: Bloomsbury.

Cundy, C. (1996) *Salman Rushdie*. Manchester: Manchester University Press.

Curtia, L. (1998) *Female Stories, Female Bodies: Narrative, Identity, and Representation*. London: Macmillan.

Dalrymple,W. (1999) *The Age of Kali: Indian Travels and Encounters*. London: Flamingo.

—— (2003) *White Mughals: Love and Betrayal in Eighteenth-Century India*. London: Viking.

Daniel, E.V. and J.M. Peck (eds) (1996) *Culture/Contexture: Explorations in Anthropology and Literary Studies*. Berkeley: University of California Press.

Dastur, A.J. and U.H. Mehta (1993) *Gandhi's Contribution to the Emancipation of Women*. London: Sangam Books.

Davies, C.B. (1994) *Black Women, Writing and Identity: Migrations of the Subject*. London: Routledge.

Dawson, T. (2000) 'Fear of the Feminine in *The Picture of Dorian Gray*' at <www.landow.stg.brown.edu/victorian/gender>.

Dean, J. (1996) *Solidarity of Strangers: Feminism after Identity Politics*. Berkeley: University of California Press.

De Beauvoir, S. (1973) *The Second Sex*. London: Vintage.

Dehejia, H.V. (1996) *The Advaita of Art*. Delhi: Motilal Banarsidass.

De Laurentis, T. (1990) 'Eccentric Subjects: Feminist Theory and Historical Consciousness' in *Feminist Studies* 16, 1.

Deleuze, G. (1990) *Pourparlers*. Paris: Minuit.

Deleuze, G. and F. Guattari (trans. B. Massumi) (1987) *A Thousand Plateaus: Capitalism and Schizophrenia*. Minneapolis: University of Minnesota Press.

Dellamora, R. (1996) 'Traversing the Feminine in Oscar Wilde's *Salomé*' in J. Freedman (ed.) *Oscar Wilde: A Collection of Critical Essays*. New Jersey: Prentice Hall.

Derrida, J. (1978) *Spurs: Nietzsche's Styles*. Chicago: University of Chicago Press.

—— (1981) *Dissemination*. London: Althone.

—— (1997) *The Politics of Friendship*. London: Verso.

Desai, A. (1990) 'A Secret Connivance' in *The Times Literary Supplement*, 14–20 September.

—— (1994) 'Cracking India: Minority Women Writers and the Contentious Margins of Indian Discourse' in *The Journal of Commonwealth Literature* 29, 2.

Devi, M. (trans. G.C. Spirak) (1995) *Imaginery Maps: Three Stories by Mahasweta Devi*. London: Routledge.

Dijkstra, B. (1986) *Idols of Perversity: Fantasies of Feminine Evil in Fin-de-Siècle Culture*. Oxford: Oxford University Press.

—— (1996) *Evil Sisters: The Threat of Female Sexuality and the Cult of Manhood*. New York: Alfred Knopf.

Dinesh, K. (ed.) (1994) *Between Spaces of Silence: Women Creative Writers*. New Delhi: Sterling.

Djebar, A. (1980) *Women of Algiers in their Apartment*. London: Quartet Books.

—— (1985) *Fantasia, An Algerian Cavalcade*. London: Quartet Books.

—— (1987) *A Sister to Scheherazade*. London: Quartet Books.

—— (1999) *So Vast the Prison*. New York: Seven Stories Press.

—— (2000) *Algerian White*. New York: Seven Stories Press.

Doane, M.A. (1989) *Femmes Fatales: Feminism, Film Theory, Psychoanalysis*. London: Routledge.

Donaldson, L. (1992) *Decolonising Feminisms*. London: Routledge.

Duncan, N. (ed.) (1996) *BodySpace: Destablizing Geographies of Gender and Sexuality*. London: Routledge.

Durix, J-P. (1998) *Mimesis, Genres, and Postcolonial Discourse: Deconstructing Magic Realism*. London: Macmillan.

Durrell, A. (1999) 'Dressing with a Difference' in *Interventions*, 1, 4, December.

Elam, D. (1994) *Feminism and Deconstruction: Ms. En Abyme*. London: Routledge.

El-Enany, R. (1998) 'The Dichotomy of Islam and Modernity in the Fiction of Naguib Mahfouz' in J.C. Hawley (ed.) *The Postcolonial Crescent: Islam's Impact on Contemporary Literature*. New York: Peter Lang.

El Guindi, F. (1999) *Veil: Modesty, Privacy, Resistance*. Oxford: Berg.

Ellman, R. (1969) *Oscar Wilde: A Collection of Critical Essays*. London: Prentice Hall.

—— (1988) *Oscar Wilde*. London: Vintage.

El Saadawi, N. (1980) *The Hidden Face of Eve*. London: Zed.

—— (trans. Sherif Hetata) (1983) *Woman at Point Zero*. London: Zed.

—— (1987) *The Death of an Ex-Minister*. London: Methuen.

—— (1988) *The Fall of the Imam*. London: Methuen.

—— (1997) *The Nawal El-Saadawi Reader*. London: Zed.

—— (1998a) *The Innocence of the Devil*. Berkeley: University of California Press.

—— (1998b) *A Daughter of Isis*. London: Zed.

—— (1999) Keynote address at Inscriptions of Identity in the Discourse on Arab Women conference, Canterbury: Kent University, 19 November.

Enloe, C. (1990) *Bananas, Beaches and Bases: Making Feminist Sense of International Politics*. Berkeley: University of California Press.

Erickson, J.D. (1993) 'Veiled Woman and Veiled Narrative in Tahar Ben Jalloun's *The Sand Child*' in *Boundary* 2, 20, Spring.

Esposito, J.L. (1995a) *The Islamic Threat: Myth or Reality*. Oxford: Oxford University Press.

—— (ed.) (1995b) *The Oxford Encyclopaedia of the Modern Islamic World*. Oxford: Oxford University Press.

Fanon, F. (1961) *The Wretched of the Earth*. London: Penguin.

—— (1965) *Studies in a Dying Colonialism*. New York: Monthly Review Press.

—— (1967) *Black Skin, White Masks*. New York: Grove Press.

Faqir, F. (trans. S. Eber and F. Faqir) (1998) *In the House of Silence: Autobiographical Essays by Arab Women Writers*. Reading: Garnet.

Feldstein, R. and J. Roof (eds) (1989) *Feminism and Psychoanalysis*. Ithaca: Cornell University Press.

Fletcher, M.D. (ed.) (1994) *Reading Rushdie*. Amsterdam: Rodopi.

Forman, R.K.C. (ed.) (1998) *The Innate Capacity: Mysticism, Psychology and Philosophy*. Oxford: Oxford University Press.

Foucault, M. (1977) *Discipline and Punish*. Harmondsworth: Penguin.

—— (1978) *The History of Sexuality. An Introduction: Volume 1*. London: Vintage.

—— (1980) *Power/Knowledge: Selected Interviews and other Writings 1972–1977*. New York: Pantheon.

Fox-Genovese, E. (1991) *Feminism without Illusions: A Critique of Individualism*. Chapel Hill: University of North Carolina Press.

Frank, K. (1995) *Lucie Duff Gordon: A Passage to Egypt*. London: Penguin.

Freedman, J. (ed.) (1996) *Oscar Wilde: A Collection of Critical Essays*. New Jersey: Prentice Hall.

Freud, S. (1919, 2000). *Three Essays on Sexuality*. London: Basic Books.

—— (ed. J. Strachey) (1961) *Beyond the Pleasure Principle*. London: Hogarth Press.

—— (1962) *The Standard Edition of the Complete Psychological Works of Sigmund Freud, vol. 3*. London: The Hogarth Press.

Gardiner, J. (1981) 'On Female Identity and Writing by Women' in *Critical Inquiry*, 8.

Gebauer, G. and C. Wulf (1995) *Mimesis: Culture, Art, Society*. Berkeley: University of California Press.

Geertz, C. (1979) *Meaning and Order in Moroccan Society*. Cambridge: Cambridge University Press.

—— (2000) *Available Light: Anthropological Reflections on Philosophical Subjects*. Princeton, New Jersey: Princeton University Press.

Ghandour, Z.B. (1999) *The Honey*. London: Quartet Books.

Ghazoul, F.J. and B. Harlow (eds) (1994) *The View from Within: Writers and Critics on Contemporary Arab Literature*. Cairo: American University in Cairo Press.

Gilbert, S. and S. Gubar (1979) *The Madwoman in the Attic: The Woman Writer and the Nineteenth-Century Literary Imagination*. New Haven: Yale University Press.

Gilligan, C. (1982) *In a Different Voice: Psychological Theory and Women's Development*. Cambridge: Cambridge University Press.

Gilman, C.P. (1892, 1981) *The Yellow Wallpaper*. London: Virago.

—— (1995) 'Hearing the Difference: Theorizing Connection' in *Hypatia* 10, 2.

Goodwin, J. (1994) *Price of Honour: Muslim Women Lift the Veil of Silence on the Islamic World*. London: Warner.

Goonetilleke, D.C.R.A. (1998) *Salman Rushdie*. London: Macmillan.

Gordimer, N. (1997) 'The Dialogue of Late Afternoon', preface to N. Mahfouz (trans. D. Johnson-Davies) *Echoes of an Autobiography*. New York: Doubleday.

Grewal, I. (1996) *Home and Harem: Nation, Gender and Cultures of Travel*. London: Leicester University Press.

Haddour, A. (2000) *Colonial Myths: History and Narrative*. Manchester: Manchester University Press.

Halliday, F. (1994) 'The Politics of Islamic Fundamentalism' in A.S. Ahmed and H. Donnan (eds) *Islam, Globalization, and Postmodernity*. London: Routledge.

Hallissy, M. (1987) *Venomous Woman: Fear of the Female in Literature*. New York: Greenwood Press.

Hammadou, G. (1999) 'Veils of my Youth' in *Transition*, issue 80.

Hanimefendi, L.S. (1994) *The Imperial Harem of the Sultans*. Istanbul: Peva.

Harik, R. and E. Marston (1996) *Women in the Middle East: Tradition and Change*. New York: Franklin Watts.

Hart-Davis, R. (1962) *The Letters of Oscar Wilde*. London: Hart-Davis.

Hawley, J.C. (ed.) (1998) *The Postcolonial Crescent: Islam's Impact on Contemporary Literature*. New York: Peter Lang.

Hawthorne, N. (1850, 1994) *The Scarlet Letter*. London: Penguin.

Hejaiej, M. (1996) *Behind Closed Doors: Women's Oral Narratives in Tunis*. London: Quartet Books.

Herbert, N. (1985) *Quantum Reality: Beyond the New Physics*. New York: Doubleday.

Holmstrom, L. (ed.) (1990) *The Inner Courtyard: Stories by Indian Women*. London: Virago.

Holton, P. (1991) *Mother without a Mask: A Westerner's Story of her Arab Family*. London: Kyle Cathie.

Hubel, T. (1996) *Whose India? The Independence Struggle in British and Indian Fiction and History*. London: Leicester University Press.

Huysmans, J-K. (1884, 1959) *A Rebours*. London: Penguin.

Ibnlfassi, L. and N. Hitchcott (1996) *African Francophone Writing*. Oxford: Berg.

Irigaray, L. (1977, 1993) *The Sex Which is Not One*. Ithaca: Cornell University Press.

—— (1985) *The Speculum of the Other Woman*. Ithaca: Cornell University Press

—— (trans. J. Collie and J. Still) (1992) *Elemental Passions*. New York: Routledge.

Jackson, S. (ed.) (1993) *Women's Studies: Essential Readings*. New York: New York University Press.

Jay, M. (1994) *Downcast Eyes: The Denigration of Vision in Twentieth-Century French Thought*. Berkeley: University of California Press.

Jayawardena, K. (1986) *Feminism and Nationalism in the Third World*. London: Zed.

Jeffery, P. (1979) *Frogs in a Well: Indian Women in Purdah*. London: Zed.

Jhabvala, R.P. (1975) *Heat and Dust*. London: Abacus.

—— (1976) *How I Became a Holy Mother*. London: John Murray.

Jordanova, L. (1989) *Sexual Visions: Images of Gender in Science and Medicine between the Eighteenth and Twentieth Centuries*. London: Harvester Wheatsheaf.

Jung, A. (1987) *Unveiling India: A Woman's Journey*. London: Penguin.

Kabbani, R. (1994) *Imperial Fictions: Europe's Myths of the Orient*. London: Harper Collins.

Kamani, G. (1995) *Junglee Girl*. London: Phoenix.

—— (2002) Address to Plenary Session, Rethinking Commonwealth/ Postcolonial Literatures Conference. Santa Clara, California: Santa Clara University.

Kandiyoti, D. (1991) *Women, Islam and the State*. London: Macmillan.

—— (1996) *Gendering the Middle East*. London: Taurus.

Kanneh, K. (1999) *Race, Nation and Culture in Ethnography, Pan Africanism and Black Literatures*. London: Routledge.

Keohane, N.O., M.Z. Rosaldo and B.C. Gelpi (eds) (1982) *Feminist Theory: A Critique of Ideology*. Brighton: Harvester.

Khatibi, A. (1990) *Love in Two Languages*. Minneapolis: University of Minnesota Press.

Khouri, N. (2003) *Forbidden Love*. New York: Doubleday.

Kipling, R. (1900) *Plain Tales From the Hills*. London: Macmillan.

—— (1901, 1994) *Kim*. London: Penguin.

Knox, M. (1994) *Oscar Wilde: A Long and Lovely Suicide*. Boston: Yale University Press.

Kouramy, J., J. Sterba and R. Tong (eds) (1995) *Feminist Philosophies*. London: Harvester Wheatsheaf.

Kristeva, J. (1991) *Strangers to Ourselves*. London: Harvester Wheatsheaf.

Lazreg, M. (1994) *The Eloquence of Silence: Algerian Women in Question*. London: Routledge.

Levy, A. (1991) *Other Women: The Writing of Class, Race, and Gender, 1832–1898*. Princeton, New Jersey: Princeton University Press.

Lewis, B. (1982) *The Muslim Discovery of Europe*. London: Weidenfeld and Nicolson.

—— (1992) *Islam and the West*. Oxford: Oxford University Press.

—— (1994) *The Shaping of the Modern Middle East*. Oxford: Oxford University Press.

—— (1997) *The Future of the Middle East*. London: Bantam.

Lewis, R. (1996) *Gendering Orientalism: Race, Femininity, and Representation*. London: Routledge.

Lewison, L. and D. Morgan (eds) (1999) *The Heritage of Sufism*. Oxford: Oneworld.

Lindisfarne, N. (2001) 'Gender Practices and Gender Rhetoric', talk at Afghanistan: Alternative Views from Anthropology seminar. Brighton: Sussex University, 5 December .

—— (2002) 'Gendering the Afghan War' in *Eclipse*, 4, 9 January.

Lindisfarne-Tapper, N. and B. Ingham (1997) *Languages of Dress in the Middle East*. London: Curzon.

Logan, H. (2002) *Unveiled*. London: Harper Collins.

Loomba, A. (1998) *Colonialism/Postcolonialism*. London: Routledge.

Lytle Croutier, A. (1989) *Harem: The World Behind the Veil*. London: Bloomsbury.

Mabro, J. (ed.) (1991) *Veiled Half-Truths: Western Travellers' Perceptions of Middle Eastern Women*. London: Taurus.

Macmillan, M. (1988) *Women of the Raj*. New York: Thames and Hudson.

Maharishi. M. Yogi, (1994) *Maharishi Vedic University: Introduction*. Vlodrop, Holland: Maharishi Vedic University Press.

Mahfouz, N. (1957, 1991) *Palace Walk*. London: Black Swan.

—— (trans. D. Johnson-Davies) (1997) *Echoes of an Autobiography*. New York: Doubleday.

Makhlouf, C. (1979) *Changing Veils: Woman and Modernisation in North Yemen*. London: Croom Helm.

Makiya, K. (1993) *Cruelty and Silence: War, Tyranny, Uprising in the Arab World*. London: Jonathan Cape.

Malti-Douglas, F. (1991) *Woman's Body, Woman's World: Gender and Discourse in Arabo-Islamic Writing*. Princeton, New Jersey: Princeton University Press.

—— (1995) *Men, Women and God(s): Nawal El-Saadawi and Arab Feminist Poetics*. Berkeley: University of California Press.

Mantel, H. (1997) *Eight Months on Ghazzah Street*. London: Penguin.

Markandeya, K. (1954) *Nectar in a Sieve*. London: Signet.

Mast, G., M. Cohen and L. Braudy (eds) (1992) *Film Theory and Criticism: Introductory Readings*. Oxford: Oxford University Press.

McBratney, J. (1988) 'Images of Indian Women in Rudyard Kipling: A Case of Doubling Discourse' in *Inscriptions*, 3–4.

McClintock, A. (1995) *Imperial Leather: Postcoloniality and Sexuality*. London: Routledge.

McClintock, A., A. Mufti and E. Shohat (eds) (1997) *Dangerous Liaisons: Gender, Nation and Postcolonial Perspectives*. Minneapolis: University of Minnesota Press.

Mehta, G. (1993) *A River Sutra*. New York: Random House.

Mehta, R. (1977) *Inside the Haveli*. London: Women's Press.

—— (1990) 'From Purdah to Modernity' in B.R. Nanda (ed.) *Indian Women: From Purdah to Modernity*. London: Sangam Books.

Melman, B. (1986) *Women's Orients: English Women and the Middle East 1748–1918, Sexuality, Religion and Work*. London: Palgrave Macmillan.

Merini, R. (1999) *Two Major Francophone Women Writers, Assia Djebar and Leila Sebbar: A Thematic Study of their Work*. New York: Peter Lang.

Meriwether, M.L. and J.E. Tucker (1999) *Social History of Women and Gender in the Modern Middle East*. Boulder: Westview Press.

Mernissi, F. (1975) *Beyond the Veil: Male–female Dynamics in a Modern Muslim Society*. Cambridge: Schenkman.

—— (1977) 'Women, Saints, and Sanctuaries' in *Signs* 3, 1.

—— (1988) *Doing Daily Battle: Interviews with Moroccan Women*. London: Women's Press.

—— (1991) *Women and Islam: An Historical and Theological Enquiry*. Oxford: Blackwell.

—— (1992) *Islam and Democracy: Fear of the Modern World*. London: Virago.

—— (1993) *The Forgotten Queens of Islam*. Cambridge: Polity Press.

—— (1994) *The Harem Within: Tales of a Moroccan Girlhood*. London: Bantam.

Milani, F. (1992) *Veils and Words: The Emerging Voices of Iranian Women Writers*. Syracuse: Syracuse University Press.

Millet, K. (1974) *Flying*. New York: Knopf.

—— (1982) *Going to Iran*. New York: Coward, McCann and Geoghegan.

Mills, S. (1992) *Discourses of Difference: An Analysis of Women's Travel Writing and Colonialism*. London: Routledge.

Milton-Edwards, B. (2000) *Contemporary Politics in the Middle East*. Cambridge: Polity Press.

Minh-ha, T.T. (1988) 'Not You/Like You: Postcolonial Women and the Interlocking Questions of Identity and Difference' in *Inscriptions*, 3–4.

—— (1989) *Woman, Native, Other: Problems Faced by the Third World Woman Writer*. London: Routledge.

—— (1991) *When the Moon Waxes Red: Representation, Gender and Cultural Politics*. London: Routledge.

Minturn, L. (1993) *Sita's Daughters: Coming Out of Purdah*. Oxford: Oxford University Press.

Mishra, P. (2001) 'The Afghan Tragedy' in *The New York Review of Books*, XLIX, 1.

Mitter, S.S. (1991) *Dharma's Daughters: Contemporary Indian Women and Hindu Culture*. New Brunswick: Rutgers University Press.

Moghadam, V.M. (1993) *Modernising Women: Gender and Social Change in the Middle East*. London: Lynne Reiner.

Moghissi, H. (1999) *Feminism and Islamic Fundamentalism: The Limits of Postmodern Analysis*. London: Zed.

Mohanty, C.T. (1985) 'Under Western Eyes: Feminist Scholarship and Colonial Discourses' in *Boundary*, 2, Spring–Fall.

Mohanty, C.T., A. Russo and L. Torres (eds) (1991) *Third World Women and the Politics of Feminism*. Bloomington: Indiana University Press.

Moi, T. (1985) *Sexual Textual Politics*. London: Methuen.

Mongia, P. (1997) *Contemporary Postcolonial Theory: A Reader*. London: Hodder.

Montagu, M.W. (ed. M. Jack) (1716, 1993) *Turkish Embassy Letters*. Georgia: University of Georgia Press.

Moors, A. (1998) 'Wearing Gold' in P. Spyer (ed.) *Border Fetishisms: Material Objects in Unstable Spaces*. London: Routledge.

Mortimer, M. (1988) *Assia Djebar*. Philadelphia: Celfan Monographs.

Mosteshar, C. (1995) *Unveiled: Love and Death among the Ayatollahs*. London: Hodder and Stoughton.

Mukherjee, B. (1990) *Jasmine*. London: Virago.

Murdoch, I. (1992) *Metaphysics as a Guide to Morals*. London: Penguin.

Naghibi, N. (1999) 'Bad Feminist or *Bad-hejabi*?' in *Interventions*, 1, 4.

Nanda, B.R. (ed.) (1990) *Indian Women: From Purdah to Modernity*. London: Sangam Books.

Narayan, U. (1995) 'Colonialism and its Others: Considerations on Rights and Care Discourses' in *Hypatia*, 10, 2, Spring.

—— (1997) *Dislocating Cultures: Identities, Traditions and Third World Feminism*. London: Routledge.

Nasta, S. (1991) *Motherlands: Black Women's Writing from Africa, the Caribbean, and South Asia*. London: Women's Press.

Nehru, J. (1967) *Towards Freedom: The Autobiography of Jawahalal Nehru*. Boston: Beacon Press.

Neshat, S. (2002) 'The Logic of Birds' at <www.connectingflights.org>.

Newton, J. and D. Rosenfelt (eds) (1985) *Feminist Criticism and Social Change: Sex, Class, and Race in Literature and Culture*. London: Methuen.

Nin, A. (1976) *Under a Glass Bell*. London: Penguin.

Okin, S.M. (ed.) (1999) *Is Multiculturalism Bad for Women?* Princeton, New Jersey: Princeton University Press.

Orlando, V.K. (1995) 'War, Women Autobiography in Assia Djebar's *L'amour, La fantasia*' in T.D. Sharpley-Whiting and R.T. White, *Spoils of War: Women of Color, Cultures and Revolutions*. West Lafayette: Purdue University Press.

—— (1999) *Nomadic Voices: Feminine Identity in Francophone Literature of the Maghreb*. Ohio: Ohio University Press.

Parameswaran, U. (1988) *The Perforated Sheet: Essays in Salman Rushdie's Art*. New Delhi: Associated East/West.

Parikh, I.J. and P.K. Garg (1989) *Indian Women: An Inner Dialogue*. London: Sage.

Parker, A., M. Russo, D., Sommer and P. Yaeger (eds) (1992) *Nationalisms and Sexualities*. London: Routledge.

Peterson, V.S. and A.S. Runyan (1999) *Global Gender Issues*. Boulder: Westview Press.

Plant, S. (1993) 'Baudrillard's Women: The Eve of Seduction' in C. Rojek and B.S. Turner, *Forget Baudrillard?* London: Routledge.

Poster, M. (ed.) (1988) *Jean Baudrillard Selected Writings*. Berkeley: University of California Press.

Pratt, M.L. (1992) *Imperial Eyes: Travel Writing and Transculturation*. London: Routledge.

Rahnavard, Z. (1990) *The Message of Hijab*. London: Al-Hoda Publishers.

Rajan, R.S. (1993) *Real and Imagined Women: Gender, Culture and Postcolonialism*. London: Routledge.

Rhys, J. (1966, 2000) *Wide Sargasso Sea*. London: Penguin.

Richards, D. (1994) *Masks of Difference: Cultural Representations in Literature, Anthropology and Art*. Cambridge: Cambridge University Press.

Rider Haggard, H. (1887, 1994) *She*. London: Penguin.

Riley, D. (1988) *Am I that Name?: Feminism and the Category of 'Woman' in History*. London: Macmillan.

Roberson, B.A. (ed.) (1998) *The Middle East and Europe*. London: Routledge.

Roded, R. (ed.) (1999) *Women in Islam and the Middle East: A Reader*. London: Taurus.

Rodinson, M. (1991) *Europe and the Mystique of Islam*. Seattle: University of Seattle Press.

Rojek, C. and B.S. Turner (eds) (1993) *Forget Baudrillard?* London: Routledge.

Rushdie, S. (1975, 1996) *Grimus*. London: Vintage

—— (1989) *Shame*. London: Vintage.

—— (1991) *Imaginary Homelands*. London: Penguin.

—— (1995) *Midnight's Children*. London: Everyman.

—— (1998) *The Satanic Verses*. London: Vintage.

Ruthven, M. (1990) *A Satanic Affair: Salman Rushdie and the Rage of Islam*. London: Chatto and Windus.

Rydh, H. (1947) 'Amongst the Women of Iraq' in *Jus Suffagii*, 41, 2, September.

Sahgal, N. (1954) *Prison and Chocolate Cake*. London: Victor Gollancz.

Said, E.W. (1979) *Orientalism*. London: Random House.

—— (1981) *Covering Islam: How the Media and the Experts Determine How We See the Rest of the World*. London: Routledge.

—— (1994) *Culture and Imperialism*. London: Vintage.

Salgado, M. (2000) 'Migration and Mutability: The Twice Born Fiction of Salman Rushdie' in A. Davies and A. Sinfield (eds) *British Culture of the Postwar: An Introduction to Literature and Society*. London: Routledge.

Satloff, R.B. (1993) *The Politics of Change in the Middle East*. Boulder: Westview Press.

Schaub, U.L. (1989) 'Foucault's Oriental Subtext' in *PMLA*, 104, 3, May.

Scott, P. (1968) *The Day of the Scorpion*. London: Panther.

Sebbar, L. (1991) *Sherazade: Missing, Aged Seventeen, Dark Curly Hair, Green Eyes*. London: Quartet Books.

Sedgwick, E.K. (1992) 'Nationalisms and Sexualities in the Age of Wilde' in A. Parker, M. Russo, D. Sommer and P. Yaeger (eds) *Nationalisms and Sexualities*. London: Routledge.

Shahidian, H. (1998) 'The Education of Women in the Islamic Republic of Iran' in *Journal of Women's History*, 2, 3.

Sharebi, H. (1988) *Neopatriarchy: A Theory of Distorted Change in Arab Society*. Oxford: Oxford University Press.

Sharpley-Whiting, T.D. (1998) *Frantz Fanon: Conflicts and Feminisms*. Boulder: Rowman and Littlefield.

Shiva, V. (1997) *Biopiracy: The Plunder of Nature and Knowledge*. Boston: South End.

—— (2000) 'The Reith Lecture' at <www.news.bbc.uk/hi/english/static/ events/reith_(2000)/lecture5.stm>.

Shohat, E. and R. Stam (1994) *Unthinking Eurocentrism: Multiculturalism and the Media*. London: Routledge.

Showalter, E. (1985) 'Feminist Criticism in the Wilderness' in *The New Feminist Criticism: Essays in Women, Literature and Theory*. New York: Pantheon.

—— (1992) *Sexual Anarchy: Gender and Culture at the Fin de Siècle*. London: Virago.

Shrivastava, S. (1996) *The New Woman in Indian English Fiction*. New Delhi: Creative Books.

Singh, J.G. (1996) *Colonial Narratives /Cultural Dialogues*. London: Routledge.

Smale, D. (ed.) (2001) *Salman Rushdie: Midnight's Children/The Satanic Verses*. London: Icon.

Smith, S. (1987) *A Poetics of Women's Autobiography: Marginality and the Fictions of Self-Representation*. Bloomington: Indiana University Press.

Soueif, A. (1995) *In the Eye of the Sun*. London: Bloomsbury.

—— (1999) *The Map of Love*. London: Bloomsbury.

Spencer, S. (1981) *Collage of Dreams: The Writings of Anais Nin*. London: Harvester Wheatsheaf.

Spivak, G.C. (1985) 'Criticism, Feminism, and the Institution' in *Thesis Eleven*, 10/11, November–March.

—— (1988) 'Can the Subaltern Speak?' in C. Nelson and L. Grossberg (eds) *Marxism and the Interpretation of Culture*. London: Macmillan.

—— (1993) *Outside the Teaching Machine*. London: Routledge.

—— (ed.) D. Landry and G. MacLean (1996) *The Spivak Reader*. London: Routledge.

—— (1999) *A Critique of Postcolonial Reason*. Cambridge: Harvard University Press.

Spyer, P. (ed.) (1998) *Border Fetishisms: Material Objects in Unstable Spaces*. London: Routledge.

Suleiman, S.R. (1986) *The Female Body in Western Culture*. Cambridge: Harvard University Press.

Suleri, S. (1992a) *The Rhetoric of English India*. Chicago: University of Chicago Press.

—— (1992b) 'Woman Skin Deep: Feminism and the Postcolonial Condition' in *Critical Inquiry*, 18, 4, Summer.

Tagore, R. (1915, 1985) *The Home and the World*. London: Penguin.

Taussig, M. (1993) *Mimesis and Alterity: A Particular History of the Senses*. London: Routledge.

Tharu, S. and K. Lalita (eds) (1993) *Women Writing in India, Vol ii, The Present*. London: Harper Collins.

Tompkins, J. (1985) *Sensational Designs*. Oxford: Oxford University Press.

Toubia, N. (ed.) (1988) *Women of the Arab World*. London: Zed.

Turner, B. (1994) *Orientalism, Postmodernism and Globalism*. London: Routledge.

Tydeman, W. and S. Price (1996) *Salomé: Plays in Production*. Cambridge: Cambridge University Press.

Viswanathan, G. (1989) *Masks of Conquest: Literary Study and British Rule in India*. London: Faber.

Viswanathan, N. (ed.) (1997) *The Women, Gender and Development Reader*. London: Zed.

Walker, B.G. (1988) *The Woman's Dictionary of Symbols and Sacred Objects*. San Franscisco: Harper and Row.

Warner, M. (1985) *Monuments and Maidens: The Allegory of the Female Form*. London: Vintage.

Warwick, A. and D. Cavallaro (1998) *Fashioning the Frame: Boundaries, Dress, and the Body*. Oxford: Berg.

Waugh, N. (1970) *Corsets and Crinolines*. London: Routledge.

Wikan, U. (1982) *Behind the Veil in Arabia: Women in Oman*. Chicago: University of Chicago Press.

Wilde, O. (1893, 1967) *Salomé*. New York: Dover Publications.

—— (1948) *The Works of Oscar Wilde*. London: Collins.

—— (1966) *Complete Works*. London: Collins.

Williams P. and L. Chrisman (1994) *Colonial Discourse/ Postcolonial Theory: A Reader*. London: Harvester Wheatsheaf.

Woodcock, G. (1989) *Oscar Wilde: The Double Image*. Quebec: Black Rose Books.

Woodhull, W. (1993) *Transfigurations of the Maghreb: Feminism, Decolonization and Literatures*. Minneapolis: University of Minnesota Press.

Worth, K.J. (1983) *Oscar Wilde*. London: Macmillan.

Yegenoglu, M. (1992) 'Supplementing the Orientalist Lack: European Ladies in the Harem' in *Inscriptions 6: Orientalism and Cultural Differences*.

—— (1998) *Gendering Orientalism: Towards a Feminist Reading of Orientalism*. Cambridge: Cambridge University Press.

Young, R. (1990) *White Mythologies: Writing History and the West*. London: Routledge.

Zoya with J. Follain and R. Cristofari (2002) *Zoya's Story*. London: Harper Collins.

Index